YAP: POLITICAL LEADERSHIP AND CULTURE CHANGE IN AN ISLAND SOCIETY

YAP: POLITICAL LEADERSHIP AND CULTURE CHANGE IN AN ISLAND SOCIETY

Sherwood
Galen
Lingenfelter

THE UNIVERSITY PRESS OF HAWAII
Honolulu

Library of Congress Cataloging in Publication Data

Lingenfelter, Sherwood G
    Yap, political leadership and culture change in an
island society.

    Bibliography: p.
    Includes index.
    1. Ethnology—Caroline Islands—Yap. 2. Yap,
Caroline Islands—Politics and government. I. Title.
GN671.C3L56   301.24'0996'6   74-23510
ISBN 0-8248-0301-9

CONTENTS

FIGURES

TABLES

ACKNOWLEDGMENTS

I am grateful for a fellowship (1 F1 MH-36, 672-01 CUAN) and a research grant (1 TO 1 MH-11213-01) from the National Institute of Mental Health, Public Health Service, and a grant from the National Science Foundation without which the research for this study would have not been possible.

I thank all persons who offered assistance throughout the project. Jane Hainline (University of Arizona) provided many helpful suggestions in preparation for the field trip and access to all of her genealogical data from Yap. John Jensen (University of Hawaii) supplied materials on the Yapese language. David Labby, who was conducting research on Yap during the writing of this work, read the manuscript and offered helpful suggestions. David M. Schneider (University of Chicago), whose research on Yap in 1946–1947 furnished the groundwork for analysis of the most difficult problems of Yapese social structure and kinship, contributed copies of publications and manuscripts that were invaluable to the project.

The administrative personnel of the Trust Territory of the Pacific Islands assisted in various ways. District Administrator George Hoover and Political Affairs Officer Tony Yinug granted access to the political development files, and John Farrell, Jr., Peace Corps lawyer, offered notes from the District and Municipal Government Study Commission.

I am especially indebted to the chairman of my doctoral committee, Alexander Spoehr, who gave many hours of assistance in preparing and sponsoring the research proposal, and in reading and offering constructive criticism of the manuscript.

My greatest thanks are extended to the many people of Yap who assisted during our two years there. For information on the traditional culture I am particularly indebted to Mooorow (Balabat village) who spent many days answering my questions. Others particularly helpful included Tamagtamdad, Tareg, Ruwepong, Gaangin, and other old men in Rull municipality; Dapoy, Figir Laarwon, Siling, Fanechoor, Pinnifen, Miregow, and Piteg, in Gagil municipality; Lukan, Urun, Tharngan, Gibma', and Tuluk in Tamil municipality; and many others in every part of Yap.

For assistance in the general program of my research and for information on present politics in Yap I thank Andrew Roboman, Francisco Luktun, and members of the Council of Magistrates, and Joachim Falmog and members of the Yap District Legislature.

Very personal gratitude is given to the people of Wonyan village who accepted us as neighbors and friends; to Fran Defngin who supplied much information and who read my manuscript, and offered suggestions and corrections; to John Iou who assisted in both the research and preparation of the manuscript; and to my wife and daughter who offered support and encouragement from beginning to end.

THE HANDLING
OF GLOSSES

English glosses for Yapese words and phrases are set within single quotation marks at their first use but occur thereafter without punctuation and Yapese referent. The reader is cautioned to remember that Yapese concepts of father, mother, sibling, and so forth, comprise relationships and functions that range far beyond those normally associated with the equivalent English term.

INTRODUCTION

The people of Yap from time immemorial have defined authority and power in terms of their land. Each individual inherited certain rights to parcels of land and to the particular sociopolitical privileges and obligations vested in them. In Yapese concepts, the land was chief and the man who inherited the land served as its voice. Thus, for politically ambitious individuals, the acquisition of land supplied the key to power, and Yapese legends and mythology abound with tales of struggle, subversion, and bloodshed in the quest for titled land.

Today, the Yapese continue their tradition of competition and rivalry for power, but in a manner altered to accommodate the impact of external forces. After over a hundred years of missionary endeavor, they are almost all nominal Christians. Secular contacts, particularly since World War II, have brought significant innovations in public administration, health, and education. The most important changes are the new concepts of equality and of election of representatives for government, the introduction of wage work and a cash-oriented economic system, and the great emphasis on and pressure for an American style of education. Consequently, new criteria for status, new personal and communal goals, new social patterns, and a dual system of politics amalgamating the old and new came into existence. In view of these intensive contacts and pressures for change, the Yapese could hardly avoid transformation into an "intermediate" society of the type found throughout much of Oceania.

Yet the people of Yap remain a relatively homogeneous group. They have been very reluctant to accept externally imposed innovations and persistently refer to the *yalen* or the "right" Yapese way of life. For these reasons they have maintained a strong sense of cultural identity and unity against the outer world.

The objectives of this book are to describe the traditional sociopolitical organization of Yap and to examine the dynamic interplay of traditional roles, rules, and values with those introduced in the contemporary situation of American-directed change. Before the Spanish established sovereignty over Yap in 1886, the Yapese governed themselves by a system of semiautonomous villages and kin groups drawn together in fragile alliances both by their need for mutual support against common enemies and by the domination of more powerful neighbors. At every level of government no individual leader was entrusted with total power, but rather decisions were made in councils of family, village, or national elders and administrative tasks distributed among three or more nearly equal leaders, balanced one against the others. The Yap-wide system of organization included two competing national alliances, or in Yapese terms "nets," coordinated by two national councils and three paramount village centers with their paramount chiefs. A Yapese proverb likened these paramount centers to the three stone pillars that held up their cooking pots; each was essential for the maintenance of the system, and the toppling of one would bring on the collapse of the whole. These councils, chiefs, and alliances conducted warfare, collected and distributed tribute, and worked to maintain control and to assure the general welfare of Yap.

In all the facets of recent change on Yap, the American administration has given its most concentrated effort to supplanting this traditional system. Change in ideology and political organization has been the carefully cultivated goal of all the district administrators who have served on Yap. The American political format—elections, a representative legislature, equal representation—was forced upon the traditional sociopolitical system. The complexities of the situation, however, extend far beyond the boundaries of the political alterations. Other changes, particularly in education and economics, have had far-reaching effects upon leaders and their selection. The Yapese initially reacted to the new political system by filling the positions with traditional leaders. However, as problems became more complex and the requirements of leadership more demanding, particularly in terms of legislative and linguistic skills, the educated moved rapidly into the fore as leaders. The traditional criteria of status were no longer adequate, and the older leaders without the new skills or the ability to cope with those who had them slowly began to drop into the political background.

Economic changes also affected leadership. As public interest in roads, transportation, and wage work increased, the demands for improved public facilities correspondingly increased. Some leaders, un-perceptive to these changes, rapidly lost ground to those who recognized such needs and initiated action to meet them.

The ultimate considerations that we undertake here are the political, social, and cultural adaptations and consequences of this directed change. The analytical focus for both traditional and contemporary situations includes the processes of succession and accession to leadership, of selection and rejection of leaders, of initiation, organization, and direction of activities, and of decision-making.

Research for this work was conducted from October 1967 through July 1969. I spent the first several months in the field in language study and in completing a household census for the whole of Yap. After gaining competence in Yapese, I conducted extensive interviews on the traditional political and social organization in all of the municipalities of Yap, but particularly in Rull, Gagil, and Tamil. Legislative sessions were observed and legislators and councilmen interviewed. Historical research was conducted in the Public Affairs and other files of the office of the district administrator. Other data were gathered through daily contact and interaction with the Yapese people.

The traditional system of Yapese politics, which began to decline many decades ago, proved to be the most difficult to research. Early reports of traders and missionaries indicate that depopulation had already had serious impact by the late nineteenth century. The recurrence of intervillage and interdistrict warfare further accelerated this decline so that by 1910 the German ethnologist Wilhelm Müller found the politico-religious ritual in a number of districts in total collapse from lack of capable leadership. It is not then surprising that Catholic missionaries successfully converted nearly 80 percent of the population during this period. In the secular sphere, however, change was slowed because German administrators tacitly recognized traditional political boundaries and leadership. The political forms were retained while the dynamics and functions of the system were changed.

These changes hampered the present research on traditional political and social organization. While time-honored statuses were still recognized, their interrelationships and functions could be discerned only through interviews with aged Yapese men who as youths had actively participated in events or who had learned about them from their elders. In a few instances I observed particular events that accorded with my knowledge of the traditional political relationships. These observations and interviews, supplemented by my readings of previous publications on Yap, made possible the following description of its traditional political system.

Apart from the accounts of the early traders and missionaries, which are of little value for a political analysis, the most significant works on Yapese culture and politics are those of Müller, who spent ten months on Yap in 1909–1910, and David M. Schneider, a member of the Coordinated Investigation of Micronesian Anthropology team who spent about the same time on Yap in 1946–1947. Müller's work is of primary value in its descriptions of the material culture and the cycle of intervillage religious ritual conducted within the major regions of the islands. Müller's data on the social and political organization are general, sometimes inaccurate, and quite brief. They are most useful as a cross-check on informants and as a starting point for further research. Schneider's work is much more extensive on social and political organization and particularly good on kinship and the family. He also supplies data on village organization and the role of the village chief, but these are not as extensive as the data on kinship. Both works lack substantial data on the Yap-wide system of economic, political, and religious interaction and leadership.

The district anthropologists for the Trust Territory government and Inez de Beauclair also have conducted research on Yap. The former gathered data on such topics as land tenure, yam and taro cultivation, and Yapese names, topics which are valuable but not directly relevant to this study. Beauclair's work provides some additional data on magic, religion, and the "caste" system.

I. YAP AND THE YAPESE: THE LAND AND THE PEOPLE

The Yap Islands are in the Western Caroline Islands of Micronesia, about 450 nautical miles south and west of Guam, 1,100 nautical miles east of the Philippines, and 1,737 nautical miles south of Tokyo. The position of the islands is 9°30′ north latitude and 138°5′ east longitude. The nearest inhabited islands to Yap are Ulithi, approximately 100 nautical miles to the northeast, Ngulu, about 50 nautical miles to the south, and the Palau Islands, about 250 nautical miles to the southwest. (See Figure 1.)

Yap is the administrative headquarters of the Yap District of the United States Trust Territory of the Pacific Islands. Included in the Yap District are the islands of Ngulu and Ulithi, and the atolls to the east and south, including Fais, Woleai, Lamotrek, and Satawal, among others. The people of these islands are linguistically and culturally different from the Yapese, but were dominated by the Yapese, politically and militarily, long before European influence was felt in the Pacific. Of the Trust Territory districts, Yap lies between Palau, to its south and west, and the Marianas, to its north, and Truk, to its east (see figure 1, inset).

The Land

The Yap Islands are an exposed portion of a large, upheaved, submarine ridge, approximately 850 miles long. The Yap portion of the

Figure 1. Location of Yap Islands, Caroline Islands
(Adapted from Hawaii Architect & Engineers 1968)

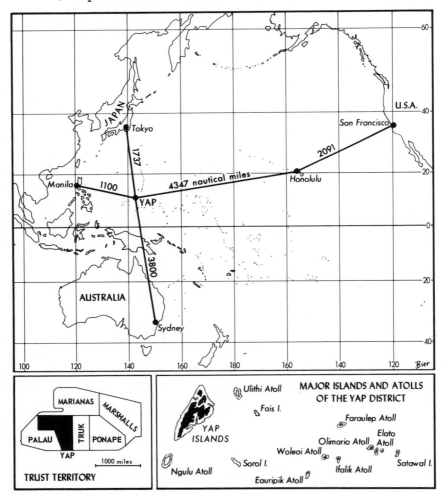

ridge (toward the southern end) slopes off steeply on the east into the Western Caroline Trench (4,122 fathoms) and on the west, gently into the Philippine basin (2,500 fathoms). There are four main high islands and six minor islands in the Yap group, separated by narrow water passages and surrounded on the perimeter by a fringing reef. The total land area is approximately 38.6 square miles, with the islands forming a chain 16 miles in length and from 1 to 6 miles in width. The islands of Yap and Gagil-Tamil,* separated by a man-made canal, form the largest land area in the group; the islands of Map and Rumung are considerably smaller. (See Figure 2.)

Topography

Much of the main island of Yap is rugged, with hills, peaks, and ridges, some as high as 180 meters (590 ft.). A central plateau occupies the northern part of Yap island and most of Gagil-Tamil. Parts of this plateau are eroded badlands of reddish volcanic clay. East of the plateau, in Gagil, is a small ridge, 60 to 80 meters high, overlooking the reef and ocean to the east. Map and Rumung are dissected into moderately steep, rounded hills. To the south, the high hills of Yap island descend abruptly into a low hilly range, which, further southward, gradually declines into a narrow, flat plateau about 15 meters above sea level (Johnson, Alvis, and Hetzler 1960).

The soils of the Yap Islands are generally quite poor and have been classified into four major groups—lithosols, latosols, planosols and soils of coastal flats, valley bottoms, and inland depressions (Johnson, Alvis, and Hetzler 1960). The lithosols are the most extensive, and are relatively fertile, but of shallow depth. They are found chiefly in hilly and mountainous areas covered with forest, grass, and pandanus. Latosols are the second most extensive soil group, and are found generally on the plateaus of southern Yap and Gagil-Tamil. These are "reddish, granular, well-drained, infertile acid clays common to tropical regions" (Johnson, Alvis, and Hetzler 1960:96) and are formed from Tamil's volcanic deposits. Most of these soils are covered with forest, grass, or with dense strands of fern. The soils of coastal flats, valley bottoms, and inland depressions form the third most extensive group. The coastal flats' soils are formed from deposition, and generally are deep and sandy, and contain considerable organic matter, silt, and clay. These soils support dense stands of coconut palms. The nearly flat valley bottoms and the narrow inland areas behind the coastal flats are character-

* While the official gazetteer for Micronesia shows Tomil as the official spelling of this area, the Yapese commonly spell the word as they pronounce it, Tamil. The Yapese preference will be followed throughout the text.

Figure 2. Yap Islands (Johnson, Alvis, Hetzler 1960:53)

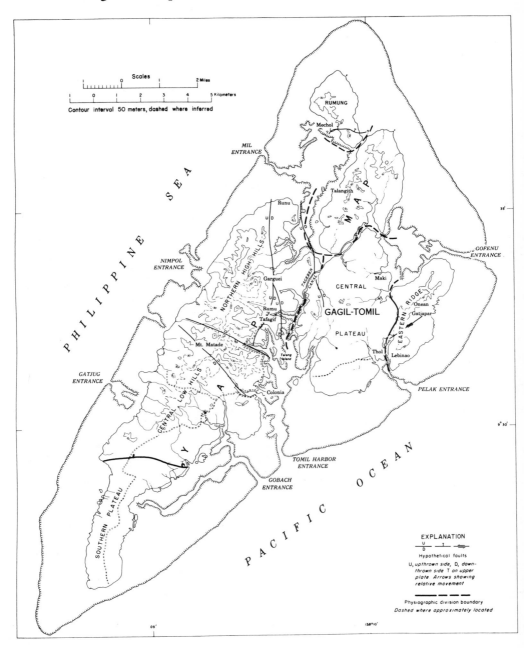

ized by deep alluvial gray clays and are generally covered with dense stands of reeds or cultivated taro. The last and least extensive of the soils are the planosols, moderately deep, somewhat fertile soils found on the gentle slopes of plateaus and hills. These are mostly covered with grass and scattered pandanus trees. (See Figure 3.)

The fertility of latosols is extremely low due to rapid decomposition of organic matter and very rapid leaching of the soil. Planosols are low in fertility, although not nearly so low as the latosols. The rugged terrain of the lithosols and the coastal flats and valley bottoms provide the most fertile soil for human exploitation.

The second most important feature of Yapese topography is the fringing coral reef, which averages over one mile in width on the eastern side and slightly less than a mile on the west. The surface features, shown in Figure 4, include the crest of the reef, the reef flat on which grow low patches of coral and coral heads, the deep holes with growing coral, and the seaweed and sand tideflats culminating in the beach, or mangrove swamps. The long reef flat and holes provide protection and feeding grounds for fish and other animal life and are thus primary resources for the human population.

Climate

The primary factor in the climate of Yap is the continual movement of warm, moist air across tropical oceans, bringing warmth, high humidity, scattered clouds, and abundant rain. Temperatures are quite uniform, averaging about 82°F in the summer months and about 80°F in the "cooler" tradewind season running from December through April. Relative humidity ranges from 65 percent to 100 percent, with an annual average of 83 percent. The average cloud cover is 74 percent, the average rainfall, 120 inches (U.S. Department of Commerce 1966).

The summer season is generally marked by frequent heavy rains, frequent calms, and light west and southwesterly winds. The tradewind season is noted for strong east-to-northeast winds and periodic drought, especially from February through April. The transitional months of May, June, and November are periods of greatest typhoon danger. Typhoons average three a year and vary in intensity, depending upon the distance between the storm center and Yap. The most damaging storms pass to the south of Yap bringing an inward surge of water that inundates and destroys coastal lands and villages.

Flora

The vegetation of Yap is similar to that of many other high islands in the Pacific and particularly to that of the islands of Micronesia. The

Figure 3. Districts and Generalized Soil Map, Yap Islands
(Johnson, Alvis, Hetzler 1960)

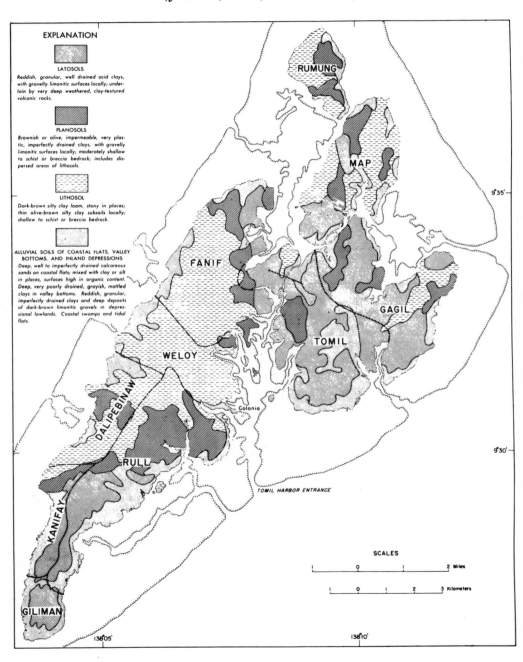

Figure 4. Coral Reef Profile, Yap Islands
(Adapted from Johnson, Alvis, Hetzler 1960)

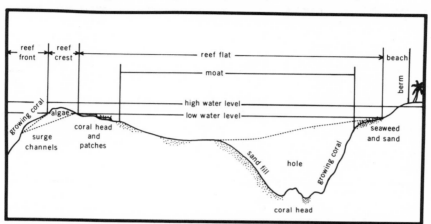

shoreline is bordered with patches of mangrove and occasionally with large extensive mangrove swamps. Coconut groves occupy the coastal flats along the beaches, and land behind the mangrove swamps and along the lower slopes of the hillsides. Marshes are scattered along the backshore areas and quite often are developed for cultivation of swamp taro. Nipa palms generally line the marshes and mangrove swamps. Valleys and the lower hillsides are usually forested, and the Gagil, Map, and Rumung highlands are covered with grasses and pandanus. The hilltops and valleys of Yap island are almost totally forested, with only scattered cleared areas, which rapidly return to bush. Scattered pandanus, grasses, and fern characterize the plateau areas. (See Figure 5.)

Forest trees include the breadfruit, banyan, mango, Tahitian chestnut, and custard nut. Areca palms (betel nut) and citrus trees are common, along with other broadleaf trees, coconut palms, and young trees and shrubs. The mountain forests are much denser than those near centers of habitation, and include thickets of bamboo, and wild hibiscus. The largest trees vary from fifty- to seventy-five-feet high and are as much as two feet in diameter. A few very old trees, such as the tamani, may grow as large as five feet in diameter.

Plants that are of some particular significance for man are those grown for subsistence (see Table 1). According to Barrau (1961), the most important of the subsistence crops is the aroid *Cyrtosperma chamissonis*. This variety of the taro family is grown in low-lying, damp, or swampy areas and cannot be profitably harvested until at least three years old. *Colocasia esculenta*, or the true taro most common

Figure 5. Land Utilization, Yap Islands
(Adapted from Barrau 1961:28)

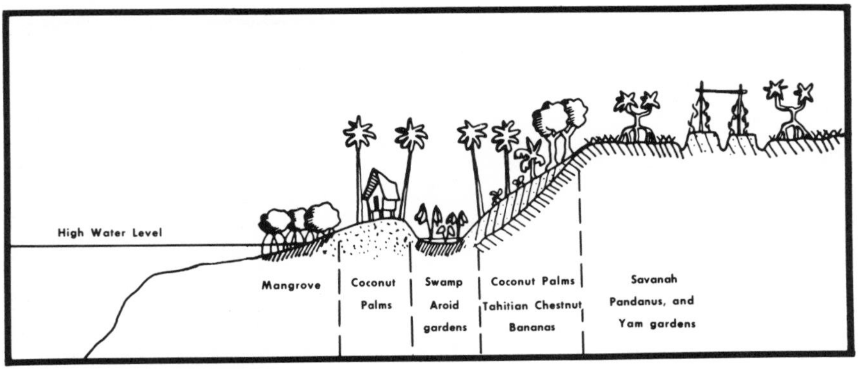

in Polynesia, is of secondary importance in Yap. Because of its softer consistency, it is generally reserved for old people who have lost their teeth.

Yams provide the second most important subsistence crop, with *Dioscorea alata* being the most important variety. *D. esculenta, D. pentaphylla,* and *D. nummularia* are also cultivated, but in lesser quantities. *D. bulbifera* is a variety eaten mostly by low-caste Yapese, and scorned by members of the high caste. Yams are grown on the high, broad ridges of the islands and on land bordering the central plateau of Gagil-Tamil. The land is generally built up into mounds surrounded by deep drainage trenches. Tall bamboo poles or other supports are used for the stems. The cultivating of yam gardens requires a rather complicated arrangement of the soil and is usually done by groups of cooperating women.

Other foods rounding out the daily diet include many varieties of bananas (*Musa sapientum, M. paradisiaca, M. troglodytarum*), breadfruit (*Artocarpus altilis*), Tahitian chestnut (*Inocarpus edulis*), and several varieties of citrus trees. The coconut palm (*Cocos nucifera*) is extremely important, not only for its food value, but because literally every part of the tree is utilized in the daily economic life of the people.

Several supplementary crops add seasonal variety to the diet. Sweet potatoes (*Ipomoea batatas*), squash, and the aroid *Xanthosoma* are the most common of these. Cassava (*Manihot esculenta* and *M. dulcis*) is cultivated but not considered a tasty addition to the diet. Mango (*Mangifera indica*), sugarcane (*Saccharum officinarum*), papaya, and pineapple are the children's delights, while the betel nut from the areca

Table 1. Economic Plants of Yap

	Scientific Names	Yapese Names	English Names
Aroids	*Cyrtosperma chamissonis*	lak'	taro
	Colocasia esculenta	mal	taro
	Xanthosoma	honolulu	taro
Yams	*Dioscorea alata*	du'og	yam
	D. esculenta	dal	yam
	D. nummularia	thep	yam
	D. pentaphylla	rowal	yam
	D. bulbifera	rok (yoy̆)	yam
Bananas	*Musa sapientum*	dinay	bananas
	M. paradisiaca		bananas
	M. troglodytarum	aray	bananas
Fruit trees	*Areca catechu*	buw	areca palm (betel)
	Artocarpus altilis	thow	breadfruit
	Inocarpus edulis	bo'oy	Tahitian chestnut
	Mangifera indica	manga	mango
	Carica papaya	babay	papaya
	Cocos nucifera	niw	coconut
Other	*Manihot esculenta, M. dulcis*	thiyogang	cassava
	Ipomoea batatas	komotiy	sweet potato
	Saccharum officinarum	makil	sugarcane
	Pueraria lobata	dinay	
	Curcuma longa	guchol	turmeric
	Hibiscus manihot	gal'	hibiscus
	Piper betle	gabuy	pepper leaf

SOURCE: Scientific names are from Barrau 1961.

palm (*Areca catechu*) and the pepper leaf (*Piper betle*) top off the daily diet of adults. The latter are mixed with lime and chewed almost constantly for the mild, relaxing narcotic effect that comes from the combined juices of the pepper leaf and betel nut.

Fauna

Mammals are rare among the Yap fauna. Fruit bats of the genus *Pteropus* are the only variety of mammal to arrive independently of man. The bats are common, but economically unimportant. Other mammals include rats, pigs, dogs, and cats. Americans introduced cattle, but the Yapese considered them more trouble than they were worth and today they are nearly extinct.

Reptiles are numerous, particularly the geckos (*Hemidactylus*), which are found everywhere, and the large harmless monitor lizard (*Varanus indicus*), which hides around the mangrove swamps and marshes. The Japanese before World War II introduced toads and they are found all over the island today. Yapese have reported that the monitor lizards have been eating toads, which poison them and thus reduce the lizard population. Sea turtles (*Chelonia mydas*) swim in the deep holes inside the reef and are considered a delicacy by the Yapese. Another food supplement is the land crab, which burrows in holes along the coastal flats and on the hillsides. Snakes and marine crocodiles are not found in Yap.

Insects are the most prolific of the land fauna and include a bountiful supply of mosquitos and flies. Cockroaches and ants add to the variety and termites are one of the most serious plagues for the people. The coconut rhinoceros beetle, which has devastated coconut groves in Palau, is not found in Yap.

Birds are largely shore and marine types, and are noticeably rare. Fruit pigeons are the only type hunted and eaten. Early Europeans introduced chickens and they are raised and eaten today by nearly every household. Some chickens that have run wild are also hunted for sport and food.

Marine fauna is the most varied and numerous in Yap. Reef fish, including parrot fish, snapper, bass, butterflyfish, and many others, provide the main source of protein in the Yapese diet. Mollusks, including the giant clam (*Tridacna*), are gathered along with lobsters and octopus to supplement the supply of fish. Trepang, once an important trade item, lines the sandy bottom of the shallow lagoon and the spiny stonefish provides one of the most painful dangers to unsuspecting, barefooted fishermen. Morays, sharks, barracuda, and rays are also numerous along the reef, but are rarely threatening to the islands' inhabitants. On rare occasions the Yapese venture into the open ocean for bonito, wahoo, tuna, sailfish, and flying fish.

The People

Physical Traits

The racial characteristics of the Yapese are varied. Yapese infants display the dark purple blot at the base of the spine characteristic of the Mongoloid peoples of Asia. Hair texture varies from kinky to wavy and straight, and hair color is dark brown or black. Skin color is brown, with some degree of variation in shade between individuals. The same is true of facial traits: some individuals have the high nasal bridges, thin lips, and very hairy faces characteristic of caucasoid groups; others have the relatively flat noses, everted lips, and flaring nostrils of the Melanesians. Stature is generally short, but varies considerably from area to area. In terms of visible characteristics, then, the Yapese seem highly varied and do not fit any one classification. Jane Hainline's forthcoming analysis of Yapese blood serology should provide some interesting insights into Yapese racial classification.

The mixture of racial groups in Yap is considered unusual in Micronesia. Yapese tales tell of people arriving in Yap from as far away as Polynesia and from Indonesia. Trips were commonly made from Yap to Palau, or to the Marianas, or east to the islands in the Central and Eastern Carolines. Other peoples surely made trips in the direction of Yap and settled there. Thus, people from all over Oceania are likely represented in the Yapese gene pool.

The cultural "appearance" of modern Yapese varies almost as much as their physical appearance. Many Yapese still wear a modern form of the traditional dress: men in loincloths and women in grass skirts. Others prefer Western-style clothes and are rarely, if ever, seen in traditional dress. Almost all Yapese, however, still chew betel nut and carry the traditional betel nut basket. Besides the narcotic effects obtained, chewing betel nut serves as a social institution that provides a well-defined means of social discourse and interaction.

Demography

The population of Yap at the time of the research, by municipality, is listed in Table 2. Perhaps the most interesting aspect of population on Yap is the reversal of the dramatic population decline (see Table 3) observed in the study of 1947–1948 (Hunt et al. 1949).

Schneider (1955) and Mahoney (1958) estimate the maximum population of Yap at about 50,000 people, based on a count of house foundations in the Rumung and Delipebinaw areas, and using an average of four persons per household. This estimate would place the population density at 1,300 persons per square mile, which is not impossible given current figures from some other Micronesian islands. However, since much of Yapese land has limited value these figures signify that in the not too distant past the Yap Islands were overpopulated. The culture had adapted itself to this condition of intensive population, and was organized politically and socially to operate with

Table 2. Yap Population, 1968

Municipality	Total Population	Male	Female
Delipebinaw	333	171	162
Fanif	495	251	244
Gagil	544	288	256
Gilman	185	104	81
Kanfay	234	132	102
Map	430	228	202
Rull	769	424	345
Rumung	190	93	97
Tamil	648	350	298
Weloy	427	221	206
TOTALS	4255	2262	1993

a large population base. (Present social values reflect these past conditions in which resources were extremely scarce and competition to obtain them intense.) Suddenly, however, the population base of Yapese social and political organization collapsed as epidemics and wars wiped out thousands of people in a relatively short period of time. By 1900 the Yapese numbered a little over 7,400, by 1946 only 2,582. In villages once teeming with people often not even enough families survived to provide one man for each position in the status hierarchy of village government. Thus, depopulation had a very far-reaching impact upon the human resources available for political activity.

Today, even with an increase in population, the human resources for traditional political endeavors are declining. One of the major factors is wage work and the concentration of people in the district center. Many people have moved into the town to work in government jobs or for economic enterprises. Others do not live in town, but commute by way of the network of unpaved roads and regular bus transportation. Many own automobiles or motor bikes. Thus, a large part of the labor force has gone off from the villages to other tasks. When weekends come and they return to the villages, they come to seek relaxation and drinking, not to engage in community projects.

With this change in orientation from the local village to the district center, traditional leadership is stripped of important authority and power. The problems of today—alcoholism, trespassing, modern roads, vehicles, money, and theft—all lie outside the sphere of traditional action. They are problems that accompany a mobile population undergoing a proliferation of new wants and dissatisfactions. New

Table 3. Population Variation, Yap, 1899–1968

Census Year	Governing Power	Total Population	Percent Change Per Year
1899	Spain	7,808	
1900	Germany	7,464	−4.4
1903	Germany	7,156	−1.4
1905	Germany	6,641	−3.7
1910	Germany	6,328	−1.0
1911	Germany	6,187	−3.8
1915	Japan	5,790	−1.6
1920	Japan	4,988	−3.0
1925	Japan	4,401	−2.5
1930	Japan	3,863	−2.6
1934	Japan	3,665	−1.3
1935	Japan	3,556	−3.0
1936	Japan	3,467	−2.4
1937	Japan	3,391	−2.3
1946	U.S.	2,582	−3.0
1947	U.S.	2,607	+1.0
1948	U.S.	2,625	+0.6
1949	U.S.	2,694	+2.4
1950	U.S.	2,720	+1.1
1951	U.S.	2,774	+1.9
1958	U.S.	3,176	+2.0
1961	U.S.	3,402	+2.4
1963	U.S.	3,508	+1.6
1966	U.S.	4,100	+5.6
1968	U.S.	4,255	+1.9
1973	U.S.	4,903	+3.0

NOTE:
  Data for the years 1899–1951 were adapted by the author from Hunt, Kidder, and Schneider 1954. Figures for the years 1952–1973 are from the Annual Reports to the United Nations on the Administration of the Trust Territory of the Pacific Islands.
  Trust Territory statistics are generally considered unreliable by scholars who have observed census procedures. I do not think Yap Islands statistics are as unreliable as those for Truk, Ponape, or the Marshalls. Communication on Yap is much better than in the outer islands of the district, so that census updating is more accurate. The figures present a problem, however, because immigrant Palauans are counted as Yapese. This may account for the extremely large increase in population from 1963–1966, as immigration from Palau jumped markedly after the completion of the Yap airstrip in 1962. The 1973 census figures distinguish for the first time Trust Territory citizens by home area from Trust Territory residents. These figures show 4,626 people citing the Yap Islands as their home area, as opposed to the 4,903 resident Trust Territory citizens.

methods of policing and control are required and the traditional leader is placed in a position of relative helplessness because the traditional ways cannot cope with the new problems. Population decline, wage work, and migration to town all have raised serious problems and at the same time have depleted the pool of support and labor necessary to maintain a viable traditional political system. Population, then, becomes an important ecological variable within the political field.

2. KINSHIP AND KINSHIP GROUPS

The Concept of Tabinaw

Tabinaw is the most basic concept in traditional Yapese leadership and sociopolitical organization. As an organizing principle for political and social relationships, it outlines reciprocal rights, obligations, and prestations between individuals of its various units. As defined in land, it assures continuity through time and a solid economic base in the community. As defined in kinship units, it provides for the exercise of authority and political succession.

Defining the nature of *tabinaw*, however, is exceedingly complex. In the Yapese language, the word *tabinaw* is used with different meanings or references. This might be fairly easily resolved were it not that the Yapese also combine these meanings with dual principles of patrilineal and matrilineal descent, and several types of kinship groups. Schneider has discussed *tabinaw* and the nature of its interpersonal relationships (1949, 1953, 1957a, 1962, 1967). The following material attempts to build upon his work in further refining the definition of basic elements and statuses within the *tabinaw* and showing their significance for Yapese leadership and political organization.

The Household or Nuclear Family

Tabinaw most commonly refers to the Yapese household. When a Yapese is asked for the location of his *tabinaw*, he cites his place of residence. When asked who stays at his *tabinaw*, he enumerates all those people who either sleep or eat at his household. The Yapese household, then, forms the elementary unit in the concept of *tabinaw*.

The household is generally composed of one nuclear family. In a complete census of Yap, 689 households were composed of nuclear families alone, while only 127 households could be classified as consisting of extended families. In 82 of the extended households a very old parent or relative, no longer able to care for himself, had children living with him to care for him. In the other cases, particular reasons were given as to why they were residing in such a manner at that particular time. (See Table 4.)

Table 4. Composition of Households by Municipality

Municipality	Nuclear Family	Old Person and Nuclear Family	Two or more Nuclear Families
Rumung	31	2	2
Map	65	7	0
Gagil	76	3	7
Tamil	79	12	6
Fanif	48	9	6
Weloy	32	4	2
Colonia*	99	11	7
Rull	155	18	8
Delipebinaw	27	7	3
Kanfay	44	5	3
Gilman	33	4	1
TOTALS	689	82	45

* Port town crossing two municipal boundaries.

In some cases a relative or close friend of one of the parents of the nuclear family lives within a household. The individual is likely to be in an unfortunate situation and has requested the help of the family for some time. If the arrangement is satisfactory to all involved it could last for a long period. However, if conflict develops, the arrangement is quickly terminated.

The primary referent of the word *tabinaw*, then, is the household, and, more precisely, the nuclear family unit comprising the household. The literal translation of the word *tabinaw* is 'one land', and the nuclear family is defined as 'people of one land', or *girdien e tabinaw*. This definition of the family reflects Yapese thinking with regard to economic resources and cooperation. Each nuclear family unit should have its own house and land for food production. In the daily routine of life, each household is independent, performing all necessary social and economic functions required for sustaining life and providing for the production, nurture, and socialization of its children. The members of the household view their relationships in terms of differential rights to the land and its produce and differential responsibilities for food production and for the nurture of the members of the group. The primary distinctions are those of age and sex, and they are clearly outlined in the spacial arrangements of the household site.

The traditional Yapese house is divided into two sections by a long log running the full length of the house. (See Figure 6.) The back side, called *tabgul* 'place of origins', is taboo and is reserved for the father or head of the household. In this area the father sleeps, stores his valuables, and deposits the sacred things for prayer to the ancestors. Women and children stay out of this section of the house unless sent there for some particular purpose.

The wife and small children sleep in the front side of the house. This side and the area around it, referred to as *to'or* 'place of many', is generally open to any member of the family. Certain restrictions do apply to low-caste visitors and to young girls who have just begun menstruation and puberty. Outsiders generally are not brought into the house, which is used mainly for sleeping and storage. Children move out of the main house when they are about ten; young boys sleep in the young men's house of the village, while young girls sleep in an adjacent cookhouse or a separate room in the main house.

At each end of the main house, a small veranda opens under the main roof. The veranda at the rear of the house, called *pe'na'un*, is taboo for women and chldren. This is usually a storage area or cooking place for old men. It is used only when aged men are visiting and have occasion to sit under the roof. The front veranda of the house, known as the *gathith*, is the family sitting area in the evening and in rainy weather. The *gathith* is divided into taboo and public sides, with the taboo side reserved for the man of the house and older male guests. This area is especially taboo for girls of menstruating age and women who have not yet passed menopause. When food is brought to the household for the man of the house, it is placed in this area as a sign of respect for him. On this same side, and in the front, stands a large stone platform, on which fish, food, or betel nut for the men are placed on ceremonial occasions or family celebrations. On the platform of high-ranking households, a smaller table called *rarow* is used for the distribution of fish and betel nut to high-ranking guests.

The back end of the house and the taboo side may have an area

Figure 6. Yap Household Ground Plans

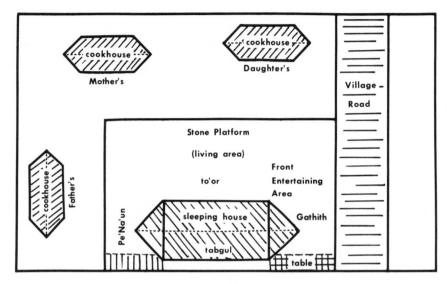

Traditional Household Ground Plan

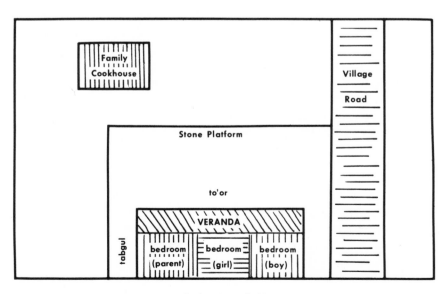

Modern Household

that is *macmac* 'supernaturally dangerous', used for making magic and growing plants for magic and medicine. These areas should be avoided at all times by all people except the practitioner of magic and medicine. Certain magicians build their houses in the midst of such an area and live alone in their sacred place.

The front end and the side of the house make up the general living area. A stone platform usually surrounds the house, and stone backrests for the comfort of the guests are placed at intervals around its edge. Again the taboo side of the platform is reserved for older men and often the backrests on this side are of upright Yapese stone money. In the daily routine, women and children of the family confine their activities to the public side of the platform and just off that platform in the cooking areas. Men, if around the house during the day, may move into any of the areas.

Most Yapese today build their houses of lumber, corrugated metal, and even cement block. These new homes are built according to the same ground plan as the traditional houses. The major change has been in the house design, which has been adapted to modern materials. Most new houses are built in a rectangular design with several rooms opening onto a long veranda, which runs the full length of the public side of the house. The various rooms provide separate sleeping quarters for the parents and the older children. The taboo area is redefined to include the section of the veranda and the house to the rear of the household plot. Parents generally take the room at the back end of the house.

Cooking in the traditional household is done in separate cooking houses apart from the main house. The head of the household has his own cookhouse and cooking utensils. His food is prepared apart from that of the other members of the household, and he eats alone or with some other male of his approximate age. The wife and the mother of the family has her separate cookhouse in which she cooks for herself and her young children. A daughter who has reached the age of puberty and has returned after two years of separation at the community menstrual house will have a separate cookhouse in which she sleeps and prepares her own food, apart from her mother and brothers. If for some reason an old man or woman is staying in the household, he has his separate cookhouse and often sleeps there. It will be located in the rear section of the household plot and as far as possible from the young girl.

Food resources also are separated in the same manner as are the cooking areas. The head of the household gets food from gardens and taro patches set aside for his use. He chews betel nut from trees set aside particularly for him. Even scarce items such as breadfruit, chestnuts, bananas, and other fruits are grown separately for him. Fish and other meat resources are divided among the family with first choice going to the male head of the household; the mother then sets aside the portion for herself and her children. Mother and children, with the exception of the menstruating teenager, obtain food resources from the same areas. Certain gardens and trees are set aside for her use and she may not go and take food from her mother's gardens. However, the mother may "throw away" food to her daughter if she so pleases. Betel nut and coconut trees are set aside for her use, if the household has enough. In the case of the household where an old relative lives with the nuclear family, his food is also obtained from separate plots, cooked in separate pots, and eaten apart from the other members of the household.

Thus, individuals are distinguished according to age, sex, and kinship status in the family and are accordingly given access to food resources and space in the household. Primary food and space resources go first to the oldest males, then to the oldest females, and on down through the hierarchy of the family. The statuses within the household will be more clearly defined and discussed later (Chapters 2 and 3) through an analysis of the kinship structure and the respective authority and responsibilities distributed within it.

It should be noted that today the restrictions on cooking and food sources are followed by less than 30 percent of the households on Yap. Most households that maintain the restrictions have older members who demand their observance. Younger families, particularly those who have commitments to wage work and the new cash economy, find these restrictions cumbersome and quietly disregard them. The effect of these changes on status relationships within the family has not yet become apparent.

The Estate and Patriclan

The household or nuclear family is the primary unit in the Yapese *tabinaw*, but quite often it is not the exclusive unit. Instead, several households may live on lands belonging to a single, named house site. Schneider (1967) has referred to these associated land parcels as an estate.

The Yapese estate may consist of several nonlocalized house and garden plots, parcels of taro patches, sections of lagoon for fishing, and ideally includes all important resources. The Yapese consider these associated land and sea resources as a single unit centered around a stone house foundation on the main house site of the estate. This stone foundation is called *kengin e dayif* 'central foundation'. It is extremely important because within it reside the ancestral spirits who have lived on the land, to whom the members of the group pray, from whom children come, and after whom parents name children. The central foundation is also the seat of all authority and political rights that by definition belong to that estate. This is especially significant in a study of leadership because titles and authority in the village are vested in particular central foundations, and not in individuals. Individual members of the estate are said to stand upon the foundation and speak for its authority. Individuals step down and die and other individuals take their places, but the authority remains in the foundation.

The other lands of an estate are called *binauan e kengin e dayif* 'lands possessed by the central foundation'. Frequently these lands contain stone foundations used by the junior households in the estate. These stone foundations are without power or authority and are subordinate to the central foundation. Lands without foundations are distributed among members of the estate group for use in food production.

In referring to the estate, Yapese use the same word that described the household, *tabinaw*. All people who live on the estate and hold rights to the land are referred to as *girdien e tabinaw* 'people of one land'. The use of identical terms for the household units and the estate units reflects the fundamental thinking of the Yapese about the nature of these groups. The relationships of individuals are seen in terms of the mutual exploitation of certain valued resources and the reciprocal obligations of cooperation and sharing. The unity of the group is defined in terms of rights to the resource unit.

Membership in the estate group for males is determined through their names, which are selected from a pool of ancestral names. Certain names belong to each estate, and, by merit of possessing a name, one possesses legal title to estate land. These names are passed patrilineally from fathers to sons. Females are also named after ancestors from the estate, but a female name does not belong to the land, nor does it confer title to it. Female membership in an estate group is determined by residence. When she resides in her estate of birth, she is a member there. When she marries, she moves to her husband's estate in patrilocal residence and becomes a member there. Following Murdock (1949), the estate group may be defined as a minimal patri-clan.

Distribution of resources among members of the estate varies according to the composition of the group. In the simplest situation only one nuclear family or household comprises the whole estate group. Thus no distribution is necessary, except as noted previously in the discussion of the household.

In the situation of father and married sons, the father resides on the most important land, the central foundation. Sons receive a minor stone foundation for their house, and food resources of all types are set aside for each of them. The ideal is that each nuclear family should have its own land. The reason offered is that the wives work the land, making gardens and taro patches. If they work on the same plots disputes are certain to arise, but if they each have their own, then family harmony will be maintained. In contrast, sea resources are shared among brothers who exploit them together. Harmony among the males of the estate is required and to a certain extent assured because of their consanguineal bonds. Also, Yapese fishing methods require both cooperation and sharing of the catch, which frequently more than one household will consume. Only minor sea resources, such as sites for small fish traps, are divided among households.

When the father of the patriclan dies, his sons inherit the land. The majority of land in Yap is passed on in this fashion. Usually before his death, the father discusses with his sons the distribution of the land. Generally, the oldest son is given the central foundation, the land with the authority and rank, and other food-resource lands to go with it. He will inherit most of the land used by his father, but must wait a period of one year until a taboo called *liw* is removed from that land. Younger brothers are given fair shares of the estate's resources and land on which to live. In the case of the younger brothers, certain particular authorities may be given by the father to the house foundations on which they reside; for example, rights to serfs, certain fishing rights, or a particular village responsibility. Each son is entitled to a fair share of the estate's resources.

In the case of estates including married brothers and their married sons, the land will again be passed from father to son. Thus, the central foundation of the eldest brother will be passed on to his eldest son. Lands of his household will be divided among his sons only, and his younger brothers will in turn pass on their household lands and authority to their sons, respectively. Thus, with the dividing of the land comes the dividing of the estate, and the forming of new central foundations. What originally was one estate ultimately becomes two, three, or as many as there are brothers with sons to whom they will pass their household's land. The division of estates is gradual, almost unnoticed; unless land is disputed, it occurs without rancor. The division occurs as a result of the development cycle of the family units through time and the nuclear family unit as the ideal for Yapese households. The latter requires a constant division and subdivision of land to provide each new household with separate resources. At the same time, leadership of the group becomes diffused through the death of the father, until the brothers assert themselves as leaders of their own incipient

clan units. Upon the death of all the brothers of an estate, their respective sons will be established in distinctive patriclans, breaking land
resources into separate estates.

The pattern of leadership as seen in land distribution in the patriclan shows the father to son, older brother to younger brother hierarchy. It should not be assumed, however, that this is an immutable
rule. A son receives land from his father as a reward for his faithful
and obedient service to him. If he shows respect to his father, cares
for him in his old age, and obeys him as a proper son, he will receive
his entitled land. However, if he is disobedient and disrespectful, and
does not provide for his father, regardless of his age and rank among
his brothers, he may receive little or no land. On the other hand, a
man can give his land to *anyone* who does care for him, show him
respect, and generally look out for his welfare. The person need not
be a son or even a relative. In this way children from a family that is
destitute may go about obtaining more land.

Females do not hold title to estates. Rather, they are said to "own
the land under their foot" meaning that in reality they possess the land
of their husbands and in bearing children they are able to pass that
land on to their children. Female names, like the women that hold
them, pass from one estate to another. A woman becomes a member
of an estate at marriage and her name becomes incorporated into the
estate names when she bears children. She will be venerated by her
children when she dies and her name will be passed on as one from
that estate, or *tabinaw*. A marriage that does not produce children,
either by birth or adoption, does not bring a new female name into the
tabinaw. The woman at death does not join the ancestral ghosts of that
estate unless she has cared for and nurtured the children of the patriclan. Her ghost would instead remain in the estate of her father.

Daughters, then, do not normally inherit the clan estate. However,
the estate *is* designated *tafen e bitir* 'possession of the children'. The
ideal rule is that male children of the patriclan inherit the estate, but
should the group have only daughters available for succession, then
the oldest girl is said to become like a man, and she may inherit the
land. Because of depopulation, large numbers of estates have gone
without heirs and the holdings of men and women have increased far
out of proportion to aboriginal expectations. The woman without
estate brothers receives land from her father and then in turn passes it
to her children. This is called *binau ni thuth* 'land in lieu of the
mother's breast'. Such a woman would be an excellent mate for a man
who wants to increase his landholdings for his children. Most often a
son of this woman will be named after her father, bestowing upon him
title to the land. When a woman does not inherit the land because she

has brothers, she may be given a small piece of land, one taro plot and one garden plot for subsistence in case she divorces her husband. A sister cannot live in the same household with her sexually mature brother after her first menstruation, thus, when she returns to the family, she resides on her own separate plot. This land is *binau ni giliungin* 'a place to put her grass skirt' when she returns to her estate of birth.

During the period of expanding population in Yap's history, land was constantly divided and subdivided among sons, as is made graphic to anyone today who tries to plot land distribution and ownership. Any sizeable plot of land on Yap is divided among many owners, with such boundaries as hedgerows, trees, or a particular bush. Because of this subdivision, many more land estates exist today than there are individual households to fill them. Many of these estates have been inherited by females and subsequently passed on to their children. As a result, one clan or household may hold as many as seven or eight estates, and some even more. In this case land from the estates will be parceled out to the separate sons, with the oldest receiving the highest-ranking estate. The example from the village of Wonyan in Tables 5 and 6 demonstrates this clearly.

The tables also clearly illustrate present-day Yapese preference for filling the extra existing estates held by the clan rather than dividing the main clan estate. Sons in the patriclan are given names belonging to extinct clan estates and in so doing the estate units are reestablished. This is becoming an increasingly common practice as the population of Yap continues to grow.

The primary functions of the patriclan are political. Rank, title, and authority assignments in the village and in Yap-wide political structures are conferred on individuals by merit of their membership in an estate group. Each estate is assigned certain responsibilities and must mobilize its economic and social resources in support of the economic, political, and ceremonial activities of the village. The patriclans compete with each other in these village activities and also in interclan activities. Each patriclan is accountable to the village for the behavior of its members.

The internal organization of the estate is more loosely structured than that of the household. The group is mobilized as a unit only when outside demands are made upon it, or when any individual household requires assistance in completing a task. The oldest male member of the estate is recognized as its leader and he coordinates activities that involve all households and members of the patriclan. Such activities would include the observation of certain life crises of clan members and large-scale economic activities such as house-building or the development of new agricultural resources. The clans are exogamous and social control among the members is maintained through social, economic, and ritual sanctions.

The Patrilineage

When a Yapese says *girdien e tabinaw* 'people of one land' he frequently includes not only the legal members of his land estate or patriclan, but also other kinsmen to whom he traces relationship by a known common male ancestor. The land estate is referred to as *barba'macaf* 'one portion of Yapese money'. Yapese brothers and their sons may hold title to several of these estates individually, but for use rights, they divide the land among themselves as they see fit. The case cited in Tables 5 and 6 of brothers from the village of Wonyan serves as an example.

All members of this group (see Figure 7) are related to two deceased brothers from the land estate called Riyeleb. Three of the five male children of these brothers were named from the estate Riyeleb. One was given a name from his mother's estate of birth, Nifara', which she received because she had no brothers, and the last was adopted into an estate in the next village of Gacpar. Three of these five men had sons, one of which was named from a fourth estate called Arcaey. Thus we find a group of kinsmen, whose names "legally" separate them into four different land estates, who nevertheless recognize themselves as people of one land. Informants stated clearly that those whose names come from land estates other than Riyeleb are not members of the Riyeleb estate group, but all are considered to have succession rights

Figure 7. Title and Genealogical Relationships of Men
from Riyeleb Estate, Wonyan

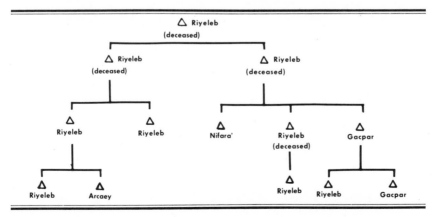

Table 5. Estates Held by Sons of Riyeleb/Godbiyel Clan Estate, Wonyan Village

| Sons | Wonyan Village | | RikenVillage | Gacpar Village | |
	Titled Estates	Nontitled Estates	Nontitled Estates	Titled Estates	Nontitled Estates
Oldest	Riyeleb/ Godbiyel	Fiten'ey	Gilminay Talal Tungthal	Numruy/ Mowal	Utunngal
Second		Arcaey	Anaeth		
Third		Nifara' Ool	Falic Bayumuc Tungunuw		
Youngest		Fanorul			Several estates from adopted parents
Son of oldest		Dulkan	Several estates from mother		

Table 6. Land Use of Riyeleb/Godbiyel Estate, Wonyan Village

| Type of Land | Plot Distribution | | | | |
| | Son | | | | |
	1	2	3	4	5
Titled Foundations	2	—	—	—	—
Other Foundations	2	1	—	1	1
Taro Lands	13	1	9	—	3
Garden Lands	4	—	1	—	6
Coconut Lands	1	1	1	1	1
Sea Rights	1	—	—	—	—

NOTE:
Sons are coded as follows: 1 is oldest son; 2 is second son; 3 is third son; 4 is youngest son; 5 is son of oldest son.

to the political power invested in Riyeleb and all share rights of access to the resources of the group's combined estates, including those obtained through their mothers. They collectively hold seven estates in Wonyan, several estates in Gacpar, and several in the adjacent village of Riken. The resources of these various estates are not held as distinctive units, but are scattered among the whole group as their needs require. Only the rights of the man adopted into the village of Gacpar were limited because his adoption, arranged before his birth, affiliated him with the estate of his adoptive parents, not his biological parents. However, adoption does not sever the relationship with the biological parents as much as it reinforces a distant kin tie between them and the adoptive parents. In this case the adoptive parents died when the child was young and he returned to live with his biological parents. His brothers recognize him as a kinsman and share family resources with him. One of his sons has been named after his biological father from Riyeleb and the other son after his adoptive father, thus claiming the estate in Gacpar into which he was adopted.

It is obvious then that the Yapese recognize a group of patrilineal kinsmen larger than the limits of the patriclan. This larger group may be defined as a patrilineage. Members of a patrilineage include kinsmen from a number of patriclans who can trace their relationship to a common male ancestor. Because this kinship tie extends beyond the legal boundaries of the land, the members of the lineage hold residual rights in their respective estates and frequently share resources and political power among the group. This is true through second, third, and fourth generations from the founder of the lineage. If serious disputes arise among members of a lineage, individuals may begin to claim all land to which their name entitles them and to evict those who lack legal rights of access to it. This kind of breach in solidarity is considered very serious and occurs very rarely.

Women born into a patrilineage are always members of that group by kinship. This contrasts to the patriclan where a woman's membership is only temporary, depending upon residence and the duration of her marriage. Female membership in the land estate of her birth is suspended at marriage, but her kinship relationship to her brothers and lineage is never suspended. She actively works for the good of the land estate of her husband, and specifically does not work for the good of the land estate of her birth. She may, however, on special occasions be called upon by a brother to render assistance as a member of his lineage.

The patrilineage is a social unit, a group of consanguineal kinsmen, while the patriclan is primarily a political and economic unit. The functions of the patrilineage are to provide support for the estate and the patriclan and to provide for succession to leadership and the exercising of authority assigned to the titles of an estate. The patrilineage plays a role in succession to leadership status primarily because of the age requirements for leadership. A young man is considered irresponsible and incapable of leading a clan. He cannot command respect nor would he desire to do so in a council consisting of older men. If he should fall heir to the leadership of his clan before reaching his old age, another old man in his lineage will act in his stead. The nature of leadership and leadership succession will be discussed in detail in chapter 4.

Finally, patrilineal relationships are extended as far as claims to land and authority can be advantageously remembered. Genealogical claims to titled land held seven or eight generations previous may be remembered by individuals, while claims to minor land may not be remembered beyond four generations. In any case, on the father's side, relatives three or four generations back are remembered because marriage to them is considered incestuous.

In his analysis of Yapese kinship (1953, 1957a, 1962, 1967), Schneider fails to distinguish between the patrilineage and the patriclan. Part of the difficulty arises from the seemingly contradictory statements by Yapese centering around the word *tabinaw*. In one breath the informant will say that so and so is *girdien e tabinaw* and then in the next he will state that they have different *tabinaw* and name the estate of the individual in question. Only after intensive questioning on the nature of relationships between individuals and their mutual rights and responsibilities do the distinctions emerge. The phrase *girdien e tabinaw* is used interchangeably for people of the household, the estate, the patrilineage, and generally for all relatives. The word *tabinaw* is used interchangeably for the household site and the land estate. When a Yapese uses these words and phrases in context, he has no difficulty determining the reference or meaning. It is the anthropologists who are invariably confused.

Müller's informants (Müller 1917) referred to the patrilineage as *bu'um e girdi*. Translated literally this means a 'group of people', and present-day informants say it may be used for any kind of group. However, it is frequently used in reference to patrilineal kinsmen. Müller failed to recognize the patriclan as an important political unit.

The Genung or Matrisib

The Sib

The second principle of kinship and social organization in Yap is that of the *genung* or the matrilineal sib. The matrisibs are named, exogamous, nonlocalized, totemic kin groups. Each sib has an origin myth and a specific place of origin located in Yap. A child is born into the sib of his mother. He is considered to belong to her *genung* because he came out of her belly. Members of each sib refer to each other as *tab ka girdi*, 'one branchy tree of the people'.

There are many clues that the sibs were once corporate, land-holding groups. Today, however, the sibs lack any formal organization and leadership and play only a minor role in the social organization of Yap. In terms of leadership, the sib is important for two of the highest-ranking titled estates in Yap. These estates are considered *tafen e genung* or land estates owned and passed from one sib member to another. They are unique, however, in the normal configuration of Yapese politics and are not representative of the pattern of ownership and succession. Certain sibs also maintain residual rights to particular land parcels, but this is not widespread.

Schneider's assertion (1962) that the seven sacred places connected with the origin myth of the Yapese are of clan origin and owned by clans is in error. None of these places are "owned" by people and only one of them (Tamil municipality) is cared for by a matrisib. In the latter case, the relationship of the sib to the sacred place is mythologically separate from the origin myth.

The weakness of the sib is seen most clearly in the fact that not all sib members are regarded as "kinsmen." Only those sib mates to whom relationships can be traced are considered as relatives (*girdirom* 'your people'). It is only these members of the sib to whom kinship terms are extended.

The Subsib

The subsib is an unnamed, exogamous, nonlocalized group of matrilineal kinsmen who hold membership in a common sib and who have a known genealogical relationship, ideally through seven generations above ego. Members of a subsib are distinguished from non-members by their mutual extension of kinship terminology to each other, and by the reference of outsiders to them as *bu'um e wolag* 'a group of siblings'.

The subsib is much more important in Yap social organization than is the sib. Schneider states that "the essence of matrilineal kinship on Yap is that of solidarity and loyalty . . ." (1962:21). In fact this is much more characteristic of the subsib (which is unspecified in Schneider's analysis) than of the sib. Distant sib relationships without any known kinship tie place little or no obligation on the people involved. Because the name of one's sib is not publicly discussed, nor known outside of one's locality, unknown relationships are not likely to be discovered. Should two individuals discover that they are members of a common sib, they are not obligated to incorporate themselves into one subsib or to accept each other as a relative. If on the other hand a relationship can be traced, the individuals will take steps to reinforce the kinship bond and to reestablish a fading relationship.

While membership in the sib extends without reference to village rank or landed/landless caste distinctions, the membership of the subsib tends to fall into general caste and class boundaries. This is caused by the practice of marrying within caste lines, as in marriages between villages of equal or adjacent rank. Marriages across caste lines are prohibited because they would break down the reciprocal obligations of class and caste observed through the ties of solidarity and support expected of members of the subsib.

Exogamy in the subsib is absolutely required and breaches of this rule are considered equal to incest in the nuclear family. In cases of incest within the nuclear family, marriage is out of the question and the participants are made to feel great shame. Partners in a marriage between sib members are believed to be punished by ancestral ghosts who will assure that all of the woman's children are boys with the result that her sib line will die out.

The primary function of the subsib is to support its members in the major life crises of marriage and death by providing economic and moral support. On these occasions, a particular old man will be recognized as the leader of the gathered members and in the distribution of goods he will receive a special gift. Leadership is determined by age and genealogical distance from the member of the subsib being honored or supported.

Members of a subsib also are expected to support each other in any need expressed by a fellow member. This support is given without stipulated reciprocity and may include loaning important property, donating valuables, assisting in a work project, or providing refuge for a kinsman in trouble. The essence of the subsib relationship is the provision of mutual support for all its members. Schneider notes that "this relationship is structurally identical with that which is defined as proper for a Yap mother and her child. A child respects and obeys his father because of what the father does for him; a child loves his mother, on Yap, and a mother loves her child and what she does for the child she does without generating the formally defined and explicit obligation to reciprocate." (1962:23)

The Kindred

For Yapese, kinship defines the most important social obligations and interests for the individual. Any prolonged and intensive social relationship is defined in terms of kinship, so that individual friends without a biological relationship may become fictional relatives. General ties of kinship are extended bilaterally through males and females, and include all individuals to whom any relationship can be remembered. It is not necessary that the exact genealogical relationship be traced. Therefore the boundaries of the unit are variable, depending upon the desire of individuals to carry on or forget distant relationships. (Ideally ego should know all collateral relatives up through the third ascending generation.) Individuals who share known relationships are referred to as *girdien e tabinaw*, and form an ego-centered kindred. Friends who are fictional kinsmen are not normally subsumed under this label, but are referred to as *girdirog* 'my people'. This latter term may be used for any individual to whom one wishes to express a real or fictive relationship.

The kindred relationship expresses Yapese interest in reinforcing and expanding their network of kinsmen. When occasion permits, distant kinship ties, through both males and females, are reinforced by making and responding to demands. Refusal of demands is considered a breach of relationship unless accompanied by a very good reason and such refusals may dissolve a relationship, even between close kinsmen. A politically astute Yapese will use every opportunity to reinforce his existing kin ties and to expand them when possible.

The kindred constitute an ego-centered support group in contrast to the patrilineage and the matrilineal subsib. The only occasion on which all members of an individual's kindred are expected to appear is his funeral. Each member comes to pay his last respects and, perhaps more importantly, to identify himself as a kinsman. An appropriate gift (cigarettes, money, or burial goods) is given to the children or family of the deceased. The gift and the giver are then publicly announced to all present. This is a public declaration of relationship, not only to the deceased, but to his children and siblings. Should a distant relative fail to appear without notifying the children of the deceased, he is signaling the end of their mutual kinship ties. Members of the kindreds of the deceased's patriclan also appear and bring gifts expressing their support.

The kindred is also important in any situation in which an individual and the members of his patriclan need to call upon their most extensive resources. This includes such ceremonial occasions as the marriage exchange, in which all relatives not members of the clan may be invited to contribute to the collection and share in the distribution. Distant relatives who wish at this time to reinforce their relationship give extra large amounts.

Adoption

Yapese informants noted three legitimate ways to have children: through pregnancy and childbirth (*fak e diyen*), by adopting a child from someone else (*fak e tefenay*), and by acquiring a child with one's wife at marriage (*fak e gilab*). The most momentous of these is the decision to ask to adopt someone else's child. Children by pregnancy or marriage just happen, but one must think about and decide to adopt a child. Yapese feel that such a decision entails great responsibility and the child in question should be considered first before any other children in the household.

Two channels exist for adopting children. A couple or person desiring a child may request a yet-to-be-born child from a distantly related or unrelated family. This is called *pof* 'the plucking of a leaf', which signifies the taking of a child from the fringes of one's kinship relations. The second channel is to select for adoption a child of a close relative. This may be done before or after the birth of the child and is accomplished with less formality. This method of adoption is referred to as *cowiy*, which signifies the taking of a child close to the core of one's kinship relations.

Pof adoption is generally arranged a few months before the birth of the child. The adoptive parents bring Yapese valuables (*macaf*) to the parents of the child and the head of the child's patriclan. The amount and kind of valuables given depend upon the rank of the family and the child. The clan head offers valuables to the clan's ancestral ghosts to ensure that they will not be angry and that the child will have a long life. The clan head then discusses the impending adoption with the senior, matrilineal relative of his deceased father, called *mafen*, who is empowered to approve or disapprove such decisions. If the *mafen* is agreeable, the matter is settled.

After the child has passed the critical postnatal period, the adoptive parents go to the home of the biological parents, at which time they are entertained and the biological father presents the child to the adoptive father. Frequently a piece of land is given by the biological to the adoptive parents to insure that the child will inherit the land of his new patriclan. This land is called *binau ni bid* 'land for wiping' (Defngin 1966), in reference to the fact that the adoptive parents will be troubled with cleaning up the feces of the child and asking their forbearance. The kin relationship between the two families is strengthened by the adoption, so that the parents establish a sibling relationship.

Cowiy adoption between close relatives is less formal. The arrangements may be made after the birth of the child and valuables need not be exchanged. The child may live with his adoptive parents, or he may remain with his biological parents, or he may alternate living with either. This contrasts with the *pof* arrangement in which the child is not told of his adoption until he reaches adulthood. However, adoption of both types is always out of the estate and clan of birth and into new ones.

The primary motive for a childless couple to adopt is to obtain heirs who will care for them in their old age. The adopted child is given a name from the ancestral spirits of the new estate and full status as a child of the adoptive father and mother. He is also considered an equal sibling with any other child born or adopted into that patriclan. Rules of age and rank in the clan follow without regard to adoption. At the same time an adopted child loses rights in his estate of birth. He may not inherit land from that estate unless all other legitimate heirs die. If he should choose to return to his estate of birth, and he may, he must forfeit his rights in his estate of adoption. Any child, born or adopted into an estate, must obey his adoptive father and care for him in his old age or face possible disinheritance.

It is obviously advantageous for a large family to give up some children in adoption, and in fact the advantages, as in the prospect of providing additional land for one's children, form one of the primary incentives for doing so. However, if the initiative for adoption begins with the biological parents, they usually approach close relatives, for to propose the adoption of one's child to a distant or nonrelative is to *oginag e bitir* 'throw him away', which is not respectable. Another reason for adoption today is to alleviate pressure on a household of too many children. A child may be given to relatives either as an adoptive or foster child. Finally, one may arrange an adoption to reestablish a kinship relationship that has nearly died out. Relationships between patriclans and between parents who have both biological and adoptive children have been reinforced in this way. The gift of a child is considered so valuable that it is not repayable. The recipient incurs a lifetime obligation to the giver; he in fact becomes a sibling of the giver, just as the child becomes a member of his family.

The kinship affiliation of an adopted child is considerably more complex than that of a nonadopted child. In most cases the adopted child lives in the household of his new parents. In all cases he is a member of their patriclan. At the level of lineage and sib, however, the child belongs to the patrilineages of both his adoptive and biological father and to the matrisibs and subsibs of his adoptive and biological mother. When the child reaches young adulthood he is told of his adoption and his affiliation with the groups of his biological parents. He is instructed to observe incest prohibitions for both sets of lineage and sib. If he lives in close proximity he will actively participate in the activities of both patrilineages and subsibs. Should a conflict of interest develop, however, his strongest ties are to his adoptive parents and their kin groups.

In his limited treatment of the *pof* type of adoption, Schneider (1949, 1953, 1962) notes that adopted children inherit the sib affiliation, totem, and eating prohibitions of both their biological and adoptive mothers. The rule of exogamy is also extended for both sibs. Schneider observes correctly that when an adopted female bears children, she will pass on only the sib affiliation of her adoptive mother. However, he fails to note that the child of an adoptive mother will still recognize members of both subsibs as kinsmen and observe subsib exogamy. It should be reemphasized that the effect of adoption is not to cut off relationships, but to reinforce and extend them for both the parents and the children.

Cases of Adoption

This complex affiliation may be illustrated by the example of one household from the village of Okaw. The parents have given four children in adoption, two by *pof* and two by *cowiy*. The oldest adopted (*pof*) child is male and lives with his adoptive parents. He is twenty-four years old and has known his biological parents for about eight years. He was married recently and works at a regular job in the town of Colonia; his biological parents, who live near the town, provide him and his wife with a small house, which they use during the week. On weekends the couple returns to Okaw village, where they stay with his adoptive parents. During my stay on Yap I was able to observe three major life crises in the clan of his biological parents, and he participated in each as if he were their son. At the same time he carried on his responsibilities to his adoptive parents and kinsmen as if he were their son. When questioned, he stated unequivocally that he belongs to the patriclan of his adoptive father and not to the one of his biological father. His legal rights to land and title come from his clan of adoption, but his kinship obligations and duties, including incest taboos, come from all four parents. This is why he may inherit his biological father's estate should the other heirs die.

The second adopted child is a girl about eighteen years old. She was adopted (*cowiy*) at birth by her biological father's brother, who himself had been adopted into another clan estate. She lived with her biological parents until she was about five years old, and then went to live with her adoptive parents. Several years later the girl was left without a mother when the adoptive parents were divorced, and so she returned to live with her biological mother and father. Later the adoptive father remarried, but the new wife declined to keep the child. She remained with her biological parents and will do so until she marries. At the same time, she considers her adoptive father her legal parent.

The third adopted (*pof*) child is a male about twelve years old. He lives in another village and does not know his biological parents, nor does he know that he is adopted. On one occasion his biological brother and I talked to him and he was unaware of their relationship. He does not visit his biological family, nor do they visit him. The other members of the two families do assist each other informally and in the three major life crises noted above, the adoptive family brought substantial contributions to assist.

The fourth adopted (*cowiy*) child is a daughter about five years old. She was adopted by a close female relative, but until she was two she lived with her biological mother. Now she stays in her adoptive mother's home, but visits in her home of birth for a few days or even a few weeks at a time. She is aware of both sets of parents, who frequently interact socially.

Irregular Adoption and Fosterage

Irregular adoptions do occur. One type is called *gilab*, which is described as a child brought in on the grass skirt of his mother (*ke 'un u bungun e ong*). In this case a child, usually without a legal father, comes with his mother to an estate and patriclan into which she marries. To make this a genuine adoption, the clan must give the child a proper name from its pool of ancestral names; this act bestows upon the child legal membership and rights to inheritance.

This type of adoption, however, is precarious for the child. In many instances other children are born to the marriage and they may challenge the right to inherit of the adopted child. Where the rights of an adopted child may be open to question, the real parents or parent may move to prevent such a challenge by giving a large piece of stone money called *mo'of* to "anchor" or "nail him down" to his new estate and clan. With the combination of a name and *mo'of*, an individual's rights in an estate cannot be challenged. Some parents who have given children in *pof* adoption also give *mo'of* to ensure their child's security in his new estate.

Informants also cited cases in which a divorced wife and her family stole children from their rightful patriclan. These children were incorporated into the wife's estate of birth and given names by the head of that estate. The act of naming again provides the child legal rights to his adoptive estate, but the child's legal bond with his estate of birth, not having been properly dissolved, is still in force. When such children reach adulthood they face a complex set of alternatives, which inevitably leads to conflict and contested claims to loyalty and land.

Fosterage is also prevalent on Yap. This occurs when a child is placed in a household and estate other than that of his birth without adoption or the legal change of name. The most common incidence of fosterage occurs when women from a patrilineage are called upon by their brothers to care for children left without a mother through the death or divorce of a wife. These women generally are married and hold membership and residence in the patriclans of their husbands. It is thus that a woman and her husband may raise her brother's children, caring for them as would a mother and father, while the children maintain legal rights and obligations to the clan and estate of their father.

Another type of fosterage reported by informants is one arranged for women who marry into distant villages and estates. Marriage, ideally, is consummated between members of the same or adjacent villages. There are a number of practical reasons for this. A woman's parents are concerned that she be well treated in her new household and patriclan, and desire that she be close so that they may observe and assist her in difficult situations. Also, a wife's family and clan have certain duties and obligations with regard to the birth of her children, and the observation of life crises in her new household. Before the present-day road system was built, long distances made these things impossible. A solution to this problem was to create a foster relationship between the daughter and some not-too-distant relatives living near her new home. The foster family would treat her as their own child, care for her needs and on special ceremonial occasions arrange for her parents to be present. This relationship would be maintained for the duration of the daughter's stay in that area.

3. KINSHIP STATUSES, AUTHORITY, AND LEADERSHIP

Certain basic principles of primary significance must be recognized in the study of Yapese leadership. First, leadership occurs within the context of kinship groups, particularly the household, the patriclan, and the patrilineage. Second, rank and succession to leadership in these groups are generally defined as functions of generation, sex, and age. Third, leadership statuses are clearly identified in Yapese kinship terminology. Through the analysis of the kinship terms one is able to define more sharply the leadership statuses within the groups and their specific rights and duties.

It should be noted initially that Yap kinship terms are used almost exclusively in reference. All kinsmen without exception are addressed by their personal names. Small children may call their father and mother *papa* and *nina*, respectively, and on occasion they address grandparents by the proper kin term, but ordinarily personal names are used.

Kinship Statuses and Authority in the Household

As stated previously, the household basically comprises a nuclear family. The kinship terms of the nuclear family clearly separate statuses and define interpersonal relationships.

Citamngin is the father and head of the household. He provides the house, land resources, fish, and Yapese valuables for the members of the household. In the celebration of life crises, in disputes between members of his household and others in the patriclan, in questions of land use, in distribution of other resources, and in all matters external to the household, he is the leader and spokesman. Within the household he is the disciplinarian of the children, and he has particular responsibility with regard to their behavior to others outside the household. He is the director of all household affairs and teacher of important family knowledge, particularly with regard to land and the rights, privileges, and responsibilities of his particular household. In the traditional household, he is also spiritual head, leading the family in prayers to the ancestors, caring for family heirlooms, and observing ritual and taboo to insure happiness for the family. He exercises and teaches the children knowledge of medicine and magic beneficial to the group.

Only one person may fill this status as father and head of the household. However, that person may not necessarily be the biological father of the children. Schneider states that the relationships within the household are socially defined exchange relationships rather than biologically defined categories (1962:5). Thus the *citamngin* of the household may be the biological father, or if he is dead, an older male relative, or if the children are adopted, a biologically unrelated individual. In all cases the status of the position remains the same; its occupant is merely replaced from among a pool of relatives when the position is vacated by death (see Schneider 1953:224–235).

Citinngin is the mother and the second-ranking member of the household. She theoretically owns no land but instead works the land of her husband to provide food for him and for the children. She is in charge of all domestic responsibilities—making gardens, preparing food, cleaning the household, and making necessities such as baskets, grass skirts, and other personal items. She represents the family in all women's affairs, and exercises any rights and obligations entailed in the land of her husband. She also provides a political alliance with her lineage of birth and may call upon it for assistance at any time. She is called the strength of the family, and in fact acts as such, always caring for the children, teaching them, feeding them, working for the good and health of the family, watching out for household affairs when the husband is fishing, traveling, or drunk. She is especially responsible for the education of her daughters in all the customs and taboos of womanhood. As in the case of the father, only one person may occupy this status in the household; however, a pool of relatives may fill this position should it be vacated by death or divorce.

Figirngin is the status of husband, *le'engin* of wife. These again are socially defined exchange relationships. The husband gives to the wife land, names for her children, and title to his land; he provides the house, assistance in heavy work projects, and fish for the family food. The

Yapese divide food into two basic categories, *thum'ag* or fish and meats, and *gagan* or vegetable and garden products. The man is responsible for providing the fish and meat diet, the woman for the vegetable-starch diet. A meal without both types of food is considered improper; thus to feed the family the labor of both spouses is required. The wife is responsible for providing the garden products for all the family, so she cultivates the gardens and taro patches. She gathers the food and cooks it in the respective places for the members of the family. She bears children for the estate, and because their names and land come from the husband, if she leaves, the children remain with him. The husband and wife share affection and love, but the wife is expected to remain faithful, while the husband feels free to have affairs. If they have no children, these affairs likely will lead to divorce. Because the children belong to the husband, and the mother is usually reluctant to leave them, the children become a major factor in the durability of marriages. The wife always may return to her estate of birth and receive land for food from her brothers.

The husband and wife statuses each normally are occupied by only one person, but a man may have more than one wife, and thus two nuclear family households. Usually this second arrangement is the result of the levirate, when the husband takes care of his deceased brother's wife and family. This arrangement is considered quite proper and the first wife cannot complain about it. Schneider notes that the matter of a second wife can be taken up with the first, and if she agrees, then the husband can have two (1953:218). She rarely agrees, however, and then sometimes only to stay with her children, knowing that if she refuses and a divorce follows, she must leave them with her husband.

Fak or *bitirrok* is the status of the children in the household. The boy child is expected to run errands, assist in fishing, and generally help both mother and father. The father in turn cares for the son, providing him with all his necessities and generally meeting most requests. For this generosity the son is expected to render obedience, respect, and when his father is old, care for him as one would a child. All productive efforts of the son, in fishing, making money, and so forth, are to be brought and given to the father who then distributes them as he sees fit. A daughter in like manner is to show deference to her father. However, her assistance is largely rendered to her mother. Sons and daughters are expected to help the father first, then assist the mother when asked.

Both sons and daughters assist the mother in the gardens and in general household tasks. A daughter is worked especially hard from about the age of eight to twelve years, helping in the care of the younger children and learning all the work of the woman in the family. When she reaches puberty, she begins a life of relative ease in terms of household responsibilities. She becomes very concerned about love affairs and spends several irresponsible years until she marries. Because she is *ta'ay* 'very contaminating' due to the onset of menstruation, she cannot assist in work having to do with her father's or mother's food, and so she is freed from these burdens. In the past she would have spent much time in the "menstrual area," learning customs and having affairs with young men. Today she attends high school and begins her courting there.

Children are not only differentiated from their mother and father, but from each other. All children of a household refer to each other as *wolag* 'siblings'. The sibling relationship is very important, for it implies a number of statuses and explicit interpersonal relations. Generally it calls for mutual care, affection, and cooperation. More specifically, the kinship system designates a series of status responsibilities. *Wolag* are divided in the household according to relative age. The oldest sibling is referred to as *ngani*, the youngest is called *wain*, and all other siblings may refer to younger siblings as *tethin*. The oldest sibling may fill the role of father or mother in the household should the death of the parent require it.

The older children are called upon from adulthood to death to care for and assist their younger siblings. Each in turn is given the respect due his age, and, in some cases, if the father dies, the oldest brother may be referred to as *citamngin* 'father' by the youngest children. As *citamngin* he would care for his youngest siblings as though he were their father, and in fact, in Yapese terms he is their father. The oldest child is the recognized leader of all his siblings from birth until his death; if a girl, she will be recognized as the most important, but she will not be able to speak in men's affairs. Her oldest brother will take charge of the male affairs of the family. Girls are said to be the strength of the family, but their power is intermittent in duration, coming to the fore only in special family functions. Intermediate siblings are ranked according to age and given responsibility accordingly. The youngest child is last in line of responsibility, usually well cared for, and pampered by the older siblings. When they reach adulthood, older siblings have first rights to land and authority, subject to their age rank. Those designated the older siblings assume responsibility for the younger and have moderate authority over them.

Brothers and sisters are not distinguished in the kinship terminology. Boys may be addressed as *tam* by their parents, and girls *tin*, but no terms used by siblings distinguish boys from girls. However, the term *rugod* 'pubescent girl' distinguishes the sister when she begins menstruation and from that point on she must strictly avoid all brothers approaching puberty and older. She must always walk downwind from them so they do not smell her body. She should conduct her love affairs secretly, and her brothers should never see her with another boy. From this point on, personal interaction between brother and sister is limited to very short, businesslike encounters to discuss matters of importance to the family. Brothers may not sit and engage in general conversation with their sister present. If she is near she will sit some distance away where she cannot hear. If her brother is in a dance that is the least suggestive, the sister may not watch, even from a distance, and a similar taboo applies to him. In fact, women should not watch a men's dance except from a distance.

Tutuw and *titaw* are grandfather and grandmother, respectively, and *tungin* is grandchild. These statuses are sometimes found in the household if the grandparents are old and require the daily care of their son or daughter. The relationship between grandparent and grandchild is affectionate and friendly. Children often address the grandparents as *tutuw* or *titaw* and they in turn may be called *tungin* or *tam* or *tin* as they wish. This free use of kin terms is a sign of informality between the statuses. In contrast a child would rarely address his father by the term *citamag* 'my father', but would use instead the personal name. To use the kinship term would be overly familiar, not showing the respect due one's father, and therefore extremely impolite. The same is true for the mother. The only exception to this rule occurs when in a very unusual situation, one wishes to show intense respect for and dependence upon one's father. At this time the term *citamag* could be used.

In the household where the grandfather is present, he will in fact be the head or *citamngin*. To the grandchildren he will be *tutuw*, but to their father he will be the *citamngin*. The end result is that of having two nuclear families in the same household, with a linear line of authority. The household has two active *citamngin*, with the oldest or grandfather overseeing all important matters and decisions regarding the household.

If only the grandmother is present, then the son is the head of the household, but the grandmother is his *citinngin* or mother. Both the son and his wife show respect and care for the grandmother, and consult her in all important matters of the family. The son, however, is the acting authority figure in the household. In contrast to his relationship of respect, obedience, and silence with his father, the son's relationship with his mother is one of respect and confidence. Thus he may feel free to discuss problems with his mother, and then act. In the presence of the father, however, he is a child and must be silent unless questioned. The children of the son have the same easy, informal relationship with their grandmother that they have with their grandfather.

A grandfather living in the household is not only its head, but also the teacher of both son and grandchildren of the old stories and the esoteric knowledge of Yap. He also teaches the important matters of the clan estate and any magic and medicine that he may know. When a grandfather and grandmother live with their married children it is usually because they are too feeble to do their own work. They contribute both material objects made by hand and their wisdom to the daily work of the household.

There are two notable Yapese customs associated with this contribution of wisdom to members of the family. If a young boy catches fish and sets apart some of the catch especially for his grandfather or father, the recipient then teaches the boy some part of Yapese custom or wisdom as payment for the fish. This reward is called *towiyeg*. In the second custom, wisdom is given in payment for keeping a fire going for the old grandmother or grandfather who cannot move around. The fire provides them warmth and its youthful maker is rewarded with some parcel of Yapese wisdom, in an exchange called *tamaror*. If at some later date the youth finds occasion to use this information in the resolution of a dispute, he is certified as telling the truth because he has learned it through *towiyeg* or *tamaror*. According to informants, this claim can always be substantiated by a sibling of the aged person who will have heard from that person of the youth's work. If the youth claims *towiyeg*, but is not backed by the sibling, his word is discredited.

In summary, the Yapese household is characterized by leadership and authority defined in relationships between father and children, mother and children, husband and wife, brothers and sisters, and grandparents and grandchildren on the basis of relative age and sex. The Yapese kin terms identifying these categories of relationship are summarized as follows:

citamngin	'father'
citinngin	'mother'
fak	'child'
figirngin	'husband'
le'engin	'wife'
wolag	'sibling'
ngani	'oldest sibling'
tethin	'younger sibling'
wain	'youngest sibling'
tutuw	'grandfather'
titaw	'grandmother'
tungin	'grandchild'

The roles or responsibilities and privileges that characterize these statuses show reciprocal obligations and respect exchanged between paired statuses. For a more detailed discussion of Yapese kin terms and status relationships within the household see Hunt, Schneider et al. (1949), Schneider (1949, 1953), and Labby (1972).

Kinship and Authority in the Clan Estate

I stated earlier that the basic political unit in Yap is the estate group or the patriclan. The discussion of inheritance of the land of the estate is very important, but by itself is insufficient for a full understanding of leadership in the clan. Quite frequently in social and political situations, members of the community outside the patriclan exercise leadership for its members. For example, in such matters as house-building, canoe-building, marriage exchanges, and other life crises, a number of statuses from both the patrilineage and the matrilineal sub-sib are accorded the leadership roles. These statuses, with their respective rights and duties, are also identified in the kinship terminology.

The Statuses of Wolag 'Sibling'

Perhaps the most important concept is that of *wolag* 'sibling'. Schneider argues that the kinship terms previously discussed for the nuclear family are exclusively applied between members of the nuclear family and are not extended to kinsmen outside unless or until they enter the family in an "active" kinship role (1953:219–232). In the course of my own research I found this true for the terms for father and mother, and to a lesser degree for child, but the term *wolag* was used freely for even distantly related individuals. Only when the informant discovered that the exact relationship was being sought would the term be qualified.

The Yapese considered it quite proper to be asked, "How many kinds of *wolag* may one have?" The responses are listed below in order of importance:

1. *beyal i wolag*—siblings from the same belly (*yo ngayal*)
2. *wolag ni fak e pin*—siblings from the same subsib
   a. *mafen ko bitir*—Si, SiCh, and SiDaCh (also *wa'ayngin*)
   b. *matam ko genung*—MoBr (also *wa'ayngin*)
3. *wolag ni fak e pum'on*—siblings from the same patrilineage
4. *wolag ni mitegruw*—siblings of one father but different mothers (two wives concurrently or serially)

(The genealogical referents of these categories are illustrated in Table 7.)

Table 7. Categories of *Wolag* 'Sibling' for Male Ego

Generation	Siblings by a Common Patrilineage		Siblings by a Common Male Parent	Siblings by a Common Female Parent	Siblings by a Common Matri-subsib	
	Male	Female	Male/Female	Male/Female	Male	Female
2nd Ascending	—	—	—	—	wolag ni fak e pin	—
1st Ascending	wolag ni fak e pum'on	wolag ni fak e pum'on	—	—	wolag ni fak e pin	wolag ni fak e pin
Ego's Generation	—	—	wolag ni mategruw	beyal i wolag	wolag ni fak e pin	wolag ni fak e pin
1st Decending	—	—	—	—	wolag ni fak e pin	wolag ni fak e pin
2nd Decending	—	—	—	—	wolag ni fak e pin	wolag ni fak e pin

NOTE:
Wolag ni fak e pum'on 'siblings who are children of male siblings'; *wolag ni mategruw* 'siblings of two wives'; *beyal i wolag* 'siblings of one belly'; *wolag ni fak e pin* 'siblings who are children of female siblings'.

A number of older informants described siblings of the matrilineal descent group as the only "real" *wolag*. This includes *beyal i wolag* 'siblings of one belly' and *wolag ni fak e pin* 'siblings who are children of female siblings'. These persons are called *tab ka girdi*, or 'people from the same tree', and as such are distinguished from sib mates who cannot trace a common relationship, forming a subsib. Patrilineage mates of different mothers are not considered real siblings, but rather *susun wolag* 'like siblings'. In this case, however, the distance of the relationship is very important. Children of the same father, but of different mothers, still consider themselves *wolag*, *as if* they had the same mother, however they are more likely to fight among themselves because of their different mothers. Although it is not considered ideal, some informants say that children of two brothers by the same father could marry, that it is better if they wait at least one more generation or two, but not absolutely required. Genealogical information shows that this kind of marriage did in fact occur in the past, but has stopped since Christianization. One may not, however, marry a matrilineal sibling.

An adopted child is recognized as adopted by other siblings in the family, but considered a "sibling of one belly." Because he gives up the sib affiliation of his biological mother and assumes the sib of his adoptive mother, he becomes "of one belly" technically, but people rarely fail to point out the adoption in discussing the relationship. An adopted sibling is not then a different kind of *wolag*, but rather a second way of entering the status.

The importance of these different kinds of siblings lies in the series of statuses and interpersonal relationships which they designate. The "siblings of one belly" is obviously the most important relationship, tying the common kinship bond of the mother with the common lineage and estate bond of the father. This relationship between siblings is marked by strong feelings of mutual responsibility and interdependence, yet tempered with mutual respect. Brothers hesitate to interfere with brothers, and brothers should never interfere in the matters of their sisters. Yet, they are all very interested in the welfare of the others. All economic needs of one or another member of the group is expected to be met readily and as generously as possible. Within the group of siblings a pattern of age, respect, and responsibility applies. The older brother is given the responsibility for the welfare and care of his younger siblings. They in turn show him the respect and obedience that one should show to one's father, yet to a lesser degree. The older sister is also important, looking out for her brothers' interests with regard to their wives and children. She may chase them from the clan-estate if they fail to care for her brothers as good wives and good children should. Brothers also look out for their sisters' welfare and provide things for their sisters' husbands and families when they are in need.

Each household or nuclear family has enough land resources to meet its daily necessities. Thus the relationships of even the closest siblings are not evident in the daily routine of life. Cooperation between brothers for fishing may occur, but it also may occur between neighbors and friends. Cooperation between women for gardening may occur between wives of brothers, but more often will occur between women who are neighbors and friends. Thus in terms of kin relationships the daily routine focuses almost entirely on the household or nuclear family. Special occasions bring into play the full network of kinship relations. In life crises such as marriage, birth, childhood rites, puberty rites, and death, the network of statuses of kinsmen are called upon to provide leaderships and assistance. The same is true for large economic or social ventures such as house-building, canoe-building, *mitmit* (ceremonial exchange) of all kinds, and religious ceremonies. At these times all statuses of siblings have their respective functions and form a leadership and cooperative hierarchy through which the whole society functions. The "siblings of one belly" are active in meeting all of their mutual needs that occur beyond the daily routine of household life. They share a mutual interest and respect, with particular authority placed on the oldest for the care of the younger.

The siblings from the subsib fall into three separate categories. The first and most important are the *mafen ko bitir* or a man's Si, his SiCh, and his SiDaCh. These people are the guardian of his rights to the care and respect of his children. *Mafen*, literally 'feeling of ownership', refers to the fact that, like the father, the *mafen* claim ownership to the land and have the right to take that land away from children who misuse the land and its related rights, or who do not care for their father. The second category is the reverse of the first in which the mother's brother has a special relationship to his sister's child. He is sometimes referred to as *matam ko genung* 'father of the sib' and acts like a father to these children. He provides them with food, Yapese money, and any other thing they may need. Because they are *wolag* 'siblings' the strong formal relationship of father and child is not present and a friendly atmosphere prevails.

The third category of *wolag* in the subsib includes all male members to whom relationship can be traced and all female members of ego's generation or below if ego is male. Female members of ego's mother's generation are referred to by the term for mother, and ego's child's generation by the term for child if ego is female. These siblings form a mutual group of relatives who assist each other on all important occasions by gathering food, traditional valuables, fish, and other goods necessary for the conduct of affairs. They also come to these occasions to lend moral support and to share in the distribution of goods. This set of *wolag* always may be depended upon to give support and food in visits to their village, and to assist in any manner in which they are able.

Wolag ni fak e pum‘on 'siblings who are children of male siblings' may be referred to as siblings in the patrilineage. Schneider (1968) notes correctly that the *tabinaw* is a land-holding unit based upon mutual exchange between father and sons, rather than upon a biological kinship ideology. Schneider argues that not biological descent but rather a spiritual descent from common ancestors and common land was recognized between members of family. The rationale given is that sexual relations are not important in paternity. It is the ancestral ghosts who give children to the wife of a man in the patriclan, and without them, children are impossible. Thus the child is the blood descendant of the mother and the spiritual descendant of the father. A male's ghost goes to the ancestors of the father, while the blood of a female is passed on to her children, and her ghost resides with her husband's ancestors. (This belief has interesting parallels among Australian Aborigines.) For present-day Yapese, however, *wolag ni fak e pum‘on* are biological siblings.

For both traditional and present-day Yapese the role of patrilineal siblings is to provide assistance in important matters as do the members of the subsib. But more important, as members of a patrilineage they are potential heirs to patriclan land should all close heirs die. Only after about three or four generations are these ties dropped and the relationships forgotten, unless friendship between two persons creates the desire to maintain the tie. The more distant the tie, the weaker the mutual obligations between the two parties.

Wolag ni mitegruw 'siblings of two wives' is a special category of sibling on which the Yapese place the stigma of dispute and dissent. These siblings are children of the same father but of different mothers to whom the father is married either simultaneously or at different times. The polygynous marriage is usually filled with tension and dissent, which is passed on to the children. The feelings of solidarity and mutual cooperation and respect expected of siblings is nearly impossible. Instead of cooperating, they fight, which is considered reprehensible. To make matters worse, usually only high-ranking men can afford two wives and thus their children fight over succession to ranking land. This situation is desired by men, but fraught with problems and dissent, making the benefits highly questionable. Probably the greatest benefit to the father is the competition between sons to take good care of him and thus win the best land.

The concept of *wolag* is basic to the understanding of leadership and succession to leadership in the estate. For patriclan and lineage members, it is a culturally defined horizontal set of interpersonal relations, which are distinguished from those of the generation above and the generation below. Leadership among these siblings is defined on the basis of their sex, age, and kinship in relationship to all others. All members of a generation are in subordination to a higher generation until all its members are dead, and on the other end of the scale, superordinate to members of lower generations. This stands in marked contrast to the subsib, in which generation distinctions for males are merged and solidarity and support characterize the relations between members (see Table 7).

The Statuses of Matam 'Public Father'

The higher generation has three basic categories of statuses: *matam, mafen, matin*. These words combine the noun prefix *ma-* 'a feeling of', and the stems for father, owner, and mother. Thus *matam* is one who "feels like a father," *mafen* one who "feels like an owner" or a trustee, and *matin*, one who "feels like a mother." The significance of these concepts lies in the fact that in the daily life of the household and patriclan they do not interfere with the lives of the members. But in any major event of that estate and clan, they all have important positions and roles. Thus they form an exact parallel with the *wolag*, who in their daily lives tend to go their separate ways, but who, in matters of importance to the estate, come together for cooperative action. These statuses are "occasional" statuses in which they act as father, owner, or mother, respectively. Schneider (1949, 1953, 1957a, 1962) in his analysis of Yapese kinship only considers the status of *mafen*, which he calls *m'fen*.

Four recognized statuses center around the concept of *matam* 'public father' (see Table 8). The first and most important is the *matam ko tabinaw* 'estate father', which is a political and ceremonial status providing leadership for the patriclan at all public affairs such as housebuilding, marriage exchange, village meetings, litigations, and so forth. At each of these occasions the holder of the status is expected to make the largest contribution of food, valuables, and other goods that are to be presented. In turn, he is the recipient of goods given to the clan and he distributes them among the members of the group and all others entitled to a share. The estate father is the key leadership position in the estate.

This status is filled by the oldest man of the patrilineage (see Table 8) with the closest relationship to the members of the patriclan. Age and generation are the primary criteria for selection. A man oc-

Table 8. Statuses of *Matam* for Male Ego

Generation	Ego's Father's Matri-subsib	Ego's Patrilineage		Ego's Patriclan	Ego's Matri-subsib	
	Males and Females	Males and Females	Eldest Male	Eldest Male	Eldest Male	Males and Females
1st Ascending	*wolagen e matam ko tabinaw*	*wolagen e matam ko tabinaw*	*matam ko tabinaw*	*citamngin*	*matam ko genung*	*wolagan e matam ko genung*
Ego's Generation	*wolagen e matam ko tabinaw*	—	—	—	—	—
1st Descending	*wolagen e matam ko tabinaw*	—	—	—	—	—
2nd Descending	*wolagen e matam ko tabinaw*	—	—	—	—	—

NOTE:
wolagen e matam ko tabinaw 'siblings of the estate father'; *matam ko tabinaw* 'estate father'; *citamngin* 'father'; *matam ko genung* 'siblings of the subsib father'; *wolagen e matam ko genung* 'sub-sib father'.

cupies the status of *matam* if he has no living older brothers and no living brothers of his father. Name and ancestral rights to the estate of the clan are irrelevant.

The second status is that of *matam ko genung* 'subsib father', who represents the wife of the head of the patriclan and her kinsmen who comprise ego's subsib. Because her children, and therefore members of her subsib, are the next heirs of estate land, they are obligated to contribute to clan functions. The subsib father, oldest male member of the group, presents their contributions to the estate father, and speaks on behalf of his kin.

The third and fourth statuses are identical in function, but different in composition. They are the *wolagen e matam ko tabinaw* 'siblings of the estate father' and *wolagen e matam ko genung* 'siblings of the subsib father'. Individuals occupying these statuses form two groups of supporting siblings from ego's patrilineage and ego's subsib (Table 8) and are present at every major function. Each individual provides support in terms of gifts. Each is asked ahead of time for those goods he is expected to contribute and he brings them as part of his relationship to the *matam*. When the *matam* dies, the closest and oldest sibling in the line of succession will take his place and marshall the siblings for all future estate functions.

For the private affairs of a patriclan, an additional leadership status is recognized, *citamngin* 'father'. This position is filled by the living father of the clan, or by the oldest living clan brother, as distinguished from lineage brother (Table 8). He has authority regarding land use, family disputes, and particularly private family affairs. He may discipline younger clan brothers who are like his children and is expected to provide constant care and assistance for them. The more he acts like a father, the more likely he is to be called *citamngin*. However, if the brothers are older and for the most part independent, he will be in a *matam* or "feeling of father" relationship with them.

It is important to recognize that the *matam* and the *citamngin* statuses are conceptually different. *Citamngin* is broken down linguistically into *ci-tam-ngin*. *Ci-* is a prefix used to designate "smallness," "intensiveness," and "importance." *Tam-* is 'father', and *-ngin, -ngig, -ngim* are the intimate forms of the possessive. Thus *citamngin* would literally be rendered as "truest intensive father to/of him". *Matam* is an occasionally invoked status, in the sense that it is important for particular, specified occasions and business; *citamngin* is an intensive, frequently invoked status involving the exchange of food and care for respect and obedience. One member of a patriclan may fill both statuses at the same time, but the statuses themselves are different. The closer the relationship of the *matam* to the clan the greater is his authority and power.

The more distant his relationship the more power passes into the hands of the oldest residing member of the clan, and the frequency of the *matam*'s involvement decreases.

The Statuses of Mafen 'Trustee'

The statuses of *mafen* arise from the Yapese conceptions of kinship and inheritance of land. As was pointed out earlier, only people of the *genung* 'matrisib' are truly of one belly or one flesh. Members of the patrilineage and patriclan are related only in terms of their sharing *tabinaw*, the unit of land/sea resources supplying common residence and nurture for them and their ancestors. Because *tafen* 'ownership' of the estate is not held by individuals, but rather by all the people born onto and nurtured by the land, when the title of the estate passes from fathers to sons, ownership passes from people of one *genung* to people of another. When a man gives estate land to his children, he essentially denies his sisters and their children any further rights of *tafen*. However, because they have shared equally their birth and nurturance from the land, sisters and their children retain rights of *mafen*, literally a 'feeling of ownership', for three generations.

The rights of *mafen* are fundamentally a trusteeship vested in a particular matrilineal subsib four generations deep, founded by a female ancestor who married into that estate and established ownership over it by developing the land and bearing her children for it. Her children occupied the estate as *tafen*, and then passed it to a new generation of children and a new subsib. Because land is passed from father to son each generation, but *mafen* rights endure for three generations, at any given time an estate may have three separate subsibs holding trusteeship of the estate. These rights, and the elder of the subsib, male or female, who exercises them, are designated *mafen ni bi'ec* 'new trustee', *mafen ni bad* 'retired trustee', and *mafen ni le'* 'final trustee',* reflecting their respective distance and weakening claims upon the estate and the subsib currently holding *tafen* rights (see Table 9).

The new trustee takes a very active role in the affairs of the clan estate. He participates in deliberations at all life-cycle functions and at important family gatherings on economic, social, and religious matters. He may also contribute goods on these occasions and receives a designated share of any distribution. His most important trust is to insure that the children of the clan meet their obligations to their father and exercise proper care of the resources of the estate. In this role, he has

---

* These terms are from the Rull area. Gagil, Map, and Rumung informants used only two terms, *mafen* and *le'*. However, informants from other districts in Yap also used three terms (see Labby 1972).

Table 9. Subsibs and the Cycle of *Mafen* 'Trustee' for Male Ego

Generation	FaFaFa Subsib		FaFa Subsib		Fa Subsib		Ego's Subsib	
	Male	Female	Male	Female	Male	Female	Male	Female
2nd Ascending	FaFa's *mafen ni bi'ec*		FaFa holds *tafen*		—	—	—	—
1st Ascending	Fa's *mafen ni bad*		Fa's *mafen ni bi'ec*		Fa holds *tafen*		—	—
Ego's Generation	Ego's *mafen ni le'**		Ego's *mafen ni bad**		Ego's *mafen ni bi'ec**		Ego holds *tafen*	
1st Descending	—	—	Ch's *mafen ni le'*		Ch's *mafen ni bad*		Ch's *mafen ni bi'ec*	
2nd Descending	—	—	—	—	ChCh's *mafen ni le'*		ChCh's *mafen ni bad*	

* This active status to ego is filled by the oldest male or female in the group when ego assumes authority as head of his clan estate.

NOTE:
See List of Abbreviations for full relationship terms.
Mafen ni bi'ec 'new trustee'; *mafen ni bad* 'retired trustee'; *mafen ni le'* 'final trustee'; *tafen* 'ownership'.
Read from top to bottom the table shows the change of *mafen* statuses within a sib from generation to generation.
Read from left to right the table shows how each subsib holds a distinctive *mafen* status for a given generation of estate owners.

the right to chase the children off the land should they neglect either their father or the land.

The authority of the new trustee begins at the death of the head of the clan estate. The children of the estate are forbidden use of their deceased father's land for a period of one year. During that year the trustee may request anything on that land. At the end of the year the children gather the produce of the land and in a small ceremony present this to the new trustee so that he will "turn away his face" and "lift the anchor" of his subsib's claims from the land. After this ritual the children may use these lands, but the interest of the trustee does not die. His rights to certain resources and first fruits remain, until the next generation of children inherit the lands and another new trustee takes his primary rights and duties.

When a new generation of children inherit and a new trustee exercises his rights to the land, the previous trustee is retired. Since his subsib has received much in the way of gifts from the clan, he is no longer entitled to first fruits. In the case of a very large ceremony, the retired trustee may be asked to make a contribution, in which case he is given a gift for his presence and assistance. This contribution and gift, however, will be less than that of the new trustee.

When another generation of children inherit the estate, the sib of the retired trustee falls to the status of final trustee. The final trustee is least important of the three and is recognized only on very important occasions by minor gifts from the estate father. He is never consulted regarding estate matters, but is treated as an honorary official of the estate. On certain ceremonial occasions in Rull, *mafen* of very important estates may be recognized for as many as seven generations, and may be given gifts. These *mafen* will be living matrilineal descendants of women who have married into and borne children to the estate.

The "falling" of *mafen* occurs logically in the developmental cycle of the clan unit. As a new generation of males inherits the estate, a new set of women and children take over the land (see Table 9). New trustees are created as the sisters move away to take up residence and ownership in other estates. Importantly, the trustee relationship is not defined as a relationship between individuals and individuals, but rather between individuals and a land estate. A woman has residual rights to the land, symbolized in her ritual gifts in all major clan functions. These rights to land are passed to her children (new trustee), to her daughter's children (retired trustee), and to her daughter's daughter's children (final trustee), each of whom retain certain rights to the produce of the estate. The rights of the new trustee, however, are the most powerful.

The people of Rull disagreed somewhat on the definition of *mafen ni leʻ* 'final trustee'. Most agreed that the final trustee is the third generation of *mafen* as described above. However, several informants said that there is also a final trustee that does not fall. Counting on the fingers of the hand, they described the hierarchical statuses of the family. The little finger is the individual or ego, next above him in authority is *matam* 'estate father', the next finger, longest and highest, is the *mafen ni biʻec* 'new trustee', then lower, the *mafen ni bad* 'retired trustee', and finally the thumb and *mafen ni leʻ* 'final trustee'. The significance of this analogy is that the final trustee, like the thumb, is short and distant from the other fingers, but very strong; it does not fall. There are indeed cases of a few estates where the *mafen* rights of a particular sib do not fall, and sib members remain in a final trustee relationship in perpetuity.

A number of cases may be cited. Seven estates in Balabat village, built long ago by sib mates from the sib Yotal, consider present members of Yotal their final trustees and say the relationship will continue until all members of Yotal have died. Members of Kanfay sib have the right to take food at any time from a taro patch in the Lan Ruʻway section of Balabat called Maʻut ko Kanfay 'taro patch for Kanfay'. Kanfay sib is also trustee of *athing* net fishing in the village of Galʻ, and from each catch, a string of fish is set aside for any member of that sib. The sib Weloblob is trustee of a stone fish trap near Bulwol, Rumung, and members may take the fish at any time. The sib Raclang is trustee of land in the village of Atiliw and holds rights to certain bananas from that land.

It should be noted that this usage of *mafen* is different from that of *tafen* in reference to permanent sib rights. There are certain lands such as Bulwol in Gacpar and Arib in Tamil that are *tafen e genung* 'possessions of the sib'. These are definitely owned by and passed on to sib members. The other cases stated here are land and resources that are *tafen e bitir* 'possessions of children', and passed from fathers to sons. For the latter the sib stands in a 'trustee' relationship, having occasional right to, but not ownership of, the land or resources in question. This phenomenon of sibs holding residual rights to land adds considerable support to the hypothesis that matrilineal sibs were once corporate, land-holding units in Yap.

Schneider argues that the *mafen* relationship "is emphatically irrelevant to the matri-lineal descent units or matri-lineal clans in the Yap view" (1962:8–13). Obviously our informants do not agree with each other, but then their disagreement may be to some extent the result of differences in the wording of the questions asked of them. Schneider discusses the concept with particular reference to a *man* and his position as owner of an estate and head of a patriclan. My infor--

mants described the relationship in terms of a *woman*, who marries into an estate, takes usufruct ownership of the land, and ultimately, through children "from her belly," takes the titles to the estate. Given this latter point of view, Schneider's argument that patrilineal siblings have equal share in the distribution of produce belonging to the *mafen* is academic. Each set of siblings gains its rights through the *mother* who bore them *and provided nurture in produce from the land* to the father of the estate. Further, Schneider errs in interpreting the kin term for sibling as applying primarily to the nuclear family, then to the patriclan, and finally to the matrisib. We have already observed that only siblings through women are considered "real" *wolag* 'siblings'. Schneider, however, correctly states that a member of the same sib as the father may not substitute for a *wolag* (member of the subsib) if all the siblings have died. Distant sib mates are not considered siblings and may not act in the role of one.

The role of the subsib in the trustee relationship is consistent with conceptions of the role of siblings in the patriclan and the solidarity of the subsib. Matrilineal siblings share loyalty and support while patrilineal siblings by different mothers are extremely competitive and their relationships are fraught with conflict. The trustee relationship of a subsib assures an individual of support and protection in this intraclan competition. In the most severe cases of conflict, the trustee may chase the children of the clan from their land.

The Statuses of Matin 'Public Mother'

The third status in the parent generation is that of *matin* 'public mother'. As with the *matam* 'public father', there are two different *matin* statuses and the respective *wolag* 'siblings' of the *matin* statuses. *Matin* is also an occasional status, referring to the highest-ranking, oldest women in the family group, who have the "feeling of mother" in their relationships with the younger members. One *matin* comes from the patrilineage and may be referred to as *matin ko tabinaw* 'estate mother', while the other comes from the mother's subsib and may be referred to as *matin ko genung* 'subsib mother'. In public functions of the patriclan these two women play a very important and active part. The estate mother, because she is from the patrilineage or the patriclan, ranks highest. The subsib mother, however, is also important and contributes heavily to the success of estate affairs. These women are the leaders in gathering the food resources for the major life-cycle events. At public meetings they are given recognition and proper payment for their work and rank in the family. They are looked upon with respect and to hold any public affair of the family without them would be considered quite improper. Like that of public

father, the positions must be filled, and when an occupant dies, someone else fills the "place."

Succession to these positions differs somewhat from those of public
father. The estate mother position is filled by the oldest sister of the
estate father. Thus sisters in order of their closeness and age to the
father fill this position. Should all the sisters be dead, the wife of the
current male leader may fill that position. The sisters of the deceased
mother of the patriclan fill the subsib mother role again in order of
their rank as siblings. As in the former case, the wife of the subsib
father may act as subsib mother should all of his close sisters be dead.

There are also two sets of supporting statuses, the *wolagen e matin
ko tabinaw* 'siblings of the estate mother' and *wolagen e matin ko
genung* 'siblings of the subsib mother'. These are women who form a
pool of potential successors to the status of *matin*, but who also act as
a strong supporting cast for all of the important patriclan affairs. The
public affairs of an estate demand a large amount of work and food
resources. The members of the estate are not able to handle this alone
and the sibling relationships in all the generations are used most fully to
project the estate's proper image and strength. Thus, while the *matam*
and *matin* statuses are prestigious, they are also very important economic positions and without their supporting siblings become quite
weak. The *wolag* are then both potential successors and holders of important and supporting active statuses.

As with the public father/father distinction, there is the lower-
ranking, but more demanding, status of head of the internal affairs of
women in the household and estate, the *citinngin* 'mother'. This position likely will be filled by the mother of the family, or by the father's
current wife, or by the father's closest sister. The mother is highly
respected by the junior members of the family and is the leader in wom-
en's affairs within the clan. She may fill the post of *matin* 'public
mother' if no other eligible older woman is available to do so. The
citinngin status, like that of father, is one upon which daily demands
are made; other members of the family are dependent upon her for
food, care, and assistance in daily matters. She may help the young
wives in the clan develop their gardens and assist in the care of their
children. She is looked upon by all as their mother and receives the
respect due her position.

One important fact about these leadership statuses is that their
formal quality, with regard to ceremonial exchanges in particular, requires that they be filled regardless of whether an eligible member is
living or not. This explains why second- and third-generation *mafen*
'trustees' may be called back into service even when they are not in
the proper relationship. When there is no eligible person to occupy

these statuses, another person of the proper age and sex, and with some general relationship to the estate, will become *madol'eg e matam*, *madol'eg e mafen*, or *madol'eg e matin*. These persons are "make-believe" *matam*, *mafen*, and *matin*, as the case may be, and fulfill the formal requirements of the particular custom in question.

The statuses of the *matam* generation demonstrate one other aspect of Yapese leadership. The highest in rank often have very little to do, but are isolated by their loftiness, treated with utmost respect, and consigned to sitting, hearing what is being said or done, and offering an opinion *if* it is requested. For example, the trustee is considered the highest authority over the estate. In matter of fact, he is quite inactive in terms of work, since the estate father conducts the affairs of the estate. He receives gifts and may give some, but the estate father does the actual speaking and exercising of authority. The power of the trustee lies in his ultimate authority to drive away negligent children.

The "child" generation has no public authority. The responsibilities of children are to assist and to obey their parents. Children have no authority to speak in public and are consulted only in matters that concern them, sometimes after the fact. Their parents may arrange their marriages and may require their divorces, as they may refuse courtships and engagements without regard to the feelings of the couple. Two matters where children are consulted and asked for their approval are in land matters and in the question of the remarriage of their father; these have far-reaching significance for the children and they are given the right to express their disapproval.

4. TABINAW LEADERSHIP IN CONFLICT

C oncerning leadership in the clan estate, two types of statuses have been analyzed, the "occasional status" and the "daily status." Both types are structural replicas of the relationships within the nuclear family, but they differ significantly in their areas of authority. The "daily statuses" of parents, children, siblings, and spouses have as referents the internal affairs and operation of the households and clan. The solidarity of the patriclan is based upon the "daily statuses" of father and mother of the group. When the parents of the clan die and leadership falls to the children, the solidarity begins to weaken. As noted, brothers tend to go their separate ways, not interfering with each other's affairs. Thus, while authority in the estate falls to the older brother, land is divided and younger brothers tend to be more independent. Cooperation shifts from the duty-bound parent-child relationship to the looser sibling relationship. Cooperation to be sure remains strong, but shifts from daily matters to the occasional matters of the clan. In the occasional matters the parent generation statuses *matam* 'public father', *matin* 'public mother', and *mafen* 'trustee' are operative and the *tabinaw* as an estate group functions as a whole. The best way to present this is to describe an "occasion" requiring full *tabinaw* cooperation. The ceremonial exchange for marriage provides an excellent example of clan leadership in action.

Marriage

Marriage Rules

The rules of marriage for Yapese are quite simple. It is considered improper to marry anyone who may be a kinsman. The rule of exogamy is applied to the patriclan, patrilineage, the matrisib, and the kindred. Marriages do occur sometimes between distant kinsmen, but they are not considered desirable, and are disapproved. Cases of incest have been reported, even within the nuclear family. Punishment for incest, however, is limited to the disgrace that comes with public knowledge and the actions of supernaturals (see Schneider 1957*a*).

Yapese preferences for marriage relate to class, caste, and personal rank. People from high-ranking clans prefer that their children marry equally ranked individuals. Everyone should marry within his caste (landed or landless), and within the same or adjacent social class. Marriage occurs between castes, but is highly disapproved by members of the higher caste. Residence at marriage is patrilocal and for this reason parents are reluctant to allow their daughters to marry into distant villages. It is preferred that they marry within the same village or one adjacent to it. In this way parents look out for their daughters' welfare and assist them in their new clan obligations. Traditionally it was more desirable for a daughter to marry into a lower-class village nearby than into an equal-ranking village some distance away. Today, however, roads provide easy access and young people meet at the central high school, with the result that marriages into distant villages are becoming increasingly common.

Marriage Exchange or Mitmit

There are several different kinds of marriage ceremony in Yap. Today some Yapese are married in the mission churches. Many, however, follow the traditional custom in which a son merely brings his girl friend home to his father. There is no ritual other than the son's declaration to the family that he and the girl are married. If the girl, however, comes from some distance and the parents are not well acquainted, a small *mitmit* may be held. The smallest, called *puf tabinaw*, involves an exchange of food between the two families and talk among the parents. A larger exchange, with brothers and sisters contributing food and other valuables, is called *towgatow*. Both of these occur immediately after the marriage.

Two other *mitmit* of marriage, called *m'oy* and *wayil*, are held at a much later time. When the families of both spouses determine that the marriage is stable, a marriage exchange may be held in which the two families compete with each other to see which is greater in generosity and in resources of food and valuables. At the *mitmit* of marriage the object is to outgive the other family in the exchange of resources, thereby demonstrating the strength of the patriclan. The *m'oy* exchange is the smaller of the two and is generally held at the estate of the husband. A *wayil* usually follows pregnancy or the birth of one or several children, and it aims to anchor the wife and children to their new land. By then the marriage appears to be durable and both families expend their best efforts to demonstrate their wealth and largesse.

In both exchanges the respective families meet separately and decide upon their contributions. The fathers of the couple meet with the respective estate father, estate mother, and trustee of their clans and decide what will be done for the exchange. Each side meets separately so as not to reveal its plans. By tradition the husband's family brings fish, green drinking coconuts, copra, and the shell money called *yar*. The wife's family brings stone money, lavalava (a handwoven cloth), taro (*Cyrtosperma*), and baskets of assorted vegetable foods. Each family may then add things such as beer, whiskey, or valuables not easily obtained. The more scarce the object, the more likely it is to outdo gifts from the rival family. The meetings among the families of each estate decide the contributors and quantity of the goods.

The collection of goods for the *mitmit* occurs through the usual channels of children and siblings. However, two special means have not previously been mentioned: the *wecma'* 'in-laws' and the *yarif* 'sister'. *Wecma'* is the term used for the spouse's relatives. The term has both economic and social connotations. The relatives of the wife are very important. They may regard the husband in a parental fashion and provide things that his own parents would provide if those positions are vacant. In particular, the wife's family provides the produce of women: vegetable foods, yams, taro, lavalava. Stone money is also considered a woman's valuable because, in the same manner that woman keep near their homes and gardens, these stones stay at the estate and show the "strength of the clan." On the other hand, a woman may call upon her husband's relatives for men's products: fish, coconuts, copra, and the shell money called *yar*. In these exchanges the objective is to test the strength of the opposite *wecma'*, which are heavily relied upon by both families for assistance. The woman's family must call upon the wives of her brothers and the wives of the estate father, trustee, and the siblings of the estate father. In the same way, the husband's family depends upon the husbands of the sisters.

The *yarif* (so called in Rull, but *gile'* in Gagil) are the sisters of the men. In a marriage exchange, the sisters of the father of the household and the sisters of the young husband are *yarif* to their respective brothers. They are very important in that they can call upon their husbands for fish and for the other needs of their brother for the *mitmit*. Significantly, the exchange may not begin until all *yarif* are present. To begin without them would be insulting and also weakening to the position of the family. If a young man does not have a sister, his family makes every effort to supply one or more. A girl may be adopted and made a member of the family, or a custom known as *pinnafen* may be applied in which the father of the young man goes to a relative who has many girls and asks him if it is possible to take one. If he gets a positive answer, sometime later he will bring some valuable shells for the father of that girl and ask him if he may take her to help his son in the *mitmit*. If the daughter is given, she becomes the *yarif* of the young man or boy. The girl does not become a member of his clan, but remains with her father. She does, however, have the *mitmit* obligation to that young man, and he to her. In the case of a girl without brothers, the opposite, called *pum'onfen*, may be done. In either case, the boy and girl exchange mutual obligations for assistance in *mitmit* and confer these upon their spouses.

The strength of the family then lies far beyond the immediate patriclan, extending to all the siblings of all generations and to their spouses and respective families. It is controlled by the estate father, estate mother, and trustee, as they decide the cases in which the family's resources will be summoned and used for the clan or its leaders. In the actual *mitmit*, the exchange is accomplished with ceremony and talk, in which the estate fathers display the wealth of their patriclans, command the youths to bring the gifts, and make the public exchanges. Once the exchange is completed, the goods are redistributed among the leaders and all who have contributed. All dignitaries present are offered something in the distribution. Some, like the chief of the village section, may refuse, but the offer nevertheless should always be made.

Case Study in Leadership

M'oy *Exchange, Rull Municipality*

The following marriage exchange was observed in Rull municipality, in February 1969. The husband's father initiated the exchange held at the estate of the wife's father. The couple, the focus of the exchange, had been married for about one year and the girl was pregnant with her first child. The couple had lived with her family because of their proximity to town and work. The husband's father was not his biological father, but the last husband of his mother's mother. When the husband's mother and father divorced, he was taken by his mother to her home. His mother died, and his grandmother refused to return him to his father as is customary, but instead brought him up in her husband's household. This man initiated the exchange and acted as the *citamngin* 'family father' to the husband in the *mitmit*. He was between seventy and eighty years old, while the husband was twenty-two years old. The wife was seventeen and her father sixty-five.

The husband's father discussed the possibility of a *mitmit* with his *matam* and *mafen*. They decided affirmatively and agreed to propose the exchange. The husband's father then went to Rull and made his proposal to the wife's father who agreed to it. After a meeting of estate leaders of the wife's family, a date was set. The two families concurred that it would not be a large affair, and that they would not compete to see who could outdo the other. Instead they would attempt to make it as reciprocal as possible. Each side was to exchange the traditional items of food, fish, stone money, coconuts, and lavalava.

The families then set about collecting goods, calling upon relatives to assist. In the wife's family, collections were completed on the proper date, but the husband's family asked for a postponement. The fishing had not been done, which prevented the full exchange. Because the food already gathered by the wife's family would spoil by a later date, the wife's father borrowed a truck and took the goods to the house of the husband's father. The perishable food and ten pieces of stone money were given, and at that time a new date was set. The food was then distributed among the members of the husband's family before the fishing had been done and before the *mitmit* ceremony took place.

On the day of the ceremony, both families gathered at the house of the wife's father. The men sat in the shade of a palm shelter built for the occasion. The women gathered by the house and around the cookhouse. The young men acceded to the directions of the wife's father, carrying baskets and performing small chores. The two fathers exchanged courtesy greetings and thanked the people present for their efforts. The visiting husband's father then presented a piece of shell money referred to as "in the baby basket," to make the ancestors happy and therefore give many children to the couple. After the shell offering, he presented fish and coconuts in a quantity equal to the goods given by the wife's family. The direction of the ceremony then shifted to the wife's father, who countered with two pieces of stone money; one for the piece of shell "in the baby basket" and one for a piece of shell given by the husband's family a year previous when they requested permission for the marriage with his daughter. He completed the exchange with lavalava for the father, the husband, and the men who fished, and then instructed the young men to serve beer and coconut toddy.

Both groups of men then sat drinking and talking briefly until the husband's father announced that they had a long trip to make, that they had been treated very well, but that now they should begin to return home. The wife's father concurred, and after thanking them for the many fish, he excused them. After they had gone, he and his wife distributed the fish and coconuts among those people present who had assisted with the *mitmit*. Table 10 notes the participants in the wife's family and the gifts presented and received.

Certain things should be noted about this collection and distribution for the wife's estate. First of all, the *mitmit* was small, thus many possible minor contributors were told that everything had been collected, that nothing else was needed. For example, the estate father was not asked for anything, although it is customary for him to give one piece of stone money. He also did not preside at the ceremony, though this would have been his job, had not the *citamngin* 'family father' been approximately the same age as he. He was not asked to help with, nor plan the exchange. He was offered a shell valuable, but refused and accepted only fish. The subsib father gave lavalava and in return was offered a piece of shell money and fish. No trustee was recognized or present, although a woman with the proper relationship did exist. Finally, the *matin* 'public mothers' were wives of the *matam*, no other *matin* existing.

In the distribution of goods, close relatives could lose something in the exchange (receive less than they gave) and no one would be offended, but more distant relatives and friends had to receive in return more than they contributed. One of the *wolagen e citamngin* 'siblings of the family father' contributed heavily in stone money because, although a distant relative, he acted in the place of a real brother of the father who had been adopted into his family and who then later died as an adult. When a child is given in adoption, the receiving family can never repay the debt incurred in the gift of the child. Thus in all needs of the family who gave the child, the "receiving family" contributes very heavily. The return in this case was also very heavy, equal to the contribution.

The *citamngin* 'family father' also directed the collection and distribution in the husband's family (Table 11). A disagreement with his son over the *mitmit* led to the son's returning to his biological father. At the same time, relatives of the old man refused to cooperate with him in the collection of goods, and he was unable to get the fishing done until he incurred the obligation of others by giving them food. The cooperative sphere here is small owing to the disputes among the relatives. The absence of *yarif* and other high-ranking figures in Table 11 indicate this. The same person filled the trustee and estate father positions. Gifts to him were very large.

Table 10. Wife's Family: Collection and Distribution, Rull Marriage *Mitmit*

Title of Status	English Gloss	Individual Relationship	Gifts Presented to *Citamngin*	Gifts Received from *Citamngin*
mafen	'trustee'	none present	—	—
matam ko tabinaw	'estate father'	FaMoSiSo	none requested	fish
matam ko genung	'subsib father'	MoMoSiSo	3 lavalava	fish, 1 shell money
wolagen e matam ko tabinaw	'siblings of estate father'	none	—	—
wolagen e matam ko genung	'siblings of subsib father'	MoBr	1 rum, 1 case beer	—
		MoBr	1 rum, 1 case beer	—
matin ko tabinaw	'estate mother'	FaMoSiSoWi	2 baskets food	fish, coconuts
matin ko genung	'subsib mother'	MoMoSiSoWi	2 baskets food	fish, coconuts
wolagen e matin	'siblings of *matin*'	none present	—	—
yarif	'sisters of family father'	MoSiDa	10 taro	fish, coconuts
		FaSiDa	2 taro	fish, coconuts
		FaAdBrDa	2 baskets food, 2 taro	fish, coconuts
citamngin	'family father'	Ego	5 stone money, beer, lavalava	shell money, fish, coconuts
citimngin	'family mother'	Ego's wife	2 baskets food	fish, coconuts
wolagen e citamngin	'siblings of family father'	Br	1 lavalava, beer, rum	fish

		MoMoSiSo	5 stone money, 1 rum	2 baskets fish
wolagen e citinngin or *wecma'*	'siblings of family mother'	MoClBrClSo	1 rum	fish
		ClBr	4 lavalava, 1 rum	1 basket fish
		WiClSi	3 lavalava, 1 rum	part of above
		WiClSi	3 taro	fish
		WiBrWi	4 taro	fish
		WiClSi	1 taro	fish
wecma'	'in-law'	BrWi	2 baskets food, 2 taro	fish, coconuts
		SoWi	2 taro	fish, coconuts
		MoClBrClSoWi	2 taro, 2 baskets food	fish, coconuts
		MoSiDaHu	5 gallons coconut toddy	fish
bitir	'child'	Da (the wife)	—	fish, 3 baskets coconuts
		So	work at *mitmit*	fish
		FaBrDaDa	1 basket food	fish, coconuts
		WiDa	2 taro	fish, coconuts
fager	'friends'	X	5 lavalava	fish, 1 stone money*
		Y	2 stone money	1 basket fish

* Contributed by *citanngin* privately.

NOTE:

See List of Abbreviations for full relationship terms.

Table 11. Husband's Family: Collection and Distribution, Rull Marriage *Mitmit*

Title of Status	English Gloss	Individual Relationship	Gifts Presented to *Citamngin*	Gifts Received from *Citamngin*
mafen	'trustee'	FaFaSiDaSo	fish	lavalava and 1 basket food
matam ko tabinaw	'estate father'	FaFaSiDaSo	—	—
matam ko genung	'subsib father'	none	—	—
wolagen e matam	'siblings of *matam*'	none	—	—
matin	'public mothers'	none	—	—
yarif	'sister'		—	—
citamngin	'family father'	Ego	shell money, 5 baskets coconuts	1 stone money, 1 lavalava, and 1 basket food
citimngin	'family mother'	deceased	—	—
wolagen e citamngin	'siblings of family father'	FaBrSo	1 basket copra	—*
		Lineage mate	2 coconut toddy	—*
		Lineage mate	5 small rum	—*
		Sib-mate	1 basket coconuts	—*
		Sib-mate	fish	1 stone money, 3 taro

wolagen e citinngin	'siblings of family mother'	none	—	—
wecma'	'in-law'	none	—	—
bitir	'child'	MoBrSoSo	fish, 1 basket coconuts	1 stone money, 3 taro
		MoAdBrSo	fish	1 stone money, 3 taro
		Sib-mates So	fish	1 stone money, 3 taro
		(Palauan) ClSo	50 bread, fish	1 stone money, 3 taro, 5 baskets food
thin	'requested help'	X	fish	1 stone money, 3 taro
		Y	fish	1 stone money, 3 taro
mafen's relative	'trustee's relative'	Z	fish, use of net	2 stone money, 6 taro

* Four baskets of food were distributed among these and other people listed.

NOTE:
See List of Abbreviations for full relationship terms.

The shares for the husband and *citinngin* 'family mother' were given to a Palauan who is currently caring for the family father. They have a very distant relationship that classifies the Palauan as a son. So we see two examples of collection and distribution, one following custom, the other adapting custom to cope with an interfamily dispute.

The exchange between the two families was very even, as planned, with the wife's family contributing women's produce and the husband's family contributing men's produce. This fits the Yapese concept of proper exchange in equal or higher amounts, but of a different, complementary substance. The overall picture of exchange between the two families is shown in Table 12.

Clan Leadership and Conflict

The pattern of leadership in the sample exchange followed ideal cultural patterns. The statuses of the parent generation were recognized in every case, with only a few vacancies in the hierarchy notice-

Table 12. Summary of Goods Exchanged, Rull Marriage *Mitmit*

Wife's Family		Husband's Family
1 stone money	*given for*	1 shell money—given in request for marriage
1 stone money	*given for*	1 shell money—in the "baby basket" to make the ancestors happy
1 lavalava for the husband		Fish—
1 lavalava for the father		2 baskets and one string for the men who gave the stone money
many lavalava for the men who did the fishing		
10 stone money and 30 taro		8 baskets for women who gathered the food and the taro
vegetable food—		coconuts—
2 baskets for *matam*		2 baskets for *matam*
2 baskets for *matin*		2 baskets for *matin*
3 baskets for husband		3 baskets for wife
5 baskets as travel gift		5 baskets as travel gift
drinks—		drinks—
5 gallons coconut toddy		1 shell money—thank you for drinks
1 case of beer		1 gallon coconut toddy
2 rum		6 pints of rum
1 bunch of bananas		

able. The most interesting insights on leadership, however, come from the observed interaction of these statuses in the light of the ideal. This interaction involved the problems of legitimacy in regard to filling the leadership status, support by those in obligation to that status, and the resulting conflicts when legitimacy was questioned and support denied.

The leader in the wife's family at the marriage exchange was very obviously the wife's father. He made all the arrangements and conducted the affairs of his estate. The estate father in this case did not handle the arrangements nor participate in the public speaking at the *mitmit* to which he was entitled. He not only did not make arrangements, he did not even contribute. The wife's father told him that everything needed had been gathered and that his contributions were unnecessary. He was honored as estate father by the gift of certain fish and by an offer of a piece of shell money, which he refused. Both the wife's father and the estate father were of approximately the same age; the estate father was slightly older, but both men were *pum'on* 'mature men' and thus able to act and lead in village and clan affairs. The kinship relationship between the two is close; the estate father is a subsib sibling (FaMoSiSo) of the deceased head of the clan, but the age and mutual obligation relationships between the two men superseded the parent/child kinship relationship. Therefore, in the *mitmit* the wife's father was the real leader, even though a higher-ranking estate father existed and had to be honored in the distribution of goods. No one questioned the wife's father's assumption of the leadership role, because he paid ritual respect to the higher-ranked estate father.

In marked contrast, in the husband's family the role of the father as a leader and estate father with the right to make a *mitmit* was seriously questioned. First of all, the son and husband questioned, on the basis of relationship, the leader's right to plan an exchange on his behalf. The son in fact had been "stolen" from his biological father by his mother and subsequently raised by his maternal grandmother and her husband, the father in question. The father chose to make the *mitmit* and to ignore all the relatives of the boy through his biological father. The son had earlier reestablished his relationship with his biological father and became angered by his "stepfather's" attempts to exclude his biological father from participation in the *mitmit*. Therefore, he ignored his own marriage exchange. Although he had a mutual care obligation to return to the stepfather, the husband chose to ignore it, in the same manner that the stepfather disregarded custom and the rights of the biological father from whom the child had been taken.

Secondly, the legitimacy of the leadership of the stepfather was questioned by his relatives, who normally would support him. His eligibility in terms of his kinship and age were not questioned, but his personal capabilities and his performance on this occasion had created a great deal of antagonism toward him. His behavior toward the husband's biological father was one point; his insistence on the exchange without the consent of the husband was another. Furthermore he had already aroused the antagonism of his relatives by previous incidences of underhanded dealing and related acts of self-interest, and in their eyes had demonstrated his instability by shifting from one to another of the religious groups present on Yap. His general behavior had resulted in a lack of confidence and respect for him, qualities which are essential for support in a leadership status.

At the time of the exchange, the husband's stepfather could not muster the support necessary to undertake the required fishing. The husband had left him and returned to his biological father, and the stepfather's other relatives refused him their cooperation. With this potential disgrace facing him, he went to the wife's family the day before the exchange saying that the fishing was not possible because of the bad weather and that he would like to delay the *mitmit* for one week. The wife's father was noticeably upset, as was the rest of the family, but agreed to the postponement. They had already gathered all their own food resources and because these would spoil in one week's time, the wife's father decided to take the food down to the village of the husband's stepfather and present it before the ceremony. The ten pieces of stone money and all of the food then were given a week before the actual *mitmit* was held. The husband's stepfather then took this food and stone money and distributed it among his relatives and other people in his and neighboring villages, and at the same time asked their assistance in the fishing for the exchange the following week. By this display of generosity and by invoking the principle of reciprocal obligation he acquired the support necessary to complete the fishing and to successfully carry out the affair. Some of his relatives, however, refused to accept the food and refused to give him support. The *yarif* refused to help saying that she had no young man to go fishing or get coconuts for him, and returned the basket of food he had brought her.

Finally, the husband's stepfather attempted to coerce the husband back into cooperation, saying that he would disinherit him if he refused. The husband had already named his son after the stepfather, and was expecting full inheritance to his lands. The threat and action did not succeed, and the husband did not cooperate. The possibility of reconciliation between the stepfather and husband still exists, but the husband will have to take the initiative at apology. He may not wish to do so, unless his biological father encourages him to apologize in order to inherit the land.

Legitimacy and Support in Clan Leadership

The legitimacy of clan leadership is grounded in three basic criteria of interpersonal relationships—kinship, relative age, and mutual obligation. The discussion thus far of the functioning of leaders such as *matam* 'public father' or *mafen* 'trustee' has noted that the more distant their kinship relationship, the weaker their power and control over affairs of the estate and clan. When distant relatives fill leadership statuses, their influence and their authority are limited to ritual expressions of honor. This was clearly evident in the case study cited above.

The relative age relationship is equally important. The authority always resides in the parent generation, and the child generation ideally shows great respect and obedience to that generation. Kinship relationships, however, often mix the relative ages of the generations, so that a classificatory parent will be younger than his classificatory child. This principle of relative age provides potential conflict within the kinship relationship system. In fact, age is most important in Yapese political life. The old men are everywhere recognized as leaders and in all public affairs young men run errands and do the bidding of old men who make the decisions. When members of the same age group are members of opposing generation groups, potential conflict exists that may override the generation kinship principle.

The mutual obligation relationship enforces the other two. When kinship and age distinguish persons, certain mutual and complementary obligations develop between them and further distinguish their respective statuses. This is most clear in the relationship between father and son. The generation and kinship relationships are clearly marked, and mutual exchanges between these two further delineate them. The father provides food and care for his son and generously meets all his needs. The son returns respect, assistance, and obedience, and when his father is old, he then returns the care given him as a child. It follows that the closer the relative age, the less likely mutual father/son obligations will be observed. Two men of approximately the same age are likely to give or receive care at about the same time, regardless of their generation differences in terms of kinship. Thus, the mutual obligation relationship between them would be more like that of members of the same generation (sibling) than that of opposing generations.

Public support of leadership statuses is grounded in legitimacy of occupancy. If legitimacy is seriously questioned, support of the leader will be withdrawn. But conversely, if legitimacy is well established, then support is given merely upon the basis of his status. Legitimacy, however, is not the only means by which a leader may gain support.

Support may be summoned through the mutual obligations of kinship relationship. The father can depend upon his sons, and siblings upon siblings. Support also may be gained by generosity and the obligation of reciprocity. If one cannot summon support by legitimacy, recourse to generosity and reciprocity may accomplish the same. Finally, support may be obtained by intimidation. An estate father may threaten disinheritance from the land, thus forcing dissenters who are also heirs to follow his wishes if they desire to have continuing interest in the land. Another type of force is the *wenig* 'pleading' by presenting shell money with a request. It is considered very impolite and socially unacceptable to refuse a plea, thus social force is brought to bear on the refuser. Support may then be obtained beyond the bounds of legitimacy, and an individual leader may operate effectively without socially recognized, legitimate authority.

Three other factors must be recognized in the maintenance of legitimacy and support—personal capability, knowledge, and performance. Because statuses such as *matam* have defined attributes of leadership and respect, the person filling that status is expected to exhibit personal capabilities that command leadership and respect. If the eligible candidate is mentally incompetent, he is quietly sidelined, even though he may fill all other criteria for leadership. Personal characteristics idealized are honesty, forthrightness vis-à-vis the clan and outsiders, fluency of speech, kindness, and generosity. Failure to meet these ideals will not damage the leader's legitimacy, but underhanded dealing and self-interest will create dissent and undermine the support necessary to the person filling the status. Performance and knowledge are also very important. The leader may be very intelligent, an excellent public speaker, but his performance in decision-making, in adherence to custom, rank, and respect patterns, and in collections and allocations are also very important. If he disregards customary channels his legitimacy will be questioned on the basis of his apparent lack of knowledge. If he disregards mutual obligation in redistribution of goods, he very rapidly will lose support.

In summary, clan leadership has been considered from two perspectives: 1) leadership statuses and their authority assignments as seen in the ideological sphere, and 2) legitimacy, support, and conflict of individuals as they occupy statuses and exercise leadership. The culture defines the statuses and the legitimate occupation of them, but within these definitions lie areas of potential conflict. Ambiguity gives rise to conflicting claims to leadership and variations in support of leaders. Support can be gained outside of "legitimate status" by other culturally defined relationships and privileges. This general picture of leadership ideal and action applies not only to the clan estate, but beyond to village and island-wide leadership.

5. LAND, LEADERSHIP, AND THE COMMUNITY

The Community

T he Yapese community is a distinctly defined, named village settlement, within which land and sea resources are developed, exploited, and protected by communal cooperation. The Yapese refer to the village as *binaw* or land, symbolizing their physical and emotional ties to the land, and they distinguish themselves from people from different lands. All land within the village is privately owned, yet its members recognize the cooperative bonds that created the community and keep it functioning.

During the periods of heaviest population the Yapese recognized over 180 separate villages. Today 91 of these villages contain at least one resident household (see Figure 8). Most of the inhabited settlements lie in close proximity to the sea. Inland villages are considered less desirable because of their distance from the sea and the lack of low, swampy taro patches. Most inland villages were of lower rank or of low caste and were the first to be abandoned when the population began to decline.

The settled area of the coastal villages is generally on the shoreline, often between the large community taro patch and the sea. These areas were once quite densely populated; people crowded into the least productive areas to free other land for gardens. Land plots are quite small, particularly those within the settlement, with distribution of land to nuclear family households reflecting population density. Today the settlements contain many empty stone foundations and a few scattered houses. The second most densely populated village outside of Colonia

Figure 8. Yap Political Subdivisions

KEY TO VILLAGE NUMBERS

( ) UNINHABITED VILLAGE

RUMUNG MUNICIPALITY
1	Buluuol
2	Mechiol
3	Gaanaun
(4)	Eng
5	Riy
6	Fal
7	Wenfara'

MAP MUNICIPALITY
(8)	Amin-Maap
9	Amin
10	Bechiel
11	Toruw
(12)	Nlul
(13)	Waref
14	Waned
(15)	Dingin
16	Wocholab
17	Chool
18	Waloy
(19)	Numdul
20	Malway
21	Malon
22	Talngiz
23	Wirilee
24	Plaw
25	Michew

GAGIL MUNICIPALITY
26	Makiy
(27)	Lay
(28)	Ruu'
29	Amun
30	Muyub
(31)	Mulolow
(32)	Mey
33	Riken
(34)	Goochol
35	Wanyan
36	Gachpar
37	Binaw
38	T'enifar
39	Leng
40	Lebinaw
(41)	Darcha'
(42)	Ul

TAMIL MUNICIPALITY
43	Madlay
44	Zol
45	Maa'
(46)	Dilag
47	Dechumur
48	Bugol
49	Af
50	Teb
51	Meerur
52	Doomchuy
53	Deboch
54	Gargey

FANIF MUNICIPALITY
55	Runu'w
56	Ayrech
57	Yiin
58	Gilfiz
(59)	Bunuknuk
60	Wulu'
61	Malway
62	Rang
(63)	Tabelang
(64)	Gurung
(65)	Bulochang
66	Rumuu
(67)	Me'reniw
68	Ateliw
(69)	Tafgif

WELOY MUNICIPALITY
(70)	Makal
71	Dugor
72	Okau
73	Numnung
74	Adubuwe'
(75)	Minef
(76)	Maa'
(77)	Alog
(78)	Gatmoon
79	Kaday
80	Mabuu
81	Mulro
82	Nimar
83	Keng

RULL MUNICIPALITY
84	Worowo'
85	Balebat
86	Benik
87	Ngolog
88	Talguw
89	Dachangar
(90)	Dinay
91	Gita'm
(92)	Baanimaut
(93)	Toraa'
(94)	Mer
(95)	Fanaliliy
96	Yinuf
97	Luwech
(98)	Firigaaw
99	Lamer
(100)	Dirikan
101	Ngof
(102)	Madargil
103	Tabinnifiy
104	Dulkan
105	Ngariy
(106)	Ley
(107)	Wgem

DALIPEBINAU MUNICIPALITY
(108)	Gaanipan
109	Magaf
110	Binau
111	Kanif
112	Aringel
113	Tagegin
114	Fedeor
115	Yaboch

KANIFAY MUNICIPALITY
116	Tafniz
117	Fara'
118	Nel
119	Ne'f
120	Gal
121	Mala'y

GILMAN MUNICIPALITY
(122)	Gacholaw
(123)	Matibuw
124	Zabez
(125)	Muru'ru
126	Tawoway
127	Anoz
128	Magchagil
129	Guror

has only twenty-five households and could easily accommodate five or six times that many on the basis of house foundations and unused land.

Within the settlement region, certain places have been set apart for community activities, such as ceremonial grounds, men's houses, menstrual areas, roads, piers, and burial grounds. These are all situated on privately owned lands, but committed to public use, from which they cannot be withdrawn. They are basic necessities for the social interaction of the community.

Certain lands are also designated for religious purposes. Each village has one or more *tiliw* "sacred place" where prayers and magic are made for the benefit of the people of the village. These sacred places are privately owned by the priest and practitioner of the religion. Magic places and other areas are set aside for the production of herbs and the recitation of magical formulas. Generally every household also has its plot for raising medicinal herbs.

Community Centers

Certain privately owned lands are set apart as social resources for the whole community. The use rights to these places are held by the community and protected by the chief who oversees the area in question. The actual owners of the land may be given certain privileges or compensation for the land, but may not claim use for their own benefit. The three basic centers of community activity are the *pebaey* or old men's house, the *faluw* or young men's house, and the *dapal* or women's menstrual house.

The Pebaey 'Men's House'

The *pebaey* 'men's house' is a large community house built for the old men of the village. The building is generally very long, rectangular in shape, and opened at the front end with a veranda under roof. It is set upon a large stone platform and has stone backrests placed at strategic places for sitting purposes. The house and foundation are actually triangular-shaped at each end, forming a six-sided platform. At the triangular ends stone money may be placed for decoration and backrests. On the sitting platform, backrests for the chiefs are placed around a small stone table called a *rarow*, which is used for the distribution of fish and other items for the chiefs. This area is especially taboo to young girls of menstruating age. Older women of childbearing age also keep a respectful distance, as the house and area are taboo to menstruating women. Directly in front of the building is the dance ground and show place (*malal*), containing some of the largest and most valuable pieces of stone money owned by particular estates. Around the dance ground are a series of sitting platforms from which village people and guests from other settlements watch the dances. A meeting area for the leaders of the village is located near the building and dance ground, while the rear of the building has an area for meetings of the women. As with the men's house, the platforms and dance ground are on privately owned lands, for which use rights have been granted the community.

All except the lowest-ranking villages have men's houses, and many villages have one for each major village section. They are generally located in the center of either the village or the respective section. Usually they are some distance inland from the sea, but not in all cases. The central road in the village runs to the house and through the dance ground.

The men's house functions as a social center of the community. It is the meeting place for the old men and may be used by them as sleeping quarters. Younger men are encouraged to stay there and to listen to the conversation, learning the patterns of custom and leadership. The building is the center of important conversation and also of daily social interaction. Parties for the old men in their respective eating ranks are also held there.

All important political activities center in the men's house. Matters of community importance are discussed in the respective meeting areas of men and women. The old men and old women conduct and dominate the meetings. Younger people refrain from unnecessary talk in the presence of the older people and come there to listen to the elders, to do some particular task to which they may have been summoned, or to attend some community-wide event in which all the community participates. If meetings are held with other villages, the place of meeting shifts from the village meeting area to the platform in front of the building where outsiders are entertained.

Collection and distribution of economic goods occur at the men's house. For lower-ranking villages who take tribute to higher-ranking villages, the collection is made at their community center, transported to the village of higher rank, and distributed from its men's house. Fishing catches in particular are distributed at the house, according to the rank and privileges of the members present. Fish are generally placed on the special stone table and the chiefs direct the distribution. Those fish pushed off the table onto the ground are distributed to the people of the village, while those left on the table are for the chiefs.

Finally, the men's house is the ceremonial center of the village, or village section. If a house is the center for one-half of a village, only ceremonies involving that half are held there. The ceremonies involving the whole village are held at the highest-ranking and main village center, and include dances, *mitmit* 'ceremonial exchanges', and traditional religious ceremonies. Dances may be held for the chief, for visiting chiefs, or for some special village occasion. *Mitmit,* in which the exchange of traditional shell and stone valuables is conducted between villagers and visitors, are extra special events to celebrate some person, occasion, or a relationship between villages. The largest of these is called the *guyuwol,* involving villages all over Yap. Others commemorate a dead chief, celebrate the completion of a community house, or honor an old person of very high rank. The traditional religious ceremonies were held both at the men's house, and in the village sacred places. The collection and distribution of foods and a feast at the community center accompanied the religious ceremonies, which are no longer observed.

The Faluw *'Clubhouse'*

The *faluw* is a clubhouse for young men, built at the seashore or on a stone platform jutting out into the lagoon. The house is similar to the *pebaey* 'men's house', except that it has no veranda. It is built upon a six-sided foundation and may display stone money and have backrests for the comfort of its occupants. In some cases the clubhouse may have a nearby dance ground where the men dance. As with the men's house, women are forbidden near or in the clubhouse. Inside the house men may remove the hibiscus fiber of their loin cloth, without which men are indecent in the presence of women. The one exception to this etiquette is the wife of the men's house, called the *mispel* 'hostess'. She is considered married to all the men of the house, within which she has free access. She cares for the house as a wife would and generally entertains the young men. (The Germans and the Japanese outlawed this practice.)

Every section of the village has its clubhouse and in some cases an association of estates or one large estate will build its own house. Therefore a village normally has many more clubhouses than men's houses. Old men are not excluded from the clubhouse and in fact many do stay there. Young and old men of the village sections sleep and work out of their respective houses.

The *faluw* is above all a social center, a residence for the young men. There they may play, shout, dance, sleep, or work without the interference of villagers. Within the village itself, young men are expected to be well behaved and quiet, but at the clubhouse, horseplay and loud noise are not prohibited. Thus it is not only a sleeping place, but a recreation center where the young men can relax and have fun.

The only aspect of life not provided for at the clubhouse is eating, which is done in the respective households. The hostess, the parties, the dancing, and the fighting are all parts of traditional clubhouse life.

One of the main activities of men is fishing and the house is a storage place for fish traps, nets, and other related tools. The Yapese believe that before he goes fishing, a man should avoid sexual relations, so the house is also the part-time residence of married men, who sleep there on nights before going fishing.

In the past the clubhouse also functioned as an educational center where young men learned fishing, rope weaving, tool making, and building. The old men staying in the house were a source of social and political as well as esoteric knowledge for the youth. Afternoons and evenings were spent discussing rank, war, and competition with rival villages, and teaching the young men to conduct these wars. Through legends and myths the young were entertained and instructed in the taboos, rules, and regulations of the culture as well as the esoteric knowledge of their past culture, religion, and magic. The clubhouse, then, provided the major center of socialization and indoctrination of youth into the culture. Young boys from eight to ten years old and even younger slept in the house, first temporarily with their fathers and then all the time as they grew older.

The clubhouse was also an important economic center, through which the young men of the village applied their energy to various village projects. The young men worked on community building projects such as roads, piers, houses, and even such major works as reclaiming land from the sea and making new taro patches. They also conducted regular and special village fishing expeditions inside and outside the lagoon.

Finally, the clubhouse was a center of political activity and defense. Guests coming by canoe arrived at the respective house of the village section they intended to visit. If they were visiting the chief, he might meet them at a clubhouse, conducting all the business there. If the meeting was considered safe and of great importance, then they moved into the center of the village to the men's house or to the house of the chief. In any case, clubhouse members were the vanguard of defense and the principal fighting units of the village. Visitors approaching them always sat down in their canoes in respect for the clubhouse and its members. To stand was to declare war, and indeed, one of the prize feats in war was to burn down a clubhouse of an opposing village. In times of war, each house would have its respective war canoe and fighters. Today, of course, these activities have ceased and the houses function primarily as sleeping quarters for young men and as social centers. Many village houses have been abandoned.

The Dapal *'Menstrual House'*

The *dapal* is the women's menstrual house. Like the clubhouse, each village had a number of menstrual houses, with usually at least one for every section. Unlike the clubhouse, however, these houses were not large, durable structures with stone foundations and seating platforms. They were small, often built on the ground, and quite low. Not built for comfort, they merely sheltered the women during their menstruation when they were contaminated (*ta'ay*) and thus set apart from the rest of the community. They did not have political functions, in that women have meeting places elsewhere. They were used for meetings, however, when women wished to discuss matters apart from the hearing of men. In that sense, then, the menstrual house was a social center. Women in menstruation were placed together for the duration of their respective periods and shared common gossip and village knowledge.

The house was also an educational center for the children. First of all, a woman usually brought her youngest children, whether male or female, with her to the area. To the young children it was very frightening because it was up on the hills away from the main village, near the burial grounds. The possibility of hearing and seeing ghosts and the actuality of hearing these stories and sharing the fright of the mother taught the child early of the spirit world of his culture. He was taught that improper behavior would surely bring these spirits down upon him and he was encouraged very early to follow the culture's standard of propriety. Mothers taught their children the patterns of respect, the taboos, and the type of behavior that helped avert a visitation of the spirits.

Secondly, the menstrual house was the place of initiation and education of the young girl in her first menstruation. These girls (*rugod*) resided in the house for a full year after their first menstruation. During this time the older women taught them all the taboos that they, the most dangerous of menstruating women, must follow. For example, the girl had to avoid old men's taro patches. She should never eat food from her father's, or any other man's, pot or garden. She had to walk on certain paths that avoided the paths of old men and old men's food. A girl had to follow rigidly these and other taboos and was given two years to learn them well. The second year was spent near the menstrual house in a place called *tarugod* 'place for pubescent girls' where she and others resided outside the main village until she had completed the second year of her isolation. After that she could move back into a separate house in her household, but she had to be very careful as she made her way through the village, following all the proper paths and often walking on her knees when coming near a high-ranking place. During the two years of isolation she was fully indoctrinated into the mores of the culture and prepared for her life ahead in the family.

Finally, the menstrual area was also used as a hospital for childbirth. Women who had given birth went to the house for one hundred days. Newborn children were kept there during the crucial period of their lives and those that died were buried nearby. Novices and other children staying at the menstrual house learned the facts of birth and of caring for the newborn child. When the one-hundred-days isolation ended, the mother and child then returned to their household.

In Yap today, only five villages, all in the municipality of Fanif, continue to use the menstrual houses. Formal education of children has eliminated the initiation rites and isolation for young girls, and church and school have undermined the religious ideology for the separation of women during this period of life. Almost all children are now born in the Yap hospital and the menstrual house is becoming only a memory in the minds of the adult women.

Other Community Areas

Some other areas within the community are relevant to our consideration and should be discussed here. First, roads also run across private land but the community holds use rights to them. The roads are generally quite narrow, and the custom is to walk single file with the man first, children in between, and the women behind. Walking abreast is considered rude and is generally impossible anyway on the narrow paths. People of high rank are given preferential treatment and people of low rank step off the path to let them pass. Women stand aside, allowing men to pass. Certain roads in the community near an important place for old men are taboo to young women and low-caste individuals. Low caste are contaminated because they bury the dead, visitors to a burial place are defiled for a time, and young girls and people of childbearing age are befouled by menstruation. These people should not go near the table for distributing fish to chiefs, taro patches for old men, meeting places for old men, cooking places for old men, and other taboo places. The paths for young women skirt these areas and low-caste and other unclean people follow these paths as well. Older women who can still bear children have alternate paths around certain taboo areas, and do not walk the low paths. Women past menopause and men have unhindered passage on the village roads. Men, however, are prohibited from the menstrual area and women from the men's houses.

Along village roads ascending into the hills where gardens are located, there are rest areas built of stone, where villagers may relax and talk en route to and from the gardens. These are also for general public use. Some families of very high rank or who are considered very taboo because of religious or magic properties of their land have a similar type of rest area adjacent to their house where guests may visit with them and yet not enter the taboo area of the house.

Children are told to be quiet in the village and, while playing is permitted, noise is kept to a very low pitch so that the old people are not disturbed. On the outskirts of the village children may play at any time and may make as much noise as they wish. These play areas are designated for children's activities, and are especially used late on moonlit nights. The children generally sit and talk, build fires, sing and start budding courtships. Courting, forbidden in daylight or in public, may begin in the play areas at night.

Every village has areas designated *tathil* 'place of fighting'. These areas, located on the outskirts of a village, were generally first and hardest hit in traditional battles. The owners of these plots often wisely utilized them for fruit trees and avoided building upon them. Villagers generally concentrated their residences toward the center of the community, leaving a buffer of gardens, fruit groves, and undeveloped

Figure 9. Map of South Section, Wonyan Village, Gagil

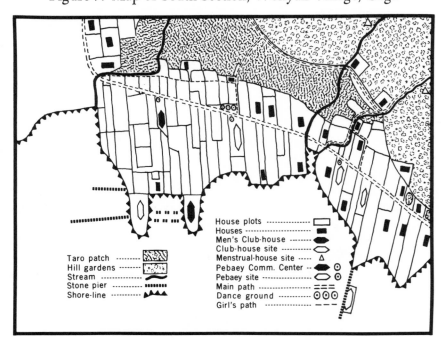

land between them and adjacent villages. For the general layout of a village see Figure 9.

Community Resources

All Yapese communities or villages are centered around two basic land resources: taro patches and garden land. The most important is the taro patch. Village taro patches vary in length from one hundred to three hundred yards, and in width according to the contour of the land. Generally they are from twenty to thirty yards wide. Most communities are limited by the size of their taro patches. More specifically, taro patches result from extensive communal labor. The site must have a water source sufficient to irrigate the patch and keep the soil constantly mud-moist. The land must be cleared, the area leveled and excavated, retaining walls built to hold the water, and proper drainage ditches dug. The hand labor required is quite extensive. The chief of the taro patch is generally the chief of the community, reflecting his role in the building of that patch. If the patch is divided into sections, it generally reflects the divisions of the community (that is, the completed patch is comprised of respective sections built by competing groups). Each estate contributing labor or other resources toward the construction of a section receives parcels as its share of the new food resources.

Obviously, the size of the cooperative unit and the community is partially limited by the size of the taro patch to be shared. Some villages have constructed several large taro patches instead of one. Separate sections of a village have built their own patches and formed smaller subcommunities. Other villages, particularly low-caste villages, have no large community taro patches. The taro patch as such does not then demarcate the community, but it does provide good insights into its organization.

The second major land resource is the garden land. Various yams and sweet potatoes are planted in gardens adjacent to the settlement area. The garden land is divided according to the sectioning of the village. As in the taro patch, individual estates own plots of land in the garden areas. There are three different types of garden areas—the sloping land inland from the beach, the valleys, and the hilltops. The sloping land is usually best in terms of soil and is generally covered with foliage. To make gardens the land must be cleared and drainage ditches dug. The soil from the ditches is spread over the garden area to enrich the soil. Family members usually do this labor; however, in the past, groups certainly developed large sections and the parcels of land were distributed among the laborers, as with the taro patch. Development of valley lands is similar, but the land is steep and not as productive. Land on the valley floor invariably contains a taro patch and is not used for gardens. The hilltop gardens have the least rich soil and are the least productive in vegetable crops. The hilltops are generally rocky, with topsoil washing away in the heavy rains. They are crisscrossed by a checkerboard pattern of drainage ditches, which appear quite clearly each dry season when the grass is burned off. Communal cooperation also developed these gardens. The sections (*falang*) have their respective chiefs and frequently a high chief over a series of sections. This organization corresponds with the general divisions of the village. These gardens are owned individually, each mound belonging to a particular estate. The clan member who owns the garden may plant when he wishes but often works cooperatively with other owners in the same section in planting the land. Each individual owner harvests his own plots.

On the hilltops (*tayid*) grow only yams and sweet potatoes, while on land lower on the slopes also grow trees and fruit trees, such as breadfruit, Tahitian chestnut, oranges, bananas, mangoes, and others. Areca palm trees are planted around the settlement areas and on the sloping garden land. Material resources as well as food resources are taken from these lands. Hill slopes and valleys are planted with timber for houses and bamboo for construction and other uses. Stone is taken from the hillsides and coral stone from the sea for the house platforms and the seating platforms. Soil in certain hill areas is used for pottery and hill streams provide water for cooking and bathing.

If the village has a sandy beach, the beach area is generally covered with a large grove of coconut trees. Coconut trees deplete the soil and thus are planted sparingly in garden areas. Villages without beaches usually have few coconut trees. Mangrove and nipa palm grow in the swampy salt water flats just off shore and provide lumber for construction, rather secluded toilet facilities with tide flushing, and nipa palm fronds for roof thatch. Coconut palm fronds also are used for thatch, but the best thatch is of pandanus leaf woven over bamboo. It is the strongest and most durable of the three. Pandanus grow on the hilltops. Today the pandanus fruit is not much used for food, but in times of greater population it was certainly eaten. Ownership of these material resources varies according to place of growth and rights of the chiefs. Generally, individual estates own the resources with chiefs holding certain residual rights.

The third major food resource of the community is the sea. Certain estates, usually of high rank, own all fishing grounds within the reef. Fishing rights sometimes are parceled out to various estates or households and careful distinction is made among methods of fishing permitted and prohibited. Rights to use nets of all kinds, to stones, to fish traps, and to particular methods of fishing all are owned by an estate. Unlike land, however, fishing resources are shared easily and the payment, though depending upon the size of the catch, is small. Communal fishing enterprises are common, and are accomplished through a similar organization to that for gardening.

Community Organization

Association of Estates

The primary units in the Yapese village are the household and the land estate. The household is the land-use group, and the estate the source of land and the basic political unit. The next larger unit in the community is an association of estates. Informants described two processes regarding the origin of such estate associations: 1) the subdivision of land among children, and 2) the award of land for service and continual allegiance.

As stated earlier, in the developmental cycle of the patriclan estate land is divided among children and these divisions emerge as new estates. The relationship of the new estates to the original form the basis of the association of estates. The new estates become "inside the house" or *lan e na'un* to the old, and together they form a cooperative association. The head of the association is the oldest titled estate in which the authority was invested.

Associations also arise through a gift of land. In certain situations a landowner may choose to give land to a poorer relative without land or with very poor land. The recipient is considered as a son because, like a son, he has received land from the father and head of the estate. He becomes part of the estate and acts as a junior member. He supports all major projects and adds to the overall power of the leading *kengin e dayif* 'central foundation'. Giving of land in this way is one method of acquiring leadership and a wider sphere of influence and power.

Not all estates belong to an association. Associations tend to form around estates that have authority and leadership power. Estates without title and without residual claims to authority lack the motivation to maintain ties with an original estate. The segmentary nature of patriclans becomes the primary factor and ties to other clans are soon forgotten. The authority and privilege of ranking estates is such, however, that estates with residual claims maintain their relationship through cooperation and mutual service. The principal function of an association is political and members share in the prestige and privileges of their leader. When the political rewards are particularly great, associations may pyramid, with a very high-ranking association encompassing several others under it.

During the period of maximum population on Yap, it is highly probable that associations of estates coincided with the boundaries of the patrilineage rather than with the estate group or patriclan. The leading estate in the association belonged to the lineage founder and his most direct descendents, and the junior estates belonged to the junior members of the lineage. It is impossible, however, to document this with present-day Yapese informants. Population has been declining for so long that the division of land has not been important for over one hundred years. Within the lifetime and memory of informants the Yapese have been faced with the problem of filling existing land estates, rather than creating new ones. Genealogical relationships that existed between estates have long since been forgotten in the extremely complex exchanges of land that resulted during depopulation and from the extinction of descent lines. It is impossible to establish the boundaries of the association of estates. Present-day Yapese have never seen such associations except in titled estates where the maintenance of ties has very important political advantages. Most associations recognized today exist because "empty land" from extinct descent lines was given to individuals who returned the reciprocal obligations that a son gives to a land-bestowing father.

The cooperative association of estates may benefit the group, for example, in the building of a small taro patch or in fishing as a group, or it also may support the wider obligations of the highest-ranking estate. If, for example, the village plans a major work project, assignments may be made to the heads of associations, who in turn call upon their members to fulfill these obligations. If the leading estate should be without a spokesman, the second-ranking would take over that job until the position was properly filled. Particular tasks of the association are parceled out to particular members so that each minor estate has some task or duties to perform for a particular job.

The estates in the association usually are located contiguously or in the same general vicinity. If they have worked cooperatively to develop certain resources, the head estate will oversee those resources. In the case of outside demands upon the association the leader may call for each member of the association to contribute from its taro patch, garden, or fishing. Associations may compete with each other to see which can most improve its land or develop resources to outgive the other.

The associations then have common historical ties to a particular central foundation and rank as junior members of that estate by common ancestry and/or inheritance of land. They share common obligations and responsibilities determined by the larger community and also share in benefits and distributions that the community may make. They are not a corporate land-holding group but rather a cooperative resource-sharing association. Failure to fulfill one's responsibilities to the group, however, can result in loss of certain resources to the association leader, for example, a section of a taro patch or gardens. At present the associations have lost much of their meaning because depopulation has resulted in a lack of people to make the cooperation network meaningful.

Village Subsections

As estates are grouped into associations, physically adjacent associations are grouped into village subsections or *gilaruc* (*barba' binaw* or *gile'* in Gagil). The subsection is a cooperative group or community in which resources are developed or exploited, or labor and taxes collected for its welfare. If the subsection is large enough, it may have developed its own separate taro patches and other food resources. If it is small, a section of a larger taro patch is the product of its cooperative effort. Certain fishing rights may be held by a subsection and shared among its associations. Hilltop gardens are certain to be developed by the subsection and controlled by its leader. Village work of major scope is parceled out to the subsections and they compete with each other to do the work with the most speed and skill. For example, construction segments of a community men's house are assigned to respective subsections. Each is expected to provide the timbers, the bamboo, the sennit (coconut-palm rope), and the labor to complete it. Each section then vies to bring the largest timbers, tie the fanciest ties, and work the hardest to complete its section first. Internally, the subsection leaders assign certain associations to provide particular materials for the building. Some provide timbers, others bamboo, others ropes, and so on. All are expected to provide labor and even may be given sections in which they compete with other associations.

Within the subsection, the associations are classified according to the rank of their leading estate. The associations are known by the name of that estate; the subsection has a name of its own. Certain estates and their associations lead the subsection; one estate is chief and its leader directs all sectional activities. He is also responsible to the high chief of the village and represents him to the estates within the subsection. The members of his association provide a pool of assistants to carry word from place to place, to gather resources, to assist in any way possible, and to fill his position if it should be vacated without proper heir. Another estate in the subsection is of second rank, and its spokesman acts as the work leader of the section. He receives the word from the leader and carries it to the people, summoning them to carry out the tasks decided upon. The members of his association provide the same immediate assistance as that of the chief.

The other associations within the subsection have minor rank, based upon the rank of the head estate in the association. These head estates form a council within the subsection, which discusses all matters of importance to its people. They discuss village affairs and make their wishes known to chiefs. When work is to be done they organize their associations and other estates to carry out their responsibilities.

The subsection may be so small that all its estates belong to the same association or it may be large enough to contain seven to ten associations, varying in size and importance (see Figure 10). The subsections, like the associations, are ranked in order of their important chiefs, thus the subsection with the highest-ranking chief has the highest rank. This hierarchical ranking of estates, associations, sections, and chiefs is characteristic throughout Yapese social organization.

Village Sections and Chiefs

Villages in turn are divided into two or three main sections or *balay e binaw*. These sections are almost separate villages except that they cooperate together for very large political events, such as war, *mitmit*, important building projects, and community-wide work. Each section has its own separate resources, chiefs, and subordinate officials. One section is of higher rank than the others and the high chief of the

Figure 10. N. Section, Balabat Village, Rull

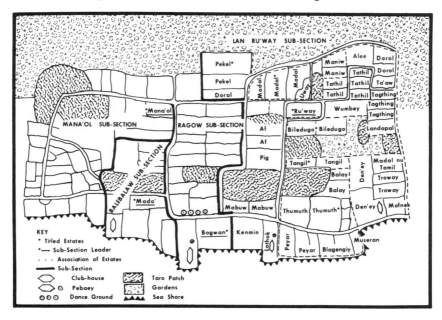

village resides in that section. Generally the members of the higher-ranking section outrank members of the other sections. Rank does not necessarily mean power, however. A villager from a high-ranking section without titled land is of higher rank but has much less power than the chief of a lower-ranking section. Rank, then, gives prestige, but titled land gives power.

Titled lands are the key to rank and power within the Yapese community. The titles are vested in the land of a particular estate, and the rank generally applies to those estates, subsections, and associated sections. Exceptions to this rule exist, but are rare. The man of proper age and family who stands upon the titled land may exercise its power and privileges. He is considered chief on the basis of the title of the land for which he speaks.

The authority that accompanies leadership in the association, subsection, section, and village is derived from the titles invested in land, and the key to leadership is the method of succession to the land and its concomitant authority. All leadership, authority, and responsibility are defined in the rights of the estate and its central foundation.

Rank, Resources, and Space

We have seen that the various divisions and subdivisions of a village are ranked in terms of all other units and that each are important economic and political entities. Economically they form organizational groups for production, collection, distribution, and consumption, while, particularly, they provide a power structure with competing and cooperative elements for the general good. The question then is raised as to the relationship of the units and their respective ranks to privileged access to space and resources.

The most obvious aspect of privileged access to resources derives from differential access to food resources within the village, section, subsection, and estate association units. As mentioned previously, the three main food resources are taro, yams, and fish, in that order. Taro is prized most highly and men always have first rights to taro. If the resources of a village are great, there will be taro patches for both women and men. But if these are scarce, men alone will have taro, and women and children will eat yams and a small amount of taro, which they grow in their hill garden plots. Men also have first rights to fish, taking the best fish and giving the rest to children and women in that order. The first and most obvious distinction, then, is between men and women, with men having access to the best taro and fish resources. The large taro patches built by village cooperation are set aside for men or for women, but are not generally shared between them. The same is true of large garden plots. The only food shared between men and women is fish, and this is separated into men's and women's portions.

The second distinction in access to food resources is relative age. Yapese men and women are divided into generational age groups as follows:

Men	Age	Women	Age
pilbithir ni pum'on	65–	*pilbithir ni pin*	65–
pum'on	45–65	*puwelwol* (menopause)	45–65
pagael	20–45	*lukanarow*	25–45
bitir ni pagael	0–20	*rugod*	12–25
		bulyal	0–12

These divisions not only designate age in the culture but are most important in the distribution of food resources. In the four men's categories none of these groups could ever domestically or publicly share the same food or pots. Furthermore, all food resources in the village are separated into units for each group. Thus one finds a taro patch for old men, one for middle-aged men, one for young men, and if enough, one for youths and their mothers together. A *pagael* 'youth' may eat with his mother or older women, but *pum'on* 'men' should not eat with women at all. In the women's age grades food resources are also separated, with each rank's resources distinct from the others and each rank obtaining and preparing food separately. The one exception is a small child, who may eat with a woman of any age. One important relationship exists here between women and men. In the household, women of an age grade higher than a man may share her food with him. Thus a middle-aged woman may share food with a young man in the household. She would act like his mother. In public feasts or eating, however, they should have separate food. Another example may be found in villages with limited taro supply: older women will usually share taro patches with younger men. Each, however, would still maintain their own plots.

One other point should be made here with regard to these age groups. The age limitations noted are approximations and are pegged generally around the transitional periods. One becomes an old man when you "act like an old man" and so the ages can vary considerably. The other important variation is the relative age of individuals in interaction. The younger always defer to the older, especially when the participants both recognize clearly the age difference.

The middle-aged women are *gelngin e binaw* 'the strength of the village'. They are the most industrious and productive workers and lead in the affairs of women in the village. They are not encumbered by childbearing as are the younger women, nor have they yet succumbed to the weaknesses that afflict the aged. Because of their economic importance they have considerable weight in the village. Without their cooperation food production in the village would come to a complete halt, and local stories indicate that women have used this power more than once.

The age ranking of men into separate resource and eating groups is related to estate rank. This is most clearly illustrated in the *yogum* 'eating classes' of men. The eating classes are founded upon three basic principles: age, rank, and access to high-ranking food resources. There are two basic sets of eating class relationships, one for men and one for male children. The latter is only active for the religious ceremony called *cef*, held in the Yapese month called Cef. This ceremony is a feast for chidren in which the boys and young men are divided into age groups and participate in separate eating ranks. Rull informants described this as play and since it is of minor importance it will not be discussed further. The eating classes for men, however, are important. First, the ranks have different names and relative positions in the myriad dialect areas of Yap. Müller lists different names for twelve different areas (1917:413–414). There is some considerable degree of variation, but the underlying determinants remain the same—that is, age, rank, and access to privileged land. The named ranks of eating classes for two municipalities are listed below in descending order of rank.

Rull	*Gagil*
1. *munthing* and *welu'*	1. *fitemalang*
2. *garkof* (or *macibol*)	2. *yamey ni pilung*
3. *matha'aeg*	3. *matha'aeg*
4. *piteruw*	4. *yangac*
5. *pagael*	5. *waltharir*
	6. *racoloy*
	7. *puth*

A boy becomes a young man when he begins to wear the hibiscus fiber with his loin cloth. Even then he is not considered a man, but only a mature youth. At this time, however, he begins to eat separately from his mother and to have his own food resources. In Rull, two things may happen at this point. If the young man has land, which entitles him to give food and participate in *piteruw* 'mature man' rank, he may present shell money and food and be initiated to that rank. If he does not have the land for that rank, he must wait until he is too old to eat comfortably with *pagael* 'young men' and then he will join the older men of the mature man rank who do not have proper land. Thus one finds two levels within the mature man rank, those who have land entitling them to initiation into the rank and those who lack the land but because of their advancing age cannot eat with the young men.

The next-highest rank is *matha'aeg* 'taboo'. The two criteria necessary to enter this eating class are maturity of age and land designated as source of food for the "taboo." A parcel in the "taboo" section of the taro patch is necessary for initiation into this rank. A majority of villagers today have this rank, but not all. Those who do not are from poor families and must remain "mature men" all of their lives.

The most elite of the general eating classes in the village is the *garkof* 'titled' rank (*talang, dagcol, munthing* in other areas). To enter this rank one should be middle-aged or a very mature young man and have taro resources in the "titled"-designated taro patch. Membership in this group is limited to the highest village elite, with all minor-ranking estates excluded. One is initiated into this group by giving the appropriate shell money and food for the "feast of the titled." Without the proper land, one may not enter this rank.

Above the titled rank two very exclusive categories are recognized in the Rull area. The first is *welu'* 'sacred', which signifies both age and prestige. Only people who pass through the titled rank may participate in *welu'*. Applicants to this rank must be advanced middle-aged or old men. It is an eating rank of high prestige but of severe limitations. The individual eats food from very taboo taro patches. He must eat only from his own garden, must always eat alone, and he cannot eat food that others prepare. These circumscriptions have definite supernatural connotations.

The final eating rank for very high chiefs and religious leaders is often called *yogum ni kan* 'class of ghosts'. In Rull this rank could only be attained by the highest chief from Ru'way, the oldest man from Rilac in Balabat, and the priest from Towol. Each must remove from their loinclothes the red hibiscus fiber representative of old men, and each must throw away his basket containing all personal belongings. In turn each puts on a new white hibiscus fiber ornament and takes a new basket. Each has special rituals and magic said over him to set him apart from other men. This sanctity (*macmac*) requires that each eat only from his own private resources, and only those fish caught and brought especially for him. The traditional taboos and restrictions upon the behavior of these men are so severe that today the observances have been abandoned. The restrictions were important in religious ritual and when the old religion was abandoned this rank was disregarded. The equivalent rank in Tamil was followed until the Japanese decreed that such religious ceremonies be stopped. The religious observations and most eating classes were discontinued because of the enforcement of this decree. Today some older men have revived the eating class initiations and observe the restrictions in public gatherings.

The eating class is a social and religious grouping of men with express reference to religious ritual, obtaining and eating of food, and the concomitant taboos accompanying rank and age. The privileges and obligations of eating classes pertain particularly to public eating at religious ceremonies and feasts, at initiation parties, and when eating at a *mitmit*, community work project, or in travels among villages undertaken for work or for other purposes. Admission to a rank depends upon one's rights in estate land and one's relative age. The criterion of age may be waived if an important political status is filled by a young man. However, without the proper land, one may not enter a higher rank than mature man. With the land, one may enter the taboo or titled ranks. If one enters the titled rank and chooses at old age to follow the rigors of the sacred rank for religious and social purposes, he may do so. Without titled rank, however, he may not go higher. Finally, a chief of high rank has privileges of collection and distribution that set him apart from all other people. He will receive first fruits from land over which he is lord, and he will receive tribute from those villages and sections of villages indebted to him for services. The class of ghosts is a rank of great prestige, but severe personal hardship, approaching the fasting and dietary limitations of a mystic.

Rank within the village is not just limited to these eating classes. As mentioned earlier, each section of a village is ranked in terms of other sections. Thus, in a village with two sections there may be two divisions of the system, one in the lower-ranking section and the other in the higher ranking. This may even apply to subsections of a village if they are large enough and contain the proper resources.

In any given village, the areas with the least actual and potential food resources invariably are the lowest ranking politically. They do not have rights to important taro patches and are also excluded from the high eating classes. In contrast, the best food resources always are controlled by the high-ranking sections of the village and owned by the high-ranking estates. Privileged access to resources creates privileged rank in a situation of expanding population. Rank also returns more privilege in terms of tribute and first fruits. Villages or sections rising in rank due to war generally receive tribute in items of scarcity in their own particular locality. Yapese rank is incorporated with privileged access to resources.

Such rights are extended to resources other than food. While stones, swamps for mangrove, and nipa palm are often found in lower-ranking areas, a chief from a higher section will oversee the mangrove swamp or nipa palms and have the right to request these from the lower section. He will reciprocate with a gift of taro or other scarce goods for the donors. The relationship is a status-defined trade relationship reinforced by the privileges accorded a dominant section over a subservient one.

6. LEADERSHIP AND AUTHORITY IN THE COMMUNITY

Leadership Statuses in the Village

Two important concepts permeate Yapese thinking with regard to leadership. The first is land, the second is voice or speech. Land is chief, all leadership statuses are vested in land estates, and particularly in the central foundation of the estate. The person who speaks for the authority of the land is the *pilung* 'voice' of the land. *Pi-* can have two possible meanings: 'person' or 'give'; *-lung* means 'voice' or 'word'. Thus *pilung* can be the "person with the voice" or the one who "gives the word." In either case the connotation is the same. The land (*binaw*) is the authority, and the *pilung* is its voice, speaking to the villagers regarding whatever is deemed to be for their good. The word *pilung* is used both in reference to land and to people. When used regarding the land it refers to the actual authority, regarding an individual it refers to his power to speak for the authority.

In the organization of the village, three particular statuses or "voices" stand out above all others: *pilung ko binaw* 'voice of the village', *pilung ko pagael* 'voice of the young men', *pilung ni pilbithir* 'ancient voice'. These are the highest-ranking statuses in any village and carry the greatest power. They are the village chiefs. Each status is assigned to a certain estate in the village and individuals from those estates sit upon that land and speak for its authority.

The Chief of the Village

The authority code or authority assignments of the *pilung ko binaw* 'voice of the village' are defined by the Yapese in terms of the things that he speaks for. He is the voice of the land; he speaks for the land in its internal and external affairs. If word comes from without his village, he conveys it to his people. He sends word from his village to other villages. If word is to be passed within the village, it originates with him. More specifically, the chief is the executive head of the village. All matters of intravillage and intervillage relationships focus upon him. Schneider states that he must decide what is good and bad for the village and then work for the good and punish the bad through supernatural sanctions or punitive warfare (1949:113–117). Importantly, however, he does not act alone but is always expected to work in consultation with or through a *puruy* 'council' of the speakers for other leading estates in the village. Should he act alone and lose the support of the council, he may be removed from office, or, as happened in the past, the other chiefs might arrange to kill him.

The council forms the decision-making body and the legal authority of the village. The chief disseminates the word of the council and represents his village in it when an offense is committed. The chief and council may intervene in disputes between patriclans that threaten to undermine the solidarity and power of the village. Mediation between fighting clans is one the chief's most important duties. His house is a place of refuge, and individuals may find protection and safety there. The chief will then plead on behalf of the individual and attempt to resolve the conflict. Schneider notes correctly that the chief mediates in kinship disputes only if invited (1949:118–119). This appears true in most interpersonal disputes. The people must always request help of a chief. If he is not told, he does not intervene. When informed, he exerts his influence and shows his skill at mediation. This is true for conflicts both within the village and between members of his village and outsiders.

The chief is also the economic leader of the village. He may be more accurately described as the village contractor. He has charge of a large portion of village resources by right of his title and thus may contract work for the benefit of the village. This contracting may be done with sections of the village or with other villages with which his village shares political ties. He initiates the work projects in the council and collects food and traditional valuables to pay the workers. He also authorizes the gathering of materials for the work project. He may initiate and contract other kinds of village work such as gardening, fishing, road building, and the building of new platforms, new taro patches, and new land on the tide flats. He must, of course, have the resources with which to obtain materials and payment for the project. Food is the most important required resource and he is able to acquire it through his status as overlord of the women producers of food.

In the social and ceremonial aspects of the community, the village chief is also the leader. Schneider notes that he must know and instruct the young in the procedures for *mitmit* 'exchanges' and other social affairs such as dances or eating class celebrations (1949:119). The community *mitmit*, a ceremonial exchange of valuables with other politically allied villages, demands the accumulation of great amounts of food and traditional valuables. Only the village chief has access to such wealth and can plan such a large affair. Of course he cannot do it alone, and must work with the council of village leaders. If a dance is in order, the village chief asks the people and the leaders of the dance to prepare it. Payments for the dance are collected and distributed by the village chief.

Finally, the village chief is the guardian of the community in religious matters. If sickness of epidemic proportions, typhoons, or other disasters threaten the community, he must go to the priest of the sacred place and request aid. He pays for such assistance with shell valuables. If the village needs blessing to assure the production of certain kinds of food crops, then he goes to the appropriate magician and pays for the magic to bring succor. He is the caretaker of community resources of all kinds and may contract them out to meet the overall needs of the community, whether they be political, economic, social, or religious.

The Chief-of-Young-Men

The authority code of the *pilung ko pagael* 'voice of the young men' is markedly different from that of village chief. First of all, although the status is invested in particular estates, the authority does not concern land, but people, namely the young men. The young men are very important in that they provide the village with labor for all major work projects, with defense against outsiders, with fish for food, and with a police force. The chief-of-young-men is the leader and *langan pagael* 'mouth of the young men' to be heard in all village councils. If the council decides upon work, the young men do it; if they decide upon war, the young men fight; if they decide upon social sanctions within the village, the young men carry this out. The chief-of-young-men represents them in the council and leads in the execution of their tasks, whether it be work, war, police action, or ceremony.

The chief of the village contracts work projects; the chief-of-young-men acts as the foreman. He calls together the young men or the young women, notifies the units of the village as to their responsibilities for the task, and then oversees the collection and distribution of the foods given in payment to the men. He inspires the workers and encourages them in competition.

The chief-of-young-men is the chief messenger (*tamel'og*) of the village, representing the village to all outside villages. In this position he carries messages on behalf of members of his village and council to the other villages of Yap. Often he carries shell valuables to reinforce the message with which he has been entrusted. In matters of highest importance or to chiefs of highest rank, the chief-of-young-men carries the word himself. In matters of lesser importance or to chiefs of lesser rank, other estates carry messages to their assigned villages. He uses this same network to communicate the decisions of the council to the village.

The chief-of-young-men is also the caretaker of all village shell valuables. When these valuables come to the village, he places them in his house. He may not use them for private purposes, but keeps them for the needs of the young men. When these valuables are distributed, he is *tu'lang* or the one who stands and makes the distribution to the various leaders of the village and to the members of the council. He supervises collections and distributions made for the visitors in the village, and for ceremonies. In a real sense the chief-of-young-men is the executive officer of the village council.

The Sitting-Chief or Chief of Ritual

The *pilung ni pilbithir* 'ancient voice', like the village chief, has authority over certain land. He commands considerable economic resources to support the needs of the village. Unlike the chief, however, he usually is not authorized to speak for the village. Rather, he is the old, wise counselor to the council and chiefs. He is entrusted with esoteric knowledge and wisdom, which he interjects into council discussions. He is responsible for keeping the power-minded leaders aware of the basic values of the culture as expressed in worship of ancestral ghosts and in behavior approved by the ghosts. He provides counsel as to the proper methods of doing things, and as to whether the will of the council is wise and to be followed, or unwise and in need of reassessment and a better solution. He is one who sits and listens, approves and disapproves, but who has no power to execute or to stop decisions. He may be characterized as the sitting-chief. His power stems from his ability either to refuse economic support of a venture of which he disagrees or to threaten supernatural sanctions.

In the past, the role of the sitting-chief included the supervision of religious ritual and ceremonial cleansings in the traditional cycle of religious observances. As overseer of the most important sacred place, he was the leader of the village feast (*togmog*), held yearly in honor of the village's founding ghosts. The preparations for the feast were his responsibility, with the support of the village chief, and he made offerings to the ghosts via the priest of the sacred place. The sitting-chief was also the leader of the highest-ranking eating class, which was prepared for these religious ceremonies and called class of the ghosts. Only the highest ranking in the village participated, and this usually meant only the sitting-chief and the highest-ranking priests. The priests were very *macmac* 'sacredly dangerous', and were set apart from the others in the village. The sitting-chief was the only nonpriest who could enter this very sacred eating class. In some villages the role of chief of ritual was so important he was called the *pilung ni ga* or highest chief.

The estate of the sitting-chief, like that of the village chief, has lines of communication with chiefs in other villages and with regional chiefs. These channels provide the sitting-chief with additional means of acquiring support for his village or his position. In leadership conflicts within a village, channels such as these are often used for political intrigue resulting in the death of a chief through warfare and a shift in power and leadership.

In his brief discussion of leadership statuses in Yap villages, Müller confuses the authority assignments for these three village leaders (1917: 407–411). First, he could obtain very little information on the role of the chief-of-young-men, and dismissed this status as unimportant. Second, he assigned authority for the internal village affairs to the sitting-chief, whom he referred to as *pilung ni ga* or *pilung ko binaw*. Finally, he defined a separate leadership status of war chief (*pilung ko makath*), following the dualistic pattern that he had observed for Polynesia. From the discussion above, it is obvious that the situation is much more complex than Müller discerned. The chief-of-young-men plays a very important role in both internal and external village affairs as the leader of the young men and chief executive officer of the village council. Furthermore, while he correctly observes the existence of two very important village chiefs, he errs in defining one exclusively as war chief. The Yapese almost universally recognized the village chief (*pilung ko binaw*) as both leader of the economic and political affairs of the village and leader and planner of war. The sitting-chief (*pilung ni pilbithir* or *pilung ni ga*) is the leader of religious ritual and a proponent of peace. He may influence other economic and political affairs, but this is normally done through judgments he makes of the decisions or actions of the village chief and the chief-of-young-men. Schneider clarifies the role of the village chief, but overlooks the importance of the sitting-chief and the chief-of-young-men (1949:108–125).

The Priest

Some of the higher-ranking villages in Yap contain sanctuaries that were important and powerful in the traditional religion of Yap. Each of

these sacred places had a priest or *petiliw* who was an important religious and political figure. The priest was the guardian of the sacred
place and made prayers and offerings to the resident ghosts for benefits
to his villagers and to all Yapese. He prayed for all kinds of food, for
children, for recovery from epidemic diseases, and for general blessings
upon the people of his village and region. The priest only performed
these ritual supplications at the request of the leaders of the village or
of the regional chiefs. A messenger brought him shell money and the
request for his services. The priest then entreated the ghosts of the
village to grant the request of the chiefs. In some cases the priest was
called upon to meet with the chiefs and to perform a ritual that
would protect the people from sickness and other plagues.

According to some informants, the highest-ranking traditional
priests often spoke a language of the ghosts and not Yapese. If a chief
wished to communicate with the priests, he obtained the services of an
interpreter or *tamananus* who would translate, for a price, the message
of the chief to the priest. This practice served to further elevate the
priest and to increase his power and influence as the source of supernatural power.

Generally the chiefs and the priest worked together for the good
of the village. Occasionally, however, they used the priest's supernatural powers to wreak havoc instead. If a chief requested, the priest
might call upon the ghosts to bring epidemics, typhoons, drought, or
famine. People who did not support the chief would be punished, and
both chief and priest were feared because of this power. At the same
time, it was believed that the power of the priest endangered himself,
and if used for evil purposes too frequently, it would destroy him.

Other Leadership Statuses of the Village

A number of lesser statuses are found in the organization of village
affairs. These have particular rights or authority for certain communal
activities. They are listed as follows:

Activity	Leader	Magician
1. gardening	*pilung ko woldug*	*tamarong ni ganiyniy*
2. net fishing	*pilung ko fita' ni nug*	*tamarong ni pisulog*
3. torch fishing	*pilung ko fita' ni magal*	*tamarong ni dafnguc*
4. war	*pilung ko mal*	*tamarong ni yaw*

In the undertaking of these activities, the leader and magician
statuses complement each other. The actions of the leader of gardening
is complemented by that of the magician of sun, rain, and food crops.
Similarly the work of the leader of net fishing is complemented by that
of the magician of net fishing, that of the leader of torch fishing by the

magician of torch fishing, that of the leader of war by the magician of war. The chiefs and magicians in these cases may often be authorities held by the same estate and the same person, in a combination of temporal and supernatural powers. It should be noted that in these cases supernatural power ensures the success of the venture of the particular village in question and assists the leader in accomplishing his task.

The authority of these statuses is confined to the activity defined. The leader of net fishing directs a fishing expedition from beginning to end, from the decision to prepare the net to the final distribution of fish. The leader of gardening directs cooperative village production and collects the first fruits of the harvest. The war leader leads the fighting expedition and the leader of torch fishing leads the night expeditions for flying fish outside the reef. The respective magicians work simultaneously to ensure success of the venture. The magician of torch fishing has a special authority called *wayarek*, which is to direct line trolling for big fish after completing a night of torch fishing.

One other type of magician, the *tamarong ni sunaniy* 'private magician', has his power not in land, but rather in his basket or *way*. He (or she) knows various kinds of magic learned from different practitioners (for example, for sickness, love, luck in war) and can be called upon by any person who needs supernatural assistance. But he has no great power in any particular kind of magic. He makes magic for the individual rather than for the chief and the people as a whole. He has no political power or status in the village, though he receives valuables for his services and may accumulate considerable traditional wealth.

The statuses discussed thus far are those having designated authority for the whole of the local community or village. No two villages are exactly the same in the distribution of these respective authorities. Some villages define the authority of these statuses somewhat differently, and some omit one particular status, or combine the function with another. However, the general pattern of the distribution of political power within Yapese villages is as described.

Leadership Statuses in Village Sections and Subsections

The subdivision of the village into smaller local units is also important in the leadership structure of the village. Each unit provides a smaller subcommunity and each is ranked relative to the others. Two levels of division have been discussed, the section (*baley e binaw*) and subsection (*gilaruc*). Each is organizational and has leadership and functions in community affairs.

Leadership in village sections is patterned upon that for the village. Each section has a *pilung* or section chief and a chief-of-young-men.

Figure 11. Organizational Structure, Balabat Village, Rull

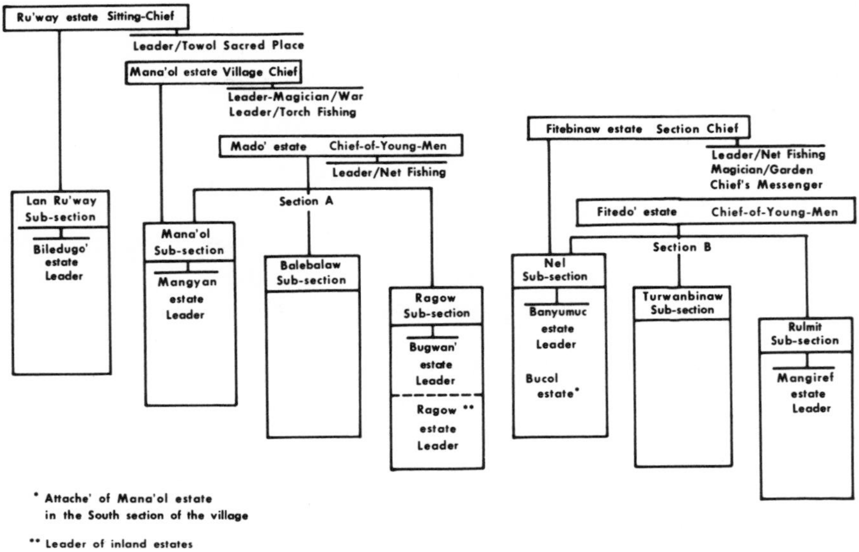

```
Ru'way estate  Sitting-Chief
                    Leader/Towol Sacred Place
               Mana'ol estate  Village Chief
                         Leader-Magician/War
                         Leader/Torch Fishing                    Fitebinaw estate  Section Chief
                    Mado' estate   Chief-of-Young-Men                    Leader/Net Fishing
                              Leader/Net Fishing                          Magician/Garden
                                                                         Chief's Messenger
 Lan Ru'way                        Section A              Fitedo' estate   Chief-of-Young-Men
 Sub-section
              Mana'ol                                                        Section B
 Biledugo'    Sub-section    Balebalaw               Nel
 estate                      Sub-section         Sub-section    Turwanbinaw
 Leader       Mangyan                                           Sub-section
              estate                   Ragow      Banyumuc                      Rulmit
              Leader                Sub-section    estate                    Sub-section
                                                   Leader
                                    Bugwan'                                   Mangiref
                                     estate        Bucol                       estate
                                     Leader        estate*                     Leader
                                    ─────────
                                    Ragow **
                                     estate
                                     Leader
```

* Attache' of Mana'ol estate
  in the South section of the village

** Leader of inland estates

The authority of these leaders is patterned after that of the village leaders, and in fact, in their respective sections the village leaders are the section leaders (see Figure 11). The section chief, like the village chief, is speaker for the estates in his section. His sphere of operation lies within the village, between the village chief and the estate leaders of his section. He speaks for the latter to the village chief, and in turn conveys the word of the village chief to them. Like the village chief, he may not act alone, but consults a section council in making decisions. As economic leader of the section he too acts as contractor of major projects, but usually in counsel with the village chief. He may initiate work projects and gather the materials and food required to accomplish them. Frequently sections compete with each other, using the incentive aroused by intense rivalry to motivate people.

Section chiefs who have *pebaey* (community centers) conduct ceremonial exchanges, dances, and other community affairs. In the planning of these events, the role of the chief is equivalent to that of the village chief, although the latter would be consulted before and honored during the occasion. In some instances the occasion may call for the services of a magician or priest. If magicians reside in the section, the section chief would request their services, but a request for the services of an outside magician would go through the village chief. The limitations of the power of a section chief lie then in the closeness of the presence of a higher-ranking chief to whom he owes certain obligations and from whom he receives support.

The authority of the section chief-of-young-men is also patterned after that of his village counterpart. He is the voice of the young men in the section council and foreman of the local work projects. He is the messenger of the section chief within the section and to other localities where his chief may have jurisdiction. He is the leader of collections and distributions in his section and follows the general executive responsibilities of the higher-ranking village chief-of-young-men.

The subsections of a village are basically dependent, interacting with other subsections within their village section, but unable to muster sufficient resources to become autonomous. Leadership within subsections is generally limited to a status very similar to that of the village chief-of-young-men. This status may be called chief-of-young-men, work leader (*gireng ko marwel*), or collection-distribution leader (*tu'lang*). In all cases the duties are the same. He leads the subsection in economic, political, and social activities assigned it by the chiefs, and represents the estates in his subsection to the chiefs. In the subsection containing the estate of a village or section chief, the chief is the subsection leader and he usually has the head of a second-ranking estate to act as work leader or executive officer. In those subsections without titled estates, the head of the highest-ranking estate is the subsection leader. Even in these lower-ranking subsections, however, the ever-pervasive theme of ranking is present and the subsection leaders have subordinate estate heads who either work as assistants or stand ready to assume leadership authority should the leading estate fall or lack a capable leader.

The status of sitting-chief (*pilung ni pilbithir*) is distinctly absent from the section and subsection divisions. This status is not duplicated at the lower levels of village organization. One reason for this omission appears to be the limited power of section chiefs. The voice of a third chief is not structurally required to balance the power of a section or subsection leader. His medial position in the hierarchy provides opportunity for control by the higher-ranking chiefs. This is not the case for the village chiefs, who are at the top of the power structure. The status of sitting-chief provides a third member to counter the power of either of the other two powerful leaders, namely, the village chief, and the chief-of-young-men. Another reason for the omission of this status at lower levels is that the village sacred places, the basis of special authority of the sitting-chief, are not usually found in the lower-ranking sections and subsections, and when they are, the village sitting-chief controls them.

One other authority may be found in the sections and subsections, the *awcaen e pilung* 'eyes of the chief'. This authority is vested in an estate with a relationship to the village chief and the status holder acts as the eyes and ears of the chief in the respective section. He enjoys high rank as the special envoy of the chief and is included in the village council as a high-ranking member of the village. He is responsible to the chief and reports the activities of the section to the chief for his information. He holds good land and is included in any important distribution of goods made by the chief.

Sections of villages may also have the minor statuses of leader of gardening, or net fishing, or torch fishing, or war. The concomitant statuses of magician might also be present, although not necessarily so. The village magician for net fishing could be consulted by the respective leaders, for example, to make good fishing magic for them. These minor statuses are not found in the organization of subsections of a village.

The Concept of Suwon Overseer

One other important leadership concept is that of *suwon*, literally defined as 'sitting erect'. The authorities designated as *suwon* sit figuratively by the item in question to see that it is handled properly and to share in the resultant benefits. Sitting is the posture of authority in Yap. All important affairs and speeches are conducted from a sitting position. Standing is the position of service and work. The concept of *suwon* connotes the concept of overseer.

The term *suwon* is applied in the estate. The *matam* 'estate father' and the *mafen* 'trustee' are overseers of all estate resources. The trustee is the higher in rank, but his role is a passive one. The estate father is second in rank, but actively uses the resources. The term *suwon* is also applied to the estate associations. The leading estate in the association is *suwon lan e na'un* 'association overseer'. This implies the same kind of authority over those estates in the association as the estate father has over the resources of his estate. The association's resources are subject to the demands of the highest-ranking (defined as the oldest of siblings) estate in the association. The second-ranking estate in the association is like the chief-of-young-men of village, section, and subsection, acting as messenger and agent of collection and distribution for the overseer of the association. The overseer is very much like a *pilung* 'voice' with one big exception. He is more than a speaker for the group, he has rights of access to its resources.

The term *suwon* is also applied to the social resources of the community. There are overseers of the men's houses, the clubhouses, the menstrual houses, and the sacred places of the village. These authorities are invested like all others in particular estates and the speakers for these estates exercise the authority. The overseer is responsible for seeing that behavior in and around these places is proper in accordance with the codes of the culture. Use of these places is guarded and benefits from usage are shared with the overseer. Offensive behavior is promptly declared to the village by the overseer and punitive action taken.

The phrases "overseer of women" and "overseer of men" sometimes refer to the authority of the village chief and the chief-of-young-men, respectively. The village chief is generally overseer of women and all activities related to women in the village. If males and females work together on a project, the village chief is the unquestioned leader. In the exclusive affairs of men, however, the chief-of-young-men is the unquestioned leader and overseer.

Another usage of overseer is with reference to the clubhouse mistress (*mispel*). When *mispel* were captured and brought to the clubhouse, generally the overseer of the clubhouse was also the overseer of the girl. She would be protected from abuse and misuse by the overseer and when she became pregnant he would make the arrangements for her marriage to one of the eligible members of the clubhouse.

The concept of *suwon* 'overseer' is applied widely to land and food resources, and the levels of overseer vary directly with the level of village divisions. There are *suwon e maʻut* (taro patches), *suwon e lawey* (valley lands), *suwon e falang* (hill-garden lands), *suwon e tayid* (hilltop gardens), *suwon e milil* (mangrove swamps), *suwon e lulʻ* (rivers), *suwon e gakiy* (trees), *suwon e day* (sea lands), and *suwon e fitaʻ* (fishing) for all twenty or so different kinds of fishing rights.

The application of this concept is best understood by example. At least three different estates may hold *suwon e falang* 'overseer for hill-garden lands' status. The largest is known as the *suwon ni malob* 'overseer who is like a flying bird'. His authority covers a large section of land located on the wooded, sloping hillsides. Within this large section are subdivisions or *gilaruc* as in the village. Each subdivision has its own leader and overseer. Finally, some sections within the subdivisions have overseers as the leaders of estate associations. Each is entitled to respective rights. If an individual makes gardens on his land, he gives first fruits to the overseer of the estate association. If the association gardens as a group, first fruits (*athalab*) go to the overseer of the subdivision. If members of the subdivision garden as a group, then they give first fruits and shell valuables to the "overseer who is like a high flying bird."

Two other kinds of tribute are paid from this land to the highest overseer. One is bananas, in particular two kinds of bananas called *yurnim* and *tengarat*, which are exclusively for chiefs and especially for an individual's chief and highest overseer. When they mature, they are given to the overseer and he returns shell money for the gift. The second kind of tribute is called *thalap* and refers to trees that may be used for constructing a house or canoe. These trees are very valuable, and if one wishes to cut one, even from one's own land, he must give the highest overseer some shell money.

Finally, the various overseers may all request food from gardens for any need of their groups at large. Thus if the highest overseer needs food to pay the laborers for their work on a new clubhouse, he calls on the leader of the village subsection to request food from the appropriate gardens. These demands apply to all food and material resources. The overseers of taro patches, gardens, sea plots, and so forth, may request produce from them as support for any community project. This authority, then, is the source of the economic power of the respective chiefs of the village, section, and subsection.

Leaders have certain overseer rights not yet mentioned. The highest-ranking chief in a village traditionally had the right of *suwon e pogfan* 'overseer of breath', the right to life and death. He did not kill people himself, but rather arranged for someone else to do it. Another authority not previously mentioned is the overseer of eating class initiation rites in which new members give shell money to the chief, and bananas, copra, and other food for the initiation feast. The chief has rights to the shell money in particular; the other goods are divided and distributed among the members of the rank.

Finally, there are minor overseer rights involving tasks in the communal work of the village; these tasks confer rights upon the worker to certain resources. The overseer of cleaning at the men's house collects refuse, especially after feasts or exchanges. In cleaning, he has rights to anything of value found upon the ground, including food. For the type of net fishing called *athing*, one estate has the responsibility for the anchor of the canoe. Each overseer of different aspects of net fishing will have certain rights to the catch for his contribution, for example, the overseer of the anchor has the right to claim the fish in the canoe he would like as payment for his work. Many other examples could be cited, and many traditional ones have been forgotten.

The Technical Specialists

Also classified among the village leaders are its technical specialists. One of the leading figures in the traditional village was the *tagac* 'renowned warrior'. Each village could designate seven of its warriors as renowned, an achievement of great honor that carried leadership status, whether entitled by land or not. The renowned warrior led in warfare with the approval of the chief, led expeditions to Palau for stone money, and even built clubhouses. In battle, he was distinguished by a special headdress and tattooing, and in his special canoe he led his fellow villagers into conflict.

Another very important traditional craftsman, the *paluw* or canoe captain and navigator for deep sea travel, led all travel from Yap to Palau for shell money or to the subservient islands of the central Carolines. His rights to these skills were not invested in land, but obtained by purchase from a previous navigator or from his father who had similar training. Along with his navigational skills he learned magic and became a magician for deep sea travel.

Building skills are also either purchased or passed on to sons. The master canoe builder is called *salap ko m'uw*, the master house builder, *salap ko na'un*, and the master platform builder, *salap ko wunbey*. Each spends years in apprenticeship to his father or to a teacher to whom he pays traditional valuables like stone or shell money. At the same time he not only learns the trade, but also the esoteric knowledge that will make him a magician. All major construction in the village requires his services, and payment is in food and valuables. It is easy to become rich as a *salap* 'master', but legend holds that masters who do so will soon die. Thus the masters are not only skilled, but very generous in distributing their payment.

Divination and diviners also are important in Yapese politics. Informants report at least twelve different means of divining the future. In traditional Yapese politics the priests of the highest sanctuaries annually observed special rituals that revealed the fortunes of war, the death of leaders, or possible impending disasters. These rituals were part of the regular cycle of religious observances and the yearly revelations were coveted by the privileged high chiefs. Village chiefs without access to such information usually turned to a local diviner called *tamanbey* to discover their fortunes in war or some other political endeavor. The *tamanbey* is expert at reading future probabilities in the random tying of a coconut frond. These diviners are still called upon today, sometimes by candidates seeking foreknowledge about election results.

Other types of divination include reading the palm of the hand or reading the future from the inside of a betel nut basket. Yapese often consult a medium to see how their problems are going to turn out. According to tradition, if one wishes to have a child, he should first go to the diviner and discover whether or not it is possible. If possible, then prayers should be made to the ancestors; if impossible, prayers are omitted as a waste of time. Other uses of divination include discovering the causes of illness, deciding if a runaway husband will return, or seeking the identity of a new lover.

Finally, villages have certain patriclans and individuals skilled in medicines. A clan estate holding the title *tataguliy* 'curing battle wounds' treated any kind of wound inflicted by weapons of war. Other types of medicine are known by every family, although some families may have acquired special skills. A patriclan with special skills is called *tatafaley* 'the place of the medicine'. Very serious ills caused by sorcery are combated by a magician, and not by medicine.

Succession to Statuses

The succession to leadership encompasses both land with its inherent authority and the status of speaker for the land. Land is inherited patrilineally, from father to sons, thus succession to the land and its authority is easily defined. All obedient faithful sons of a given father, who have received names from the estate's pool of ancestral ghosts, have rights to the estate land and its authority. To be named after one of the ancestral ghosts is to become a son. The mode of becoming a family member, whether by adoption or birth, makes no difference. To inherit, a son must be faithful and obedient, and especially must care for his father in his old age. A particularly disobedient son may be disinherited.

Succession to the status of voice of the land may be more complex. The genealogy of the estate of the village chief in Balabat, called Mana'ol (Figure 12), shows *voice* consistently passed from father to oldest son. According to informants, this is the rule of inheritance. The

Figure 12. Line of Succession to Mana'ol Estate, Balabat, Rull

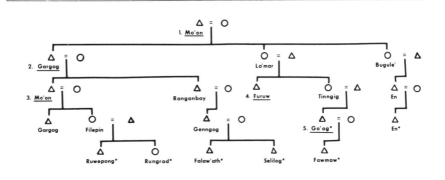

Note: The heirs to the authority of the estate, numbered in order of succession, are underlined.

* Indicates living persons.

oldest son receives the land with the highest authority, younger sons receive land with lesser authority. Land is divided among the sons. Should the oldest son die an early death, his younger brother would become the voice of the land, but the land would pass to the oldest son's son. When this son reached middle age, he would then speak for his own land.

Two factors are very important in the succession of sons to the rank of voice of high-ranking land: relative age and absolute age. The eldest son has the right to the authority of the estate land. However, if his absolute age has not yet placed him in the category of mature man, he may not act as chief nor assume the authority of his land. Rather, the *matam* 'estate father' would speak for him and would exercise the authority of the estate. This estate father is one of the younger brothers of the son's father, who owns other land, but speaks for the authority of the land of his older brother. The right of the estate father to speak for the land is lifelong, regardless of the age of the legitimate heir.

If, however, the son is middle aged at the death of his father, he in all likelihood will assume the authority of the land. He may use an older man as spokesman if he has just entered the category of mature man, or he may do his own talking. In either case he is recognized as the spokesman of the land and the exerciser of its authority. The older spokesman fulfills a ceremonial propriety; the power lies with the actual heir.

Should the land and the voice of the land be without proper heir, that is, if the sons of the chief all die before the father, or if the chief has no sons, then the land reverts back to its potential heirs. First among these are the patriclan brothers of the deceased chief; the second are the *mafen* 'trustees' or matrisib brothers of the deceased chief's father. In the case of Mana'ol estate (Figure 12), the chief died after his sons and brother. His brother's son was too young to succeed, and so his trustee or father's sister's son succeeded to the voice of Mana'ol. When this man died, the original chief's brother's son had already died and so the trustee or FaSiDaSo inherited the voice of Mana'ol. There are grandsons of the chief's brother living, and after the death of the trustee who now speaks for Mana'ol, the oldest may succeed to become the voice of that land.

In all cases of succession, the village has some word as to who will be the chief. The dying chief tells the village whom he feels is capable of the job. If the council agrees, the matter is settled, but if they disagree, then the chief must choose again. He may designate one son as his heir, but if the people say no, he must select another son or brother. In most cases, however, a good son will be a good chief and a very bad son is likely to be disinherited anyway. Should an important piece of land be completely without heirs, as happened with the estate Pebinaw, chief-of-young-men, in Me'rur, Tamil, the village council may select someone to fill that position and take ownership of the land. A man who is very hard working, *madangdang* 'wealthy', and of very high character is usually selected to take the land and the voice.

Sometimes when a chief dies without proper heirs, a leader from another high-ranking estate will assume the authority of the land. He is known as *madol'eg e pilung* 'make believe chief', or *pilung ni misi'uw*, a derogatory term. He has not been given authority, but has merely assumed it.

Succession to the three leading estates in the village is extremely important, and although patrilineal primogeniture is the rule, exceptions occur when the qualifications of the candidate are questionable. A chief is said to merely stand on the land and speak for it. If he is incompetent, tyrannical, or deceitful in his conduct, he can be removed from that land (usually through assassination) and someone else is selected in his place. The new chief will always be selected from the pool of legitimate heirs, following the proper line of succession, unless the potential successor is considered as bad as the previous chief.

Decision-Making Procedures

Decision-making on Yap is rarely, if ever, a one-man affair. The power of a chief is tempered always by the power of the *puruy* 'council' of important leaders in the village. The council is found at all levels of village organization. It includes the three leading titles—village chief, chief-of-young-men, and sitting-chief—their highest-ranking associated estates, and the section and subsection leaders of the village. Depending upon the subject of the discussion, word is carried to the village sections and subsections where additional councils are held and decisions are passed on and executed. Proposals from the top are more frequent than those from the bottom. Chiefs, wishing to compete with other chiefs, seeking to raise their own and their subjects' rank, plan projects of prestige and war. They present these ideas to the council and seek its support; once this is obtained, the leaders urge the people on to accomplish the goal.

In a public council all members of the village may come and listen, but only the ranking estate leaders of the village and sections may talk. If a lower-ranking individual wishes to express an opinion, he quietly speaks to his leader who relays the idea to the general meeting. Speakers are artists at circumlocution, presenting ideas in such a way as to avoid commitment to a particular viewpoint until a feeling for consensus is obtained. Decisions of the council are reached by consensus. Issues are discussed until public consensus is reached, or until a consensus is deemed impossible and the issue is dropped.

The council functions in all aspects of public decision-making that require the expenditure of village resources. Thus exchanges, dances, religious feasts, and all major projects are decided in council. In the usual procedure a leader will introduce a suggestion, the group will discuss it thoroughly, and, when a consensus is reached, the village chief will declare the decision and if the proposal is approved begin to ask for contributions. The ideas of the three leaders, village chief, chief-of-young-men, and sitting-chief, weigh heavily with the other leaders and if they present a consensus the others are certain to follow.

The task of the chiefs is to see that all things in the village are maintained in good order. Thus when the roofs fall into bad condition or foliage grows in roads, a chief points out the needs and proposes a solution. The other leaders quickly support the chief on such matters and rally the people to the task.

On unusual matters, however, the chiefs do not have such open-ended power. Major new projects, such as taro patches, land fill, or massive house or road building, may be broached by a village chief, but then must survive extensive discussion. To leave a project unfinished is a shame to both village and chief, and so serious tasks requiring high expenditure of labor and goods must be decided in council. No chief has enough economic power to accomplish such major works alone and needs the support of all the council. Furthermore, the hardship exacted upon the people of the village must be considered, for, if the people become greatly discontented with the drain upon their personal resources, the chief may lose his support.

Another matter calling for serious consideration by the council is war. In past cases a chief would introduce a proposition to make war against another village. When a war was being planned, preparation for it was made in a small closed council. Assistance requested from allies could be granted without a council meeting, with a chief hastily gathering together his forces and joining the fight.

In matters of law, social control, and public sanctions, the council is the functioning legal body of the village. Any theft, destruction of property, breach of custom regarding respect of taboos, or failure to meet village responsibilities are brought before the council. The individual is considered guilty if summoned, and his father comes to beg on his behalf and to offer retribution for the crime. Small thefts may be fined in stone and shell money. Serious breaches of custom, such as men visiting the menstrual house, may be punished by seizing the culprit's land. In either case, the father of the offender comes before the meeting and makes his case. The better he is at pleading, the less he is likely to pay. The village chief speaks on behalf of the village and suggests that the offer of stone or shell money given in the plea is enough or not enough. The council may discuss this if they desire and decide upon the sanction.

In cases of murder or adultery when the offender's life is in serious danger, he may run to the house of the chief and request refuge. If the chief wishes he may take the offender inside and protect him. Then the chief becomes the pleader before the council. He takes shell money of considerable value to the chief-of-young-men and requests that the offender be forgiven and be permitted to return free of harm to his home. The chief-of-young-men receives the shell money and returns to the estate of the victim. Presenting the shell money to the head of that estate he tells him that the chiefs wish the matter to be settled peacefully. To disregard this request is considered a serious insult to the chiefs and invariably it will be accepted. Other devious means of revenge, such as sorcery, may be visited upon the offender by the victim's family, rather than through public violence. The chiefs cannot stop this. In certain cases the chief-of-young-men may refuse the shell money, in which case the offender must remain in the house of the chief or flee the village.

In matters requiring the supernatural intervention of the village priest and/or magicians, only the village chief or the sitting-chief has the authority to request such assistance. The council, however, may discuss the necessity of such a measure and request that the chiefs make gifts on the behalf of the people of the village. As the magician is normally a member of the council, he also has some comment to offer as to the necessity of his services. If the council decides to call in the magician, the chief proceeds to the house of the magician at a later time, presents the shell money, and formally requests the services already discussed in the council.

Leadership Legitimacy and Support

The legitimacy of a candidate's claim to leadership status is defined by at least four major criteria. Foremost is ownership of titled land, which allows its owner to speak for its authority. The only exception to this occurs when an eligible, legitimate heir is not available and the village council agrees upon an alternate person for the duration of his lifetime. The second criteria is legitimate succession to the voice or *lungun* of the land. This particularly refers to the oldest son having first rights to the title of authority, and maintaining the right to pass it on to his oldest son. Third, a man must be about fifty years of age and felt to be capable of handling a man's work. Finally, he must know the rights and procedures for exercising the authority of his land. Yapese believe that all leaders should follow the code of right action (*yalen*) handed down from their ancestors. Knowledge of this code is imperative, and adherence to the code is required for legitimate action and decision-making. The code of right conduct assures that leaders will act in accord with the best interests of the village. To act contrary to the code is considered illegal and raises questions about the legitimacy of the leader's occupation of the status.

After land, political power and leadership are perhaps most sought after in Yap. Case after case may be cited of attempts to challenge the legitimacy and the power of particular chiefs. Presently, one of the most frequent areas of conflict is in the question of legitimate ownership of titled land. In the rapid and devastating depopulation of Yap, many estates suffered from a lack of legitimate heirs and even a lack of old men who could speak for their authorities. In such cases the office of chief has often fallen by default to one of the elder, higher-ranking men of a village. Because of the constant rivalry between old men for such unclaimed positions, however, the villagers tend to say that there is no chief, but that so and so acts like a chief because there is no one to do the job. The village council often cannot agree upon a successor because the members of the council, limited in number, usually all want the job. The older or more dominant of the group frequently acts as leader, but his support is critically weakened because his claim to the position is questionable. When a council is large enough and powerful enough to support a selected candidate, then he is recognized as the legitimate chief.

Another area of conflict lies between younger and older brothers. Informants tell of one high chief in Rull whose younger brother tried to usurp his authority. Expressing their rivalry in exhibitions of power, the older brother and chief built a house six-arm-spans long, and then the younger brother built one seven-arm-spans long and higher. The older brother called in warriors from an adjacent village and the younger brother sent them home. The rivalry was concluded by the arranged death of the younger brother in a planned battle. In such showdowns between rival brothers, the older brother likely will emerge on top, unless he has particular weaknesses that question his legitimacy and support.

The problem of a young heir is solved more easily. If the legitimate heir is still a young man, but not a child, he can succeed to the voice of the land. His success, however, depends upon his own behavior and wisdom. One of his most important moves is to find an older man, preferably a classificatory brother, who will speak for him in village affairs, and who will reflect his own views. The best arrange-

ment is to select a brother who is of low rank; he will feel very honored at being asked and will acknowledge that he is not the leader, but
is merely speaking for the chief of the village. At the same time, he
carries the weight and respect of an old man, which is added power for
the younger legitimate heir.

Finally, a chief who is out of harmony with the village and the
code of right conduct is in serious trouble. A case in point is a chief
from Gagil who secretly arranged with an adjacent village to enter his
village and kill a number of the people. He further assisted the enemy
by dispersing the young men of his village. The attack was successful
but when the people of his village discovered the treachery, the young
men surrounded his house and killed him.

The question of legitimacy leads to the question of support. A
village chief is recognized as the voice of the land and the village. Thus,
when he directs, the people should follow, for he is speaking as the
land, and his words are for the best interests of all. Though his decisions may be costly and difficult to carry out, as long as they increase the
pride, prestige, respect, power, and productivity of the village, he is followed.

If the leader's direction is questioned, support for him given for
the sake of the village may be dropped in terms of more personal interests. And, if the decision-making of the chief violates the trust the
people have placed in him, he will lose support. Prior to German rule*
he would have lost his life. In general, however, the mere fact that he
is chief commands the support of the people. It is considered a very
serious action not to follow the word of the chiefs.

A village chief does not rely merely on his title in land for his
power. He has considerable authority to back up his decisions with
force. First, he is the "overseer of breath." He can very easily have
killed any low-ranking figure who does not follow his decisions.
Higher-ranking leaders are more difficult to dispose of, but can also be
eliminated by a very crafty chief. Through his control of the young
men of his village, a chief can exercise political control over his rivals.
In conflicts with higher-ranking rivals, he usually depends upon extravillage allies, arranging wars with the clear purpose of eliminating a
particular individual.

Leaders also have recourse to considerable psychological and social
force. The Yapese are very competitive and leaders use this desire to be
foremost (and the associated feeling of shame at not being so) to push
people to productive activity. Lower-ranking leaders are especially

---

* German colonial rule sharply curtailed the power of chiefs. The ethno-
graphic present is based upon the period before 1900.

controlled in this manner; they are given praise for good work and public reproach for failure.

Chiefs also have considerable economic force. The power of a chief to seize land in cases where an individual has failed in his obligation to the chief already has been cited. This is one of the primary motivating forces for people whose lands are under the "overseer" authority of a chief. Land is life and to lose it is extremely serious.

Finally, a village chief has that unknown, mysterious power of the supernatural, which he controls through his control of the magicians. If the people are constantly uncooperative, he may make magic to summon a typhoon to destroy the resources they have been withholding from him (or if not a typhoon, an epidemic sickness).

While Schneider is correct in stating that a chief's power is limited by his lack of technical competence with the supernatural, he overemphasizes the limitations of the power of the village chief (1949:117). This is in part due to the anarchical tendencies of his informants from Rumung, who are rather well known in Yap for spitting in the face of power. The assertions of Schneider's informants that chiefs may not seize land, banish people from the village, or levy punishment for breaches of custom are denied by informants from other areas of Yap. A chief may do these things as long as they are not done arbitrarily, but in accord with customary codes of correct behavior and just recompense for breaches of these customs. Generally such decisions or punishments are decided upon in a council meeting, with other ranking leaders of the village, in which the village chief acts as prosecutor and judge for customary law.

The most successful chief builds support through the mutual obligation relationships of generosity and reciprocity. The generous leader is praised, while the stingy is criticized, questioned, and even scorned. If a leader is very generous, he will reap the obvious support to be gained in a reciprocity relationship and the people may feel favorably enough toward him to overlook his other faults. It is worthy of note that today titled estates actually consist of very small amounts of private land. Their ancestors had been so generous in giving it away that in many cases very little is left but the myriad obligations and overseer authorities of the land. These obligations, however, provide strong support.

The leader not only gives for private needs, but rewards for services. He may give as rewards aspects of his own authority, for example, he may give a particular fishing right to a family who served in a special way, or overseer rights to a parcel of land or sea with title to first fruits and support from the individual owners. He may also give the services of his low-caste serfs, and in some cases even give the total rights to those serfs. He may give status to estates by granting them certain authorities. In the village of Balabat, one estate has been designated the "eyes" of the chief for a certain area. Such status would be given as reward for service. Finally, the chief may reward with the traditional valuables of shell, stone, or other kinds of money. Besides enrichment, these valuables also grant prestige to their owners.

The same general criteria for legitimacy and support apply to the lesser leaders of the village. While these estates may lack extensive resources to effect force or reward, they may acquire necessary additional support from the village chief. As long as they maintain the support of the high chief, they have not only their own authority, but also that of the high chief.

Support is crucial in leadership competition and conflict within a village, and may be gained outside the bounds of legitimacy. Two different cases illustrate this point. In the village of Wacolab, Map, the present high chief of the village is in fact the traditional sitting-chief. The transition in power resulted from a war with Gacpar in Gagil in which Wacolab village suffered an attack and severe losses. The chief of Wacolab had been allied with Gacpar and because of his treachery lost complete support in the village. The sitting-chief had been allied with friendly forces in Tamil who gave assistance to Wacolab in the battle and to the sitting-chief in the power struggle with the village chief who lost not only support, but his authority. Legitimately the sitting-chief had no right to assume the village chief's powers, but the village council decided to abandon the old authority and alliances for new ones in the best interests of the village.

The second example is from Rull. The paramount estate there was left without sons and direct heirs. The authority for the land was passed to the *mafen* 'trustee' who, however, was greatly indebted to a lesser-ranking chief because of that chief's extreme generosity. The trustee gave the land and authority of the estate to the subordinate chief who then divested himself of claims to his lower-ranking land. The legitimacy of this move is questioned by Yapese informants, who argued that it is against the "code" to give away the ranking land of a patriclan. However, the lower-ranking chief gained and maintained support by extensive generosity and reward for services. Subsequent inheritance then established the legitimacy of land ownership and the legitimacy of the patriclan ceased to be a question.

Thus, support for village leaders may be acquired by legitimate or illegitimate means. Effective leadership is that which can maintain support. Legitimacy and support are interdependent, and one may be used by leaders to establish the other. Ideally Yapese leaders acquire legitimacy through ascribed leadership status and support through adherence to a code of personal and public conduct.

7. THE POLITICAL STRUCTURE OF THE YAP ISLANDS

The village is the most important single unit in Yap-wide politics. The villages, like the sections and estates within them, rank in relation to each other. This ranking defines a hierarchy of dominant/subordinate relationships with inherent reciprocal obilgations. These reciprocal obligations create the series of mutual exchanges and alliances of the political structure of Yap.

The village chief is the focal point of extravillage interaction and the official representative of his village. He is the voice of the clan estates that make up his village, and intervenes for their good or evil in the relations of his village with other villages. His voice is generally the most important and the strongest in his village, but it is not the only one. Invariably at least one other clan estate, and often two, have channels of communication to different outside villages. In the past these estates sometimes have led their village sections into affiliations with opposing alliances, and have engaged in life and death struggles for power and rank. Leaders of opposing sections have plotted to have each other killed. When fighting occurred among opposing sections within a village, allies were necessarily different, because both could not obtain support from the same groups. To provide flexibility and power within their alliance, the village chief, sitting-chief, and chief-of-young-men all maintained distinctive ties outside their village. This diversity of political ties restricted the individual power of any one chief and introduced stability by balancing the power of chiefs against each other.

This chapter describes the traditional relationship of Yapese villages and their leaders in the Yap-wide political structure; most of its data has not appeared in any of the earlier literature.

The Paramount Villages and Chiefs: Delipi Ngucol

The Yapese describe the highest leadership in Yap in terms of the cooking implements in which three stones form a pedestal for pots placed over a fire. Yap is the pot and the three highest-ranking villages and their chiefs are the *ngucol* 'stone pillars' upon which the other villages rest. Significantly, if one potstand falls, the pot falls over. This is the basic philosophy of Yapese politics. There are three paramount villages and three paramount chiefs. Each is important, and none should become so strong as to cause another to fall.

The three highest-ranking (*bulce'*) villages in Yap are Ngolog in Rull municipality, Teb in Tamil municipality, and Tholang section of Gacpar village in Gagil. Each of these three have a counterpart (*ulun*) or right-hand assistant: Balabat village in Rull, Me'rur village in Tamil, and Ariap section of Gacpar village in Gagil. These three pairs are considered the *delipi ngucol* 'three pillars' of the Yapese political structure. Each of the three has a paramount chief who is head over the paired villages and their respective chiefs. He is like the father of these villages, the *pilung ni pilbithir* 'sitting-chief' of each respective place. These leadership statuses belong to titled estates, with authority invested in land and not in people. The estates are Ru'way in Rull, Arib in Tamil, and Bulwol in Gagil.

The development of power in these three areas cannot be documented. The mythology of Yap, however, does provide some interesting insights into their actual functioning and respective importance. In the mythology of Yapese origins, the first human beings set up a household in the Rull area. The first chiefs of Yap lived at Towol 'sacred place' in Rull, which is currently under the authority of the paramount chief of Ru'way. After considerable time had elapsed, a large typhoon devastated Yap, killing most of the people and washing a mythical mountain in Tamil down to the area now known as Nimgil in southern Yap and creating a new land. One man and his wife survived in Tamil, and they are progenitors of present-day Yapese. They had seven children. When dividing their land among the children, they gave the oldest son the land of the parents, as was the custom, and gave the others choice land in the other areas of Yap. The youngest son, however, refused to leave Tamil, his birthplace. The parents felt this was very bad, but rather than cause fighting among the children, they asked the oldest son to settle in Gagil. Because he was entitled to stay in Tamil, but agreed to go to Gagil, he was given sovereignty over Map, Rumung, and all the islands to the east (the central Carolines). The youngest son stayed in Tamil, the smallest area, and the oldest daughter went to Rull.

Three things stand out in the story. Rull is the oldest area of the highest chiefs of Yap, but was supplanted by Tamil after the typhoon. Tamil is the place of origin for the present political alignment, the *"tabinaw"* of the first family of present-day Yap. Gagil has dominance over all the islands east of Yap.

The Paramount Chief from Arib

The estate Arib in Tamil is considered the *pilung ni pilbithir ko nam* 'the old wise chief of Yap'. Like an old man, its chief does not work, but rather voices his approval or disapproval of the actions of others. His title is sitting-chief for the villages of Teb and Me'rur. The people and chiefs of these villages are his servants, building his house and meeting his requests.

Arib estate derives its major authority from its position as overseer of the sacred places Ta'ag, Cen, and Amun, site of the origin of the first family of Yap. The chief of Arib presides over the religious ceremonies for these places, which are held once every two years in the month called Yan e Duw. The ceremonies include one hundred days of religious observances, including the rebuilding of the fences around the sacred places, rebuilding the fence and house at Arib, and then making the appropriate prayers, offerings, and ritual for the duration of the period. Five priests from the estates of Magif (1), Magif (2), Dal'aw, Fanfaraew, and Fitewar direct the religious observances, while the chief summons the people and resources for the tasks. The observances climax with a large eating class feast for the men of Tamil and the visitors from the other high-ranking villages in Yap.

Arib is also the overseer of the priests and power of the sacred places. Those chiefs who desire certain blessings for all of Yap must place their requests through Arib. The chief of Arib may instruct the priests to perform ritual to bring plenty of fruits (*galwog*), and fertility of women, or he may request disasters such as typhoons or epidemics to punish the people for wrongs.

The other powers of the chief of Arib are very limited. He may hear the plans of the subordinate chiefs in Teb and Me'rur, and approve or disapprove them. He is like a woman, however, in that he does not take an active part, he merely sits and listens. Should the subordinate chiefs desire to exclude him from secular matters, they may do so.

Succession to Arib estate is a matter for the council of chiefs in

Teb and Me'rur to decide. Arib is owned by the matrisib called Fanif and succession to its land and voice is limited to members of that matrilineal sib. The council of chiefs from Teb and Me'rur select a low-ranking member of Fanif sib to speak for the authority of Arib. Informants named two men, Nuuan and Mo'on, from the commoner village of Af, as the two most recent chiefs of Arib. Today the land is without a leader because its religious functions are defunct and its political functions are minor. Care of the land falls to the estate in Teb called Magif, the first assistant to Arib.

Historically, the chief of Arib did come from the paramount village of Teb. Informants said that these chiefs had such great power that the people suffered from the burden of providing support for the chiefs' decisions. The last high-ranking chief of Arib was Tamanfal'-ethin from Gireng estate in Teb. Gireng is the chief of men in Teb, and Tamanfal'ethin held both the authority of Gireng and Arib. Using this power, he created hardship for the people, overextending their resources for public works and warfare. He ultimately was killed by a chief from Okaw village when he started a ceremony (in violation of protocol) before the Okaw chief arrived. After his death, the council of chiefs in Teb selected a low-ranking man from the sib Fanif to be chief of Arib. Because of his low rank, the chief was meek and afraid to seize power and bring hardship upon the people of Tamil.

Undoubtedly the chief of Arib was once an important figure in the council of chiefs of the highest-ranking villages of Yap. The authority, however, has been usurped by the chiefs of Teb and Me'rur and the power of Arib diffused by placing weak, low-ranking persons in the position of authority. When the Japanese forbade the practicing of traditional religious ceremonies, the last vestige of the position's meaning and authority died, leaving the chiefs of Teb and Me'rur the sole leaders in Tamil.

The Paramount Chiefs from Bulwol and Ru'way

The chief of the estate Ru'way in Rull is sitting-chief of Balabat and Ngolog, and leader of the Banpilung alliance of villages in Yap. This alliance is defined as the "side of the chiefs" (or "wise old men"). The chief of Arib in Tamil is also a leader in Banpilung, but in the role of counselor, rather than an active executive. In contrast, the chief of Bulwol estate in Gagil is sitting-chief of Gacpar village and the leader of the Banpagael alliance. Banpagael villages are defined as young and strong as boys, but not so smart as the chiefs. The sphere of power of the three paramount chiefs is demonstrated by Yapese informants on their fingers. Tamil is the thumb, short but strong; Rull is the first finger, much longer with power over the longest island, referred to as

Yap island; Gagil is the longest finger, with power extending all the way to Truk in the central Carolines.

Both the chiefs of Bulwol and Ru'way represent their respective areas in the *puruy ko bulce'* or council of highest-ranking villages of Yap. Each sits on the councils of his local paramount villages, hearing from both of the pair. As is the case with Arib, each has overseer authority over certain sacred places and supervises ceremonies and makes requests for rituals to bring either blessing or disaster upon Yap. Each is overseer of the highest ceremonial eating rank in his respective area.

The power of the chiefs of Ru'way and Bulwol is in their words. They sit in the council of chiefs in their area and listen and give their approval or disapproval. The execution of decisions of the council lies with the lesser chiefs of the two villages under them. Their power is more secular and stronger than that of the chief of Arib. Both chiefs have channels of communication and spies in different localities to keep them informed. Both preside over estate associations that provide support and participate in distributions made by the chief. Both, then, have a secular power and authority not enjoyed by the paramount chief of Arib in Tamil.

Presently, both Gagil and Rull make claims of being paramount in Yap. The chief at Bulwol sails in a canoe around Yap in a demonstration of his power and allies. En route he is received by each village along the shore; the receiving village gives gifts of fish to those bringing the chief and then carry him on to the next village along the line. The trip requires considerable preparation, necessitating that each village fish in advance to present the carrying village with the appropriate gifts. The last chief from Bulwol to try this was Tithinyow, who began a progress during the Spanish occupation of Yap. He reached Bulwol village in Rumung and then stopped when a spy informed him of a plot to kill him at Gilfith on the west side of Yap.

The extent of the power of the chief at Ru'way is demonstrated by the technique of net fishing called *yartan*. When the chief of Ru'way sends out the word, men from all the villages on the east side of Yap from Maa' in Tamil to L'ey in Gilman gather at the seashore to fish with a net stretching for several miles along the shoreline. The catch is brought to Ru'way and distributed to Ngolog and to other villages of the *bulce'* rank. A *yartan* has not been carried out within the memory of living informants.

Bulwol, like Arib, is owned by a matrisib, and succession is limited to members of the matrilineal sib called Waloy. When the chief of Bulwol dies, the other leaders in the village of Gacpar meet together and decide which member of Waloy sib in Gacpar should fill the vacancy. Known chiefs from Bulwol are:

Yo'lang—mythical first chief
Defngrad
Fanapiliw
Tethinyow (died around 1900)
Fithingmow (died around 1950)

Today no old men in Gacpar are from Waloy sib. Siling, from Dachngar estate (first in the association of estates under Bulwol), was asked by the wife of the last chief, Fithingmow, and his sib mate from another village to take care of Bulwol and speak for the authority when necessary.

Ru'way is inherited by the children of the owner. From a mythical genealogy it appears that Ru'way was once passed alternately between two sibs called Ngolog and Ngabinaw. In recent history it has been passed from father to son.

The respective roles of the three paramount chiefs are defined in the same terms as the chief statuses in a village: voice of the land, ancient voice, and voice of the young men. Ru'way is leader of the Banpilung alliance, the side of the chiefs, and controls the largest area of land resources in Yap. Arib is the guardian of the sacred places of Yap and strong in terms of wisdom and supernatural power. Like the sitting-chief in the village council, the chief of Arib provides a third mediating voice between the other two. Bulwol is leader of the Banpagael alliance, or the side of the young men. Like the chief-of-young-men, Bulwol's chief is strong in manpower and has extensive allies for war. Together the chiefs and their supporting villages maintain a balance of power in Yap politics. Each struggles in his particular sphere to gain the advantage over the others, but each is controlled in turn by the other two. The symbol of the pillars for the cooking pots illustrates the interrelatedness of all three. If one fails or becomes weak, the whole system collapses.

The Paramount Villages: Bulce' and Ulun

The three paramount centers of Yap are dual, matched units, called *bulce'* and *ulun*, symbolizing chiefs and warriors, respectively. The organization of each of the paramount centers is based on the same ideology and definition of status as is found for the three paramount chiefs. For example, the village of Ngolog in Rull is considered the "female" village, with chiefs having overseer authority over land and resources; the village of Balabat is considered the "male" village, with chiefs having overseer authority over the sea and warfare. Ru'way section in the village of Balabat is the domain of the paramount chief, who sits in the position of "wise old man" over both villages, approving and disapproving decisions and actions. The roles of these villages are very clearly defined. In any major political function in Rull involving economic resources, Ngolog provides garden produce (involving women and land) and Balabat provides fish (involving men and sea), while Ru'way supervises, seeing that obligations are met in the proper extent and order. The village of Ngolog, being like a woman, does not go to war with other villages. If fighting is called for, Balabat will do it. Any young men of Ngolog who wish to fight will do so as members of Balabat, the warrior village.

The dual units of the paramount villages are the highest-ranking in Yap, and each unit has a particular role in the administration of land, resources, and power for the paramount chief. The *bulce'* villages play the roles of chiefs and women, the strength of Yap, sitting above the fray of battles, planning what will be done, and watching it happen. The *ulun* villages take the male role, active, mobile, executing the decisions of the *bulce'* and the paramount chiefs. Ultimate leadership over the whole of Yap clearly lies in a committee of chiefs, each with definite specified authority and power. Each paramount chief and the village chiefs of the respective villages or sections preside over a council of ranking men and estates. These councils share a large part of the power and a chief is severely handicapped without them. The basic formula of this system is a council of seven. Each of the *bulce'* villages has seven estates, referred to as *cath*, which play major roles in the decision-making process and which share in the collections and distributions authorized by the high chiefs. Some *ulun* villages and the paramount chiefs also have supporting councils of seven. The actual composition of the councils are often disputed by informants because certain estates have gained or lost this authority in the unceasing competition for status and power. Table 13 illustrates the distribution of power in the leadership structure of the paramount center at Rull. This distribution and balancing of power is the primary theme of Yap leadership and is seen at every level, from the lowest-ranking patriclan to the paramount chiefs.

The Paramount Villages and the Dual Alliances

Certain other ranking villages allied to the paramount chiefs are also called *bulce'* and *ulun*. These villages, grouped into two competing unions, Banpilung and Banpagael respectively, represent the paramount chiefs to a series of lesser-ranking, but allied villages. Gagil is the undisputed leader of the Banpagael alliance, while Rull is the leader of the Banpilung. Traditionally, Tamil balanced between the two alignments, shifting from one to the other as the particular case may require. Today, however, Tamil is considered Banpilung and allied with Rull. This shift appears to be the result of the increasing power of Gagil, brought

Table 13. Leadership Statuses and Authority of Paramount Villages in Rull

Territorial Divisions	Titles	Estates	Local Authority	External Authority
	Paramount Chief	Ru'way	Sitting-chief; *suwon* of Ngolog, Balabat, and Rull sacred places	Chief, Balabat, Ngolog; chief, Atiliw, Rumu'; chief, Adibuwe', Kaday; chief, Yanuf, Luwec
LAN RU'WAY SUBSECTION*	Councillors WOLCATH**	Biledugo' (1) Pekel Banyumuc Thumuth Madal' Tangil Biledugo' (2)	2nd to Ru'way 3rd to Ru'way Association leader Association leader Association leader Messenger Assistant to Biledugo' (1)	Chief, Ngof, Gal' Chief, Rulmit subsection, Balabat; chief, Af (Tamil)
	Village Chief	Mana'ol	War chief; *suwon* of women, *yogum*, sea, and torch fishing	Chief, *ulun* villages, S. Yap; chief, 14 villages, S. Rull; chief, Dachngar, Gitam, Talguw
BALABAT VILLAGE	Chief-of-Young-Men	Mado'	Chief of village land activities; chief, N. Section of Balabat	Chief, subsection of Mulro'

	Fitebinaw	Chief of village fishing, gardening; chief, S. Section of Balabat	
Councillors			
Oob**	Mangyan	Assistant to Mana'ol	
	Towar	Association leader	
	Pun'ew	Association leader	
	Magabac	Association leader	
	Debecig	Association leader	
	Falmarus	Association leader	
	Bucol	"Eyes" of Mana'ol, S. Section	
Messenger	Bogwan	Messenger between Ru'way and Mana'ol	Chief, Nimar
NGOLOG Council of Chiefs	Tidirra'	*Suwon* of men	Chief, *bulce'* villages, S. Yap; chief, Kanif
	Magcug	*Suwon* of women	Chief, section of Yanuf
VILLAGE Cath**	Pegal' (1)	Assistant to Tidirra'	
	Pegal' (2)	Assistant to Magcug	
	Mager	Section chief	
	Gubiyel	Section chief	
	Marmog	Section chief	

* See Figure 10 for a map of this subsection with its leading estates and associations of estates.
** Local designations for the councils.

about by the distribution of wealth obtained from its tribute relationships with the inhabited atolls to the east. Gagil had a source of tribute wealth unavailable to the other paramount chiefs and used this to expand its sphere of allies. The structure of the alliances is outlined in Table 14.

Table 14. Paramount Villages and the Dual Alliances

delipi ngucol 'Three Pillars'	Rull	Tamil	Gagil
Paramount chiefs	Ru'way estate	Arib estate	Bulwol estate
bulce villages	Ngolog village	Teb village	Tholang section, Gacpar
ulun villages	Balabat village	Me'rur village	Ariap section, Gacpar
Alliances	Banpilung—*bulce* rank		Banpagael—*ulun* rank
Allied villages of Chief Ranks	Gilfith village, Fanif		Co'ol village, Map
	Kanif village, Delipebinaw		Bugol village, Tamil
	N'ef village, Kanfay		Okaw village, Weloy
	Guror village, Gilman		Anoth village, Gilman

NOTES:
>Informants disagree as to the particular villages ranked *ulun* or *bulce*. The ranking system was quite dynamic until the German government stopped warfare. The above villages were apparently on top at that time, but others may lay claim to *ulun* or *bulce* ranks. In some cases it is undoubtedly true that once in the village's history it may have been one of either, but the fortunes of war effected a change.

Under the *bulce* and *ulun* concept other important but lesser-ranking estates have a direct representative relationship to the paramount chiefs, increasing the range of the leadership and communication network. Two particular statuses should be defined—the *yalung samol* and the *teyugang ni rod ni pilung*. The *yalung samol* are particular estates representing the paramount chiefs located in a low-ranking village considered strategic. They are given the rank of *bulce*, although the remainder of the village in which they reside is considerably lower. The following estates are reported by informants as *yalung samol*: Bileyow, Magcagil village, Gilman; Bileydid, Magaf village,

Delipebinaw; Tefaenfel', Dachngar village, Rull; Macngod, Madalay village, Tamil; Ba'anngel, Alog village, Weloy.

The concept of *teyugang* is not too clear to present-day Yapese, but is definitely a part of the traditional system. The *teyugang* villages are neither *bulce'* nor *ulun*, but rank just below these and play a leadership role in the alliance of a group of villages to the paramount chiefs. Like the *ulun* and *bulce'* they have subordinate villages beneath them. They act as regional leaders, but are not high enough in rank to sit on the councils of *ulun* or *bulce'*.

The dual alliances function primarily in times of warfare and when mobilization of support is required in situations of conflict. Their roles are always competitive, whether they involve economic exchanges, religious ceremony, or actual fighting. In the past, wars were arranged by leaders of villages in competition with each other or by competitors within a village. These arranged wars required that each village have a representative from the opposing alignment who could communicate the desires and plans of the chief to those who would execute them.

The Authority of the Bulce', Ulun, and Paramount Chiefs

Channels of Communication—The Tha'

The Yapese concept of *tha'* is perhaps the most important element in differentiating the power of separate political statuses. *Tha'* is literally 'a series of things, tied together with string'. For example, the term is used to classify a string of shell money—*tha' e yar*. When used in Yapese politics, the concept of *tha'* designates a long line of communication that ties together the various geographical and political units of Yap.

As mentioned earlier, the essence of Yapese politics is verbal communication or the passing of the word. Any legitimate request or message must follow the channels of communication, or *tha'*. This is a very serious matter to the Yapese and if word is passed improperly, regardless of its importance, it may be disregarded. On the other hand, a properly communicated message has the force and power of the highest chiefs and to disregard it brings serious consequences. This hierarchy of communication is one of the keys to the power of the paramount chiefs.

An example from the village of Gacpar illustrates the concept of *tha'* as it is applied in the political field. There are two major *tha'* out of Gacpar to the islands of Map and Rumung—Damanman *tha'* for the alliance of Banpagael, and Bilemalob for the alliance of Banpilung. The first originates from Tagabuy estate in Ariap section, *ulun* rank, and the second from Pebinaw estate in Tholang section, *bulce'* rank. The leaders of the two estates are respective chiefs of their sections, and second in rank only to the leader of Bulwol, the paramount sitting-chief. Any message to allies in the islands of Map or Rumung must begin with the word from the chiefs of one of these two estates. The chain of communication links may be seen in Figure 13.

In addition to this type of *tha‘*, certain lines of communication are designated for a specific purpose. One example is the *tha‘* Wolangel, which runs from Fanawol estate in Gacpar to the four villages on the southwest side of Map. The sole purpose of this *tha‘* is the collection of tribute at a certain time of the year.

The concept of *tha‘* includes all types of relationships for communication between villages. The most important are the *tha‘* of *bulce‘* and *ulun* with their respective alliances of Banpilung and Banpagael. All important matters, including war, work, religious ceremonies, or requests for support and assistance, are handled "on top of" (*dakaen e tha‘*) the lines of communication. Breaches of custom regarding marriage or even murder may be carried to the high chiefs on the *tha‘*. In such a case, the accused pleads with his chief for support and intervention. The chief then takes a piece of shell money and presents it with his plea to the next higher chief on the *tha‘*, who passes it on to the highest chiefs, with each chief adding a piece of shell money if he approves, until it returns to the victim's family. To refuse such a plea passed along the *tha‘* of all the high chiefs of Yap would be utter folly. It is invariably accepted and pardon given.

Figure 13. Channels of Communication (*tha‘*), Gacpar, Gagil

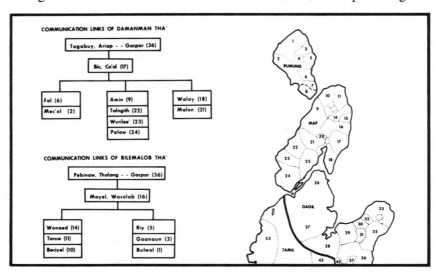

The function of the various *tha'* in the political field is of primary importance. The *tha'* provides the channel for acquiring or withdrawing economic and political support for the chiefs. It is the basic framework for collection of tribute and for mobilizing forces in warfare.

The power of the paramount chiefs is limited and balanced by the distribution of the *tha'*. Each of the three paramount chiefs from Gagil, Tamil, and Rull must go through subordinate chiefs to send messages to allies. The two subordinate chiefs in the paramount centers are also controlled in that both have respective *tha'* and neither has exclusive power. In the case of a dispute among the three chiefs of Gagil, two of them may work together to outflank the third. Therefore, no one chief is capable of exerting total power or influence over his locale. The power is distributed among the three chiefs in each of the three paramount centers. Support is maintained through cooperation and consensus within the hierarchy of the system.

An incident in the village of Anoth in Gilman municipality provides an excellent example. The people of Anoth had seized an automobile belonging to men from Balabat, Rull, because they created considerable disturbance on the road going through the village. The young men returned to their village and requested assistance from the paramount chief of Ru'way. Because Ru'way is *bulce'* the chief could not send word directly to Anoth, which is Banpagael and *ulun*. Instead he sent his messenger (Tangil estate) to Mamfal estate in Guror village (*bulce'*), which has a *tha'* relationship with Anoth. The messenger from Ru'way gave the chief of Mamfal a piece of shell money and requested his assistance in obtaining the release of the car. The chief of Mamfal accepted the shell money, and taking a much more valuable piece of stone money in its place, went to see the sitting-chief of Bileyow, Magacagil, who acts as intermediary between Guror and Anoth. The sitting-chief of Bileyow added another piece of stone money, and they both presented the pieces of money to the village chief of Anoth, with a plea to release the car. Such a plea, coming on the power and legitimacy of the *tha'*, could not be ignored, and reluctantly the people of Anoth released the car. If, however, any of the intermediary chiefs between Ru'way and Anoth had been omitted, the request would have been considered illegitimate (improperly made) and denied.

The *tha'* also provides a means of recognizing legitimacy—legitimacy of a new chief, a decision, a change in rank, or a tribute relationship within the political field. For example, when a new chief plans a ceremonial exchange in honor of the deceased chief he has replaced, the word is sent out on the *tha'* and the new chief performs the duties of a chief—organizing the village, collecting, distributing, and so forth.

The response of other chiefs in attending the ceremony and participating in the exchange articulates public recognition of the new chief's
succession and of the support of the allied chiefs of his position and
authority. Maintaining support and recognizing legitimacy are two of
the primary functions of the *tha'*.

Alliance and Rank

Complementary to the concept of *tha'* is that of *nug* 'net'. The
Yapese describe regional alliances in terms of a fish net. The *tha'* originates with the leading village in the net and leads to the lower-ranking
member villages. Each of the two areas in the example given earlier of
the *tha'* from Gacpar to Map and Rumung would be defined as a net.
The *tha'* from Gacpar passes to the head village of each of the nets,
the head village being determined by the particular channel, Banpilung
or Banpagael, used. The villages of Co'ol in Map and Fal in Rumung
are the primary leaders of the respective nets. However, word from
Banpilung alliance would come to the second-ranking villages of
Wacolab in Map and Riy in Rumung.

The alliances of Banpagael and Banpilung are described as nets.
The spheres of each of the three paramount chiefs are nets, and within
these three are other smaller nets with their respective leading villages.
The nets have geographical as well as political ties and, as illustrated
above, it is frequently the case that nets may be divided along lines of
the two major political alliances. The geographical nets and their leaders are listed in Table 15 and illustrated in Figure 14.

Table 15. Geographical Nets and Their Leaders

Rull Net		Gagil Net		Tamil Net	
Local Net	Chief Village	Local Net	Chief Village	Local Net	Chief Village
Rull	Ngolog	Gagil	Gacpar	Tamil	Teb
Malew	Lamaer	Weloy	Okaw	Fanif	Gilfith
Likaycag	Dulkan	Map	Co'ol		
Delipebinaw	Kanif	Rumung	Fal		
Kanfay	N'ef				
Gilman	Guror				

The ranking of villages within each net is quite complex. Ranking
first of all should be understood as an ongoing, dynamic process. It is
a waste of time to ask the rank of a particular village in Yap. The

Figure 14. Paramount Villages and Geographical Nets

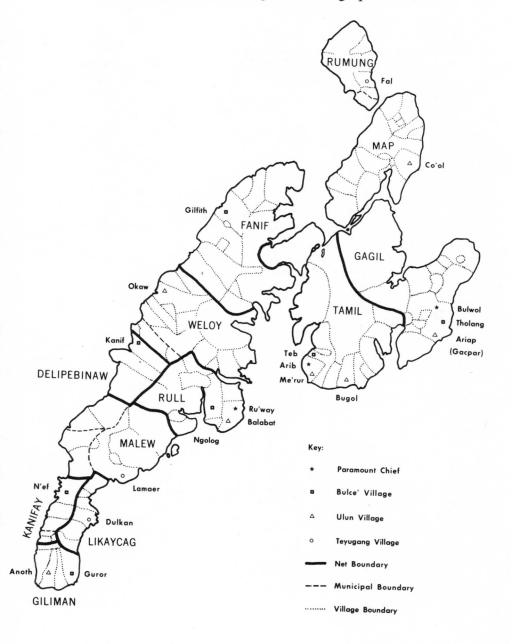

answer given is always the highest rank ever enjoyed by that village and, if that is not very high, quite often the informant will up it one notch. Traditionally ranking was a dynamic of war, work, service to the paramount chiefs, and subsequent reward for such services. Villages were constantly rising and falling in rank according to the tides or fortunes of war. To obtain a ranking of villages today, similar criteria must be used as were used in the past, namely, which villages have managed to ride the political crest to leadership in their respective nets and how do the other villages rank in relation to them? Questioning informants as to the rank of their village is an interesting historical exercise, but totally confusing when one tries to establish the so-called correct ranking of Yapese villages.

The traditional ranks are not clearly understood by informants today. There is no hesitation about the existence of the *bulce'* and *ulun* ranks and that there are seven of each, but upon naming them, nine or ten villages usually appear on the lists, depending upon where the questions are asked. Again this reflects the dynamics of the system; villages rose and fell, but no one likes to admit that it was his village that fell. Another problem is that the meanings of some of the lower ranks have been forgotten. The categories of the ranking system are listed in Table 16.

Table 16 illustrates that the eight rankings of Yapese villages fall into five different general groupings: 1) the chiefly villages, 2)

Table 16. Categories of Rank

	Levels of Ranking	Yapese Categories of Rank
	Chief	*bulce'* division *ulun* division
pilung "high caste"	Nobility	*methaban* division *tethaban* division
	Commoner	*daworcig*
	Chief's servants	*milngay ni arow*
pimilngay "low caste"	Serfs	*pimilngay* *yagug, milngay ni kan,* etc.

their closest and highest-ranking allies, or nobility, 3) the common villages, the most numerous on Yap, 4) the servant rank, and finally, 5) the serfs. It must be remembered that villages and sections of villages are classified by named rank, but *nug* or the 'nets' of allies are ranked only as they are represented by a high- or low-ranking village. No net or municipality on Yap is led by a village lower than the *methaban/tethaban* 'nobility' rank. The villages within each named rank, however, are also ranked, with some holding higher prestige and privilege than others. The interrelationship of rank, net, and *tha'* is seen in Figures 15 and 16.

There is considerable confusion today as to the difference between the second-level ranks of *methaban* and *tethaban*. Some say that *methaban* is an old rank of villages that were defeated in war, and consequently have almost ceased to exist. Others say that *methaban* villages support *bulce'* villages and that *tethaban* villages support *ulun* villages. Others reverse this formula. One old informant argued that *methaban* comes from the two words *methilin* and *ban*, meaning respectively, 'between' and 'side'. Thus *methaban* villages mediate between the sides of *ulun* and *bulce'*. If this was true, however, the functions have been dropped for so long that informants no longer remember them. The same informant said that *tethaban* comes from the words *tethith* and *ban*, and means a "side which renders badly needed assistance". This is not incompatible with the actual functions of *tethaban* villages. They generally do form first-ranking assistants to the higher-ranking and related *ulun* or *bulce'* villages. The general consensus, if one can come close to consensus, is that villages of the two ranks, *methaban* and *tethaban*, refer to respective assistants for *bulce'* and *ulun* villages, and whether this was the usage long ago is quite irrelevant at the present.

Teyugang is another status with implications that are no longer remembered. How is *teyugang* different from *methaban* and *tethaban*, or is there no difference? The word connotes a strong chief, and appears to apply to those villages in which the chief was the representative of the paramount chiefs over a number of other villages, or a leader of the net. This is not always true of the *tethaban* and *methaban* villages. It appears then that *teyugang* is not a special rank, but rather a delineation within the ranks of *tethaban* and *methaban*.

Rank depends upon a number of factors, the most important being ownership of land. The lowest-ranking strata in the system, *pimilngay* and *yagug*, comprise landless serfs. The *milngay ni arow* 'chiefs' servants' have land, but it is land whose title belongs to a high chief to whom the people give first fruits of its produce. The second most important factor in determining rank is victory in war. The rise and fall of villages is chronicled in the stories of battles, and serious defeat

Figure 15. Banpilung Alliance—Power Structure and Communication Networks

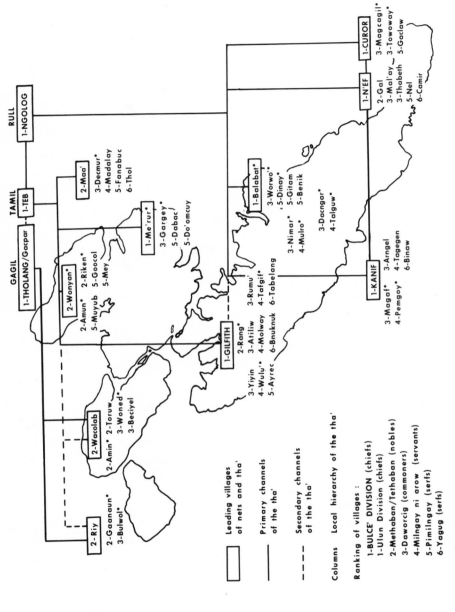

Columns   Local hierarchy of the tha'

Ranking of villages :
1-BULCE' DIVISION (chiefs)
1-Ulun Division (chiefs)
2-Methaban/Tethaban (nobles)
3-Daworcig (commoners)
4-Milngay ni arow (servants)
5-Pimilngay (serfs)
6-Yagug (serfs)

Leading villages
of nets and tha'

Primary channels
of the tha'

Secondary channels
of the tha'

* Villages in both Banpagael and Banpilung tha'

Figure 16. Banpagael Alliance—Power Structure and Communication Networks

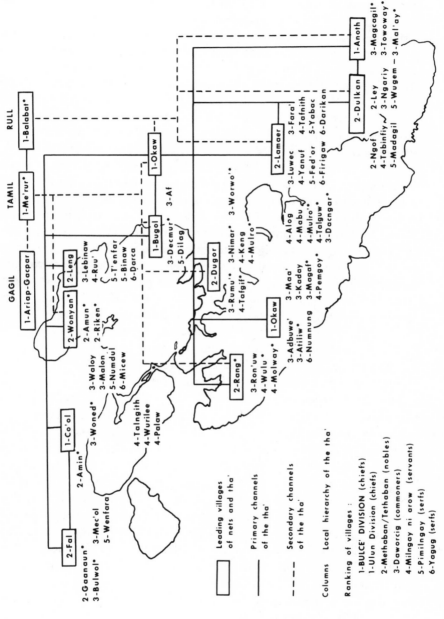

GAGIL   TAMIL   RULL

Leading villages
of nets and tha'

Primary channels
of the tha'

Secondary channels
of the tha'

Columns   Local hierarchy of the tha'

Ranking of villages :

1-BULCE' DIVISION (chiefs)
1-Ulun Division (chiefs)
2-Methaban/Telhaban (nobles)
3-Daworcig (commoners)
4-Milngay ni arow (servants)
5-Pimilngay (serfs)
6-Yagug (serfs)

* Villages in both Banpagael and Banpilung tha'

resulted in loss of both status and land. Success in war provided access to higher rank, and coupled with extensive service to a paramount chief or to one of the villages of *ulun* or *bulce'* rank, yielded status privileges such as tribute from lower villages and overseer authority over certain lands. Even the lowest serf villages have upon occasion risen to higher rank in the status system. The crucial factors were survival in war and, in recent times, survival from the ravages of epidemics. Villages without people very rapidly lose whatever status and prestige are attributed to them. Ranking is dynamic by nature and those who manipulate the system the most effectively are those who rise or stay at the top.

The variations in the ranks are defined clearly in privileged access to resources. The villages of the paramount chiefs are located on some of the best Yapese land resources. These villages pay no tribute, but rather collect tribute from other villages and then redistribute to their own. In terms of rank the *daworcig* 'commoner' villages pay the heaviest tribute in the high-caste ranks and the *milngay ni arow* 'servants' rank are the virtual servants of their overlords. The *methaban/ tethaban* 'nobility' ranks both receive and pay tribute. They receive tribute from commoner and servant villages, but also pay tribute to the paramount villages. The lowest ranks of *pimilngay* and *yagug* form a low caste of landless serfs, which does not pay tribute, but actually serves its overlords from commoner and higher villages.

Marriage, as influenced by the system of rank and alliance, has important implications for leadership. Chiefs who wish to reinforce ties with other powerful chiefs will arrange marriages between the two families. These marriage alliances serve to consolidate the power of a chief by establishing more stable and dependable external ties. The nature of the relationship changes from mere political bonds to the stronger kinship bonds, especially when children are born to the marriage. For the same reasons, a marriage between the families of higher-ranking and lower-ranking chiefs is considered undesirable by the chief of higher rank. This type of alliance provides no prestige for the high chief and very little political gain. The lower-ranking chief reaps the benefits through the reciprocal obligations brought about by the marriage. Marriage of women into lower-ranking villages is undesirable unless the lower-ranking village is geographically very close; then the marriage is thought good for the girl because she can be near her parents. If the adjacent village is of too low a rank, an effort will be made to raise its rank if frequent intermarriages are desired. Marriage between the landed and landless castes is prohibited, but such marriages do sometimes occur.

Tribute: Economic Authority and Support

Tribute is an expression of the mutual obligations that exist between the various chiefs and their subordinates and an economic affirmation of political ties and dominant/subordinate relationships. Tribute also serves to reinforce the authority allocations and balances set forth in the structure of the *tha'*. The act of tribute has two important facets—the collection and the redistribution. Collection is the positive assertion of power on the part of the chief and a display of subordinance on the part of the donor. Distribution provides the opportunity to reward service, recognize status, show generosity and incur further obligations, and demonstrate wealth and power.

The Yapese conceptualize these obligation relationships in the following ways:

1. *tha'*—obligations for support in work, *mitmit* 'exchanges', and warfare
2. *suwon/lungun tafen*—obligations for food, service, and resources
3. *athalab*—obligations for first fruits of produce
4. *thariyeg*—obligations for traditional valuables (*macaf*)
5. *wolbuw*—obligations in return for past services
6. *maybil*—obligations for religious observances

It was noted earlier in the discussion of the *tha'* that certain communication channels are designated to elicit support of work projects. When important chiefs begin to plan a major construction project, they send out word via the *tha'* to collect materials and laborers to do the jobs. A leader may not send word to all of his allies, but only to those who have the obigation of contributing assistance to work. Some channels of *tha'* are designated exclusively for support in warfare, or support in the ceremonial exchanges, while others include all three types of obligations. The obligations of each channel depend upon the particular historical relationships that were established between the participants. For example, the men's house of Lothok in Ru'way section of Balabat belongs to the paramount chief of Ru'way and the *bulce'*. During the construction of this building, the villages of Ngolog and Kanif, both *bulce'*, were obligated to provide labor support for the project. Other *bulce'* villages were not asked to help because they are not on the work *tha'*, but belonged to the *tha'* for warfare and policy councils.

Another type of tribute is that rendered because of a political dominance/subordinance relationship. These are defined as rights of *suwon* 'overseer' and obligations of *lungun tafen* 'estate's voice'. The overseer rights were defined earlier as the authority to collect food, service, or resources from subordinate villages or clan estates over which one is *suwon*. Estate's voice is the responsibility that a village leader or leader of a clan estate has to fulfill the obligations of his land and title toward a higher-ranking overseer. Yapese distinguish two kinds of relationships toward an overseer: those estates and villages of slightly junior rank considered *wolag* 'siblings', and those of inferior rank considered *fak* 'children'.

The overseer rights of a chief toward estates and villages of slightly junior rank are usually specified as to the kind of tribute required. For example, the paramount chief at Ru'way is entitled to tribute from all net fishing done by the *ulun* village of Balabat. In this case the catch from the first two days of fishing (called *mar* and *tithymar*) are brought to Ru'way before Balabat village may take fish for itself. The chief of Ru'way may also request fish from Balabat when he has a special need, but he may not demand garden produce. If he needs garden produce, he would request this from the *bulce'* village of Ngolog over which he has overseer rights to produce. The specific rights of an overseer over junior estates and villages vary widely with regard to kinds of demands and their volume and frequency. The rank of the chief and his geographical distance from the subordinate villages and estates are important variables in the frequency and volume of tribute.

The *fak* 'child' relationship occurs between a high chief and a village of commoner rank or lower. One such relationship for the chief of Ru'way is called *gal'ud* and includes the villages of Rumu' and Atiliw. The relationship is formalized with the gifts of fish and firewood brought once a year for the religious ceremonies in the month of Tafgif. Each village is then required to meet additional responsibilities. Rumu' brings the fruits of yam harvest once a year (*lamar*), and repairs the roof on the sacred men's house Tabaw, where Ru'way gives prayers to the ghosts of the island. Atiliw brings the first catch of a fish called *buy*. Both villages may be called upon by Ru'way for assistance in matters other than specified in the regular offerings. If Ru'way needs economic support for a ceremonial exchange, or for a construction project, these villages may be called upon for assistance. The lower the rank of the village, the more dependent it is upon the high chief and the more demanding he may be with regard to support and obligations.

The most commonly defined child relationships are those between chiefs and their servant or serf villages. All chiefs in Yap have certain villages that provide services and goods without the competitive reciprocal obligations due to villages of the higher ranks. These rights were obtained during periods of severe population pressures in which land became extremely scarce and access to it limited to patrilineal inheritance and gift. Individuals who were disinherited became vagrants and beggars and gradually formed a landless class. These people eventually became organized into serf villages, working for wealthy landowners in return for the use of the land. The relationship between these people and their landlords was defined as the relations between a father and his children, following the ideology of the clan estate in which obedient and helpful children are granted land by their fathers. The disobedient were disinherited or expelled from their land. Low status, prohibition of marriage between men of the serf group and women from higher ranks, and the stigma of always being children, dependent upon and protected by the chief or father, served to solidify the poor group into a serf caste.

Individuals or villages whose lands are not considered ritually contaminated may bring first fruits (*athalab*) of produce to their chief. This gift of first fruits recognizes the position of the chief as the overseer of the land. A chief may not punish an individual for failure to present first fruits but it generally benefits the donor to do so. The chief usually rewards such a gift with a shell valuable and feels obligated to assist such faithful followers in any particular need that might arise in their households or patriclans.

Another type of tribute relationship is *thariyeg*, designating the right of a chief to request traditional valuables (*macaf*) from subordinate villages and chiefs. Collections are made in preparation for the large *mitmit* in which equally ranked villages compete with each other in the exchange of valuables to determine which is the most wealthy and therefore the most powerful. Villages and chiefs that contribute in the collection also are entitled to a share in the distribution after the exchange.

The last two types of tribute have both ritual and economic functions. The first is called *wolbuw* 'gift' and refers to large ritual gifts of food or service offered at a specific time during each year. Many of these gifts are designated as rewards for particular service in warfare or assistance in revenging the death of a member of the patriclan or a chief. Generally the donating village gives from their most valuable and/or scarce resources. For example, Co'ol village in Map brought the yam called *dal'*, grown almost exclusively on Map, to a village in southern Yap as a reward for assistance in warfare. The economic function of this type of gift is to give a wider distribution of scarce resources. The ritual function annually reinforces the political bonds established through cooperation in the past. Such ties are considered quite valuable and either member may be called upon for help at any time.

The most common gift symbolizing allegiance to a high chief is the giving of turtles and large fish. The paramount chief from Bulwol in Gagil, for example, has rights to all turtles, whales, and very large fish caught in Map and Rumung. These items are brought to Bulwol as a symbol of loyalty and respect. The chief bringing them is rewarded with important gifts and acquires more economically in the transaction than the paramount chief. He, on the other hand, has obtained his reward in status recognition. To fail to bring turtles, in particular, is a declaration of disrespect and arrogance, and in the past has incited punitive warfare from the village of the paramount chief.

Another aspect of the ritual functions of *wolbuw* 'gift' is the collection of food for the major religious ceremonies called *togmog* 'feast'. The feasts are large annual religious celebrations frequently involving many allies and having strong political overtones. Maragil feast in Okaw for the sanctuary at Alog is an excellent example. The village of Okaw provides the taro (*Cyrtosperma* and *Colocasia*) for the celebration. The chiefs of Okaw collect bananas from all the lower-ranking villages in the Okaw net. Villages in Gilman are invited to attend in recognition of their aid in constructing the Okaw taro patches. The Gilman villages contribute fish and coconuts. The political significance of this ceremony lies in the fact that all villages in the island of Yap with *tha'* relationships to Okaw attend, including Banpagael villages from the nets of Gilman, Likaycag, Malew, Weloy, and Fanif, extending from one end of the island to the other. The religious ceremony is not only an occasion for offerings to spirits, but a demonstration of political alignments, rank (in the distribution of food and eating relationships), and alliance solidarity. These same villages may on other occasions be called upon to cooperate in warfare, support a decision or a chief, or to offer economic assistance for a major project in Okaw.

The last type of tribute is the *maybil* 'offerings' to the spirit of a sacred place in Yap. Numerous kinds of gifts are collected for all the sacred places, priests, and religious ceremonies held in Yap. One example is the cycle of prayer ceremonies held for the sanctuary of Numruy in Gacpar. Four months of the year are devoted to prayers for the spirit of Numruy. In each of these four months, one important titled estate in Gagil will collect bananas, fish, betel nuts, and coconuts from their village and bring them as an offering to the sacred place. Taking this offering, the old leaders from seven clan estates, including the priest at Numruy, make an offering to the spirit of the place and then divide the bulk of the gifts among themselves. Each portion of the collection will in turn be distributed among the lesser-ranking estates under each of the seven leaders. These collections are ritual and political. The participating estates are leaders in adjacent villages, who at times are hostile to each other. The ritual expresses cooperation and solidarity. At the same time, the leaders are praying for good things for all the people.

The chiefs do not collect for the sake of collecting. Collections are made for ritual or political ends, to assure the good of the people through religious observances or to achieve some political goal. This is not to say that the chiefs are not self-seeking, but rather that the desire to remain in power curbs any self-seeking tendencies. One present chief stated very clearly that a chief cannot just collect things for himself but must be very generous to the people, working hard to bring as many benefits as possible to them. This fact is rather obvious when one observes the tribute situation. On a men's house construction project in Rull, the chiefs who received assistance from subordinate villages spent a great deal more in labor and gifts than did those who assisted. Indeed, in order to sponsor the labor party, the chiefs incurred great debt among their own villagers. When asked why they did not request more assistance, they replied that they could not afford it. To maintain political power and dominance is expensive, and the brunt of the effort falls upon the highest-ranking villages. The use of servant villages provides some relief from the burden of reciprocal obligations.

Without doubt the chief who receives tribute is under considerable pressure to provide some reciprocal service or gift to the donor (see Table 17). This aspect of tribute provides part of the pressure and dynamic that leads to changes in ranking, to maneuvering in warfare, and to flexibility in the structure of the system. Furthermore, the tribute/distribution network provides an opportunity for trade, with certain areas contributing to the chief resources plentiful in their area and receiving in return items of scarcity. One example of this type of trade occurs when villages with large stands of coconuts pay tribute in coconuts and receive in return yams or taro, or specially produced items, such as pots or woven cloth from the banana fiber, which they may be lacking. When European traders came, the chiefs used the collection networks to gather coconuts for copra and then paid back the lower-ranking chiefs with gifts acquired from the sale of copra. Large pieces of stone money were transported on traders' ships to Yap with copra being used to pay the freight. Cannons and guns were also bought and then presented to subordinate chiefs.

By 1968 most of the formal tribute relationships had ceased to be observed. Observation of the traditional religious calendar stopped shortly before World War II and was never resumed. Many gift obligations had been ignored and even forgotten before the demise of the traditional religion. Gifts of first fruits may still be given by a few in-

Table 17. Tribute for the Paramount Chief, Ru'way, Balabat, Rull

Village	Local Net	Type of Tribute	Contributed	Received
Balabat	Rull	Suwon-wolag[a]	fish, labor	food
		wolbuw[b]	fish, turtles	—
Worwo'	Rull	suwon-wolag	fish, labor	food
		wolbuw	fish, turtles	—
Ngolog	Rull	tba'[c,e]	labor	fish, food
Kanif	Delipebinaw	tba'[c]	labor	fish, food
Arngel	Delipebinaw	wolbuw	fish	—
Rumu'	Weloy	suwon-fak[a]	yams, betel nut, labor	coconuts
		atbalab[e]	yams	valuables
		wolbuw	fish, firewood	—
Atiliw	Fanif	suwon-fak	fish	coconuts
		wolbuw	fish (buy)	—
Adbuwe'	Weloy	suwon-fak	yams	coconuts
		tbariyeg[f]	valuables	coconuts
Kaday	Weloy	suwon-fak	yams, tarugod[g]	coconuts
Yanuf	Malew	suwon-fak	coconuts, fish	yams
Luwec	Malew	suwon-fak	coconuts, fish	yams

a. *suwon-wolag*, contributions from estates of slightly junior rank; b. *wolbuw*, contributions from allies in the channels of communication; c. *tba'*, contributions in return for past services; c. *tba'*, contributions from villages in servant relationship; d. *suwon-fak*, contributions from villages in servant relationship; e. *atbalab*, contributions of first fruits; f. *tbariyeg*, contributions of traditional valuables; g. *tarugod*, place for menstruating daughter from Ru'way.

dividuals who wish to gain the favor of a leader, but generally the custom is ignored. Ceremonial exchanges are occasionally held, but the collection of shell valuables usually is confined to relatives and other friendly chiefs. The only persistent obligations are those of the *tha*ʻ and overseer/estate voice relationships. Warfare between villages has, of course, ceased but the *tha*ʻ relations may still be used for community projects and exchanges. The power of the overseer is now ambiguously defined, and individuals either meet the obligations reluctantly or frequently disregard them altogether.

Gagil and Outer Island Tribute

One other category of tribute should be considered—that of the special relationship of the villages of Gacpar and Wonyan in Gagil to certain atolls in the Carolines east and south of Yap. The atolls included in this relationship are Ulithi, Fais, Woleai, Eauripik, Sorol, Ifalik, Faraulep, Lamotrek, Elato, Satawal, Pulusuk, Pulap, and Namonuito (see Figure 17). The atoll of Ngulu south of Yap was once included in the sphere, but was given to the chief of Guror in Gilman as a marriage gift accompanying the daughter of the chief from Ethow estate in Gacpar. The inhabitants of these atolls are bound to the people of Gacpar and Wonyan by ties of kinship, tribute, and economic trade and interdependence.

The relationship of the people of Wonyan and Gacpar to the Carolinians is defined on a kinship basis: the Yapese are fathers and the outer islanders children. This father/child relationship is best expressed by the giving of food and shelter while the outer islanders reside on Yap and supplying lumber and other of Yap's resources not available on the atolls. Whenever these people come to Yap they are cared for by particular clan estates as if they were children of that patriclan. In return the Carolinians present prayer offerings (*maybil*) to the ancestral ghosts of the Yapese (as any good child would) and give gifts to the family.

As *fak* 'children' of the Yapese, the Carolinians are also tenants, with Yapese claiming ownership of their land. Their tenant relationship requires tribute or *sowai* 'trade' from them. This tribute is generally in the form of woven cloth called *bagiy* (lavalava), coconut rope, coconut oil and candy, coconut syrup, mats from pandanus, and shells of various types. In return these people receive canoes from the Yapese, turmeric, food, flint stone, and other Yapese resources.

The Carolinians are required to wear white loincloths while residing in Yap and to assume postures of respect like the Yapese low caste. They also are prohibited from marrying Yapese women. How-

Figure 17. Map of Western Caroline Islands and Gacpar-Wonyan "Empire"

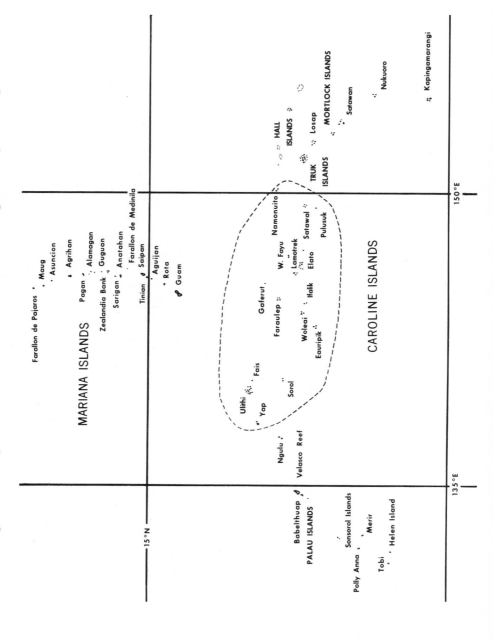

ever, their lot is much easier than that of the low-caste serfs, and many have been adopted into Gacpar and Wonyan and become Yapese.

The formal characteristics of these exchange relationships are viewed by Yapese in terms of the clan estates in Yap. Particular land estates in Gacpar or Wonyan have relationships with particular land parcels in the outer atolls. The Yapese define these land segments as *tabinaw* 'estates' and the relationships between clan estates in Yap and *tabinaw* on the atolls are relationships between estates. The different systems of kinship and inheritance described by Lessa (1966) and Alkire (1965) are either unknown or ignored by the Yapese and appear to be insignificant in Yapese conceptions of the system. An individual from the atolls who comes to Yap brings gifts to and resides at the clan estate that is the overseer of his household and land in his home atoll.

To describe the formal power structure of Gacpar and Wonyan over these outer islands, it is necessary to discuss the political statuses and authority structure of these two villages. The roles of Gacpar as one of the three paramount centers of Yap and the leader of Banpagael alliance have been described. The paramount chief of Bulwol presides over the *bulce* section called Tholang and the *ulun* section called Ariap. Each of these sections is led by a section chief and each has *tha* to Banpilung and Banpagael respectively. Tholang section, *bulce*, contains the estate of the paramount chief and the sacred places for Yangolab, the mythical chief and founder of Gagil and the first chief of the outer islands. Within Tholang section are two councils of chiefs—one called *cath*, which is responsible for decision-making, and the other called *gile*, which is responsible for collections and distributions in support of the chiefs (see Figure 18). Immediately north of Tholang is the section of Wonyan called Galpagael, within which are the estates of the high chiefs of Wonyan. The village chief in Galpagael is the overseer of northern Gagil and is immediately subordinate to the chiefs of Ariap section of Gacpar.

Authority over the outer islands does *not* follow the local authority structure of these two villages. The high chief of the outer islands is not paramount at Bulwol, nor are the section chiefs of either Tholang or Ariap; it is rather the chief of the estate Ethow, a member of the council of *gile* 'support' in Tholang, who holds that position. Ethow is the ancient house of Yangolab, the mythical ancestor through whom the relationship to the atolls is traced, and holds a *sowai* 'trade' relationship with Fasulus, Mogmog, the Yap-defined residence of the paramount chief of Ulithi. The estate Pebinaw, chief of Tholang, is second in Gacpar to Ethow with regard to the outer islands and maintains a trade relationship with the house at Falaglow, Mogmog.

Figure 18. Political Structure of
Gacpar and Wonyan Villages, Gagil

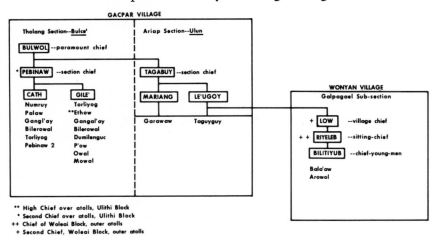

In Wonyan, the chief of Riyeleb estate (who is also sitting-chief of Wonyan) is high chief over trade from the outer islands and second in rank to Ethow. The chief of Riyeleb is the chief of the atolls east of Ulithi and has direct trade relationships with the chiefs of Fais, Woleai, (Wotagay and Fananus sections, respectively), and Ifalik (Lugalop section). The chief of the estate Low, who is also village chief of Wonyan and head of the *tha‘* for Banpagael, is second to the chief of Riyeleb, and maintains trade relationships in Fais and Woleai. Other titled estates in Wonyan and Gacpar have trade relationships with particular islands or sections of islands in each atoll.

The leadership hierarchy just described for the Yapese side of the Yap/atoll relationships parallel closely that described for the outer island hierarchy as recorded by Lessa (1950, 1966:35–39). Lessa reports that Ulithian informants see the "Yap empire" as three separate blocks —Gagil district, Yap; Ulithi; and "Woleai." The term "Woleai" includes all of the related islands to the east of Ulithi, except for Fais. Ulithi is subordinate to Yap and "Woleai" to Ulithi. When the chiefs in Yap demand tribute, the demands follow a regular chain of authority very similar to the Yapese concept of *tha‘*. Ulithi forms the head of the chain, and Woleai atoll is second in rank, leading the Woleai Block. All other atolls receive demands through these two leaders, and tribute is channeled back up through the chain. Lessa states that protocol is strictly observed throughout the hierarchy, from atoll chiefs to lineage heads and demands outside the regular channels are ignored (1966:38).

In comparing Lessa's description with the data above, certain parallels become obvious. The chiefs of Ethow and Pebinaw estates in Gacpar are the Yapese chiefs over Ulithi; the chiefs of Riyeleb and Low estates in Wonyan are the Yapese chiefs over the Woleai Block. Demands from Riyeleb must pass through Ethow to Ulithi and then to Woleai Block; tribute would return through the same channels. Riyeleb cannot communicate to the Woleai Block independently, but must go through Ethow and Ulithi (see Figure 19).

The control held by Ethow and Riyeleb is seen clearly in the protocol that must be followed by canoes arriving from the east. All canoes coming to Yap must first stop in Ulithi. According to Yapese informants, navigators from islands to the east of Ulithi did not know how to come to Yap and therefore had to stop and obtain the services of an Ulithian navigator. Upon their arrival at Yap, the canoe must proceed directly to the clubhouses Faltamol and Siro', located side by side on the shoreline at the border between Gacpar and Wonyan.

The high chiefs from Ethow and Riyeleb are first to receive the visitors, Ethow at Faltamol, and Riyeleb at Siro'. The travelers identify themselves, make their tribute payments to the chiefs, and give prayer offerings for Yangolab. Then they request that word of their arrival be sent to their respective trading partners in the villages of Gacpar and Wonyan. Certain other titled estates in Wonyan and Gacpar hold rights to receive incoming canoes from the atolls and these chiefs bring shell money to the chiefs of Riyeleb or Ethow respectively to obtain the release of the canoes. Once this payment is made, the canoe proceeds to its assigned clan estate. The Yapese clan estate whose trading partner

Figure 19: The Chain of Tribute Relationships
in the Gacpar-Wonyan "Empire"

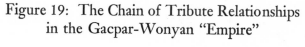

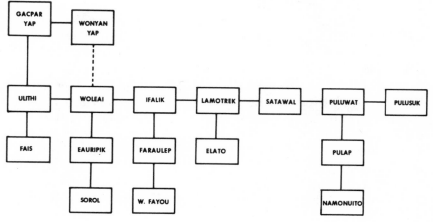

has come brings shell money to the intermediate chief for the release of the partner and his cargo. The intermediate chief ordinarily is the trading partner of the chief of the canoe and the area from which he came.

All trade relationships held by other estates, whether in Gacpar or Wonyan, are subordinate to Ethow and Riyeleb on the basis of the place of origin of the trade. Trade from Ulithi passes directly through Ethow, trade from Fais and the Woleai Block passes first through Ethow, then through Riyeleb. The chiefs of Pebinaw and Low share in the distribution of tribute given to Ethow or Riyeleb respectively. The intermediate chiefs who receive the individual canoes also collect tribute and distribute it among their immediate assistants.

It may seem strange that the paramount chief of Bulwol has no trade relationship with and collects no tribute from the outer atolls. It is even more odd that while the chiefs of the *ulun* and *bulceʻ* sections of Gacpar have important trade relationships, the ultimate authority is given to a minor titled estate in Tholang, which is not even a member of the *cath* or decision-making council. Yet, in the context of the Yapese fear of too much centralized power, the structure makes perfect sense. The high chiefs again have been forced to depend upon the members of the village councils for support. Ethow estate and several other estates rich in trade form the *gileʻ* or council for collection and distribution in Tholang. The wealth of tribute brought from the outer islands is channeled through this council and may or may not be used in support of the paramount chief of Bulwol or the chiefs of Tholang and Ariap. This control of wealth places an effective curb on the personal power of any high chief. To obtain the wealth necessary to maintain the complex alliances with other villages in Yap, he is increasingly obligated to his subordinates in his own village. If he refuses the counsel of these subordinates, they may withdraw support and reduce his outside power.

Using the outer island tribute, the high chiefs of Gacpar were very effective in expanding their alliances through distribution of that wealth. The Banpagael alliance of which Gacpar is chief was without question the most powerful, with the most extensive network of allies. The deciding factor in the accretion of power appears to be the distribution of trade goods from the outer islands and the reciprocal obligations incurred by that distribution. Even in present-day research, informants were quick to mention that one *thaʻ* coming to their particular estate had a part in the trade distribution from Gacpar. Furthermore, informants in Tamil tell the story of a chief who prayed earnestly that foreigners would come to Yap and bring a new trade to Tamil and Rull. It seems significant that early traders were received readily in Tamil and Rull, but with hostility in Gagil. The chiefs of Rull and

Tamil welcomed new trade goods that might swing the balance of power in their favor again.

In summary, tribute relationships were a primary source of political capital, particularly with reference to increasing support for a chief. Chiefs used collection and distribution of tribute as a trading mechanism, shifting goods from areas of plenty to areas of scarcity. In the process of this exchange, the chiefs gained and maintained political obligations and power, particularly through demonstrations of generosity and the concomitant obligations of reciprocity. Certain tribute goods such as pottery in Yap and lavalava from the outer islands were translated by chiefs into political capital, using scarce goods in distribution to increase the indebtedness of subordinate chiefs and to draw others into their orbit. Finally, the ceremonial aspects of tribute served to redefine the status and rank relationship of individuals and villages and to mark these positions and individuals with legitimacy. Legitimacy was not only formally marked, but sanctioned supernaturally through the performance of the religious ceremonies and the participation of all related villages and chiefs.

A number of questions remain regarding this outer island "empire" of Gacpar and Wonyan. How did it originate? Why did it persist over time? What impact have foreign administrators had upon it? The question of origin is a mystery, only slightly revealed in the oral traditions of the past. The myths and legends assert that the Yapese held eminent domain over the atolls and that both areas share certain common ancestors. Warfare is also reported in the legends, but the extent to which tribute is related to conquest cannot be documented.

The persistence of the relationship is more easily understood. Trade appears to be one of the primary functions of the network, and in the economic exchange between the two groups the Carolinians invariably received greater economic benefits from the exchange than the Yapese. However, the benefits for the Yapese were counted in terms of political rather than economic gains. The goods received from the outer islands, particularly lavalava and certain shells, were scarce on Yap and, because of this scarcity, of much greater value to the chiefs in Gacpar than regular Yapese tribute. Gifts of lavalava were much more valuable than coconuts, yams, or even pots, which could be acquired on Yap. Lavalava became part of the *macaf* 'valuables' and were presented as important gifts in marriage exchanges and other village ceremonies. The high chiefs from Gacpar were able to turn this tribute relationship into political capital to the extent of shifting the balance of power to a permanent alliance of Rull and Tamil.

Alkire argues that the relationships between the atolls and Yap, and within the atolls themselves, are more than mere trading relationships;

they are a "complex of socio-economic ties" that are adaptive toward sudden alterations in the environment (1965:135–174). The nature of the atoll environment is such that periodic typhoons or epidemics might decimate social groups or devastate the meager resource base. The interatoll systems of economic exchange, through trade and tribute, personnel exchange through marriage and adoption, and alternate methods of inheritance and land tenure are cultural responses to the environmental conditions. Alkire suggests that Yap is the ultimate source of relief for these environmental disasters, and that the same ties that unite Lamotrek, Elato, and Satawal into a single social system are the basis for the political network tying all of these atolls to Yap.

From the perspective of the Carolinians, Alkire's arguments are certainly valid. The Yapese, in contrast, are in no way dependent upon the atolls for survival. This is probably one reason why the relationships are limited to Gacpar and Wonyan. Probably through historical accident kinship ties were established between Yapese from Wonyan and Gacpar and the early settlers of the atolls. These Yapese, being the earliest inhabitants of the area, would have claimed eminent domain over the atolls, even though they may have only visited them periodically in search of turtles and other food. Intermarriage between Yapese and Carolinians was probably not uncommon until the system crystallized into its present form. The constant pressures of typhoon disasters would have kept the Carolinians in fairly regular contact with the Yapese, and yet because of the unique kinship ties, the relationship was limited to Gacpar and Wonyan. Other Yapese had absolutely nothing to do with the Carolinians. By the time the Yap political system had evolved to the form described here, the tribute-trade relationship had become an extremely valuable political asset to the leaders of Gacpar and a powerful argument for maintaining the obligations of assistance and typhoon relief.

While the coming of foreign administrations had limited impact on the atolls (Alkire 1965:163–169), the Japanese prohibition of long ocean voyages in canoes effectively stopped the flow of tribute into the administrative center of Yap. When typhoons were severe enough to require assistance from Yap, the Japanese administrators provided it.

During the postwar period, the U.S. administration (under the aegis of the U.S. Navy) tried to get all the municipalities of Yap to provide food for Carolinians who were visiting Yap for medical care, but they were not too successful. These tasks were ultimately taken over by the present civil administration of the Trust Territory of the Pacific Islands. Today many Carolinians come to Yap on the government field trip ship and visit their trade partners. Exchanges of food and goods are still common between partners, but the formal acts of tribute to chiefs and prayer offerings to Yangolab and the clan estate ghosts are no longer observed.

The Pimilngay *Caste and Yapese Political Structure*

One of the most critical distinctions in Yapese social structure is that between the landowning high-caste villages called *pilung* 'those who give the word' and the low-caste "tenant" or serf villages called *pimilngay* 'those who run to do it'. The Yapese said such villages came into being when a beneficent chief gave parcels of land to the starving poor in return for service. The poor established households on the least productive land and formed organized villages of serfs. These villages, like the high-caste villages, are all ranked in terms of each other.

There are two major ranks in the low caste: the *milngay ni arow* 'servants' of the high chiefs, and the *milngay ni kan* 'serfs' of any member of the high caste from whom land has been obtained. The servants work for the chiefs of paramount villages of the high caste. Some sections of these villages may give service to a high chief in a nobility ranked village, but this occurs much less frequently. Servant villages enjoy some prestige over the lower-ranking members of their caste. They have much better food resources and have a much better chance to climb out of the low caste through extraordinary service to their paramount chief. They also at times may wear the comb in their hair, which is a symbol of the high caste.

The serf villages are the lowest ranking on Yap. These villages have both high-caste chiefs who are overseers of the village sections and minor high-caste overseers who are landlords and require extensive services from their low-caste tenants. These landlords may come from even the most common villages in the high caste, but may not come from a servant village. The low villages do not wear the high-caste comb and are seriously restricted as to movement and posture in the presence of high-caste people.

The terms *pimilngay, milngay ni arow,* and *milngay ni kan* are not used in the presence of the members of these ranks and caste. Such terms are extremely embarrassing to these people, and so the term *fak* 'child', connoting affection and a father/child relationship, is used instead. Furthermore, the members of the low caste rarely refer to themselves as members of such and such village. If asked where they are from, they give the municipality and avoid using the name of their low-caste village. The village designates rank and caste, and to say that one is from a village considered of low caste is again embarrassing.

Several names are applied to the serfs of lowest rank. These names have generally derogatory references and are a variation of terms used for something low and not to be respected. With regard to relative rank, *yagug* villages are likely lower than those referred to as *milngay*. However, any system to this ranking has been forgotten. The relative ranks are remembered, the relative derogation of the terms are remembered, but a placing of villages into the titles is very difficult to achieve from informants. Most high-caste Yapese consider all those of lower rank than servant as being of the same rank. The serfs, however, do differentiate among themselves and note variations in rank.

Milngay ni Arow 'Servants'

To understand the low-caste villages, one must first consider their overlords. As stated above, the servants attend the chiefs of the highest-ranking high-caste villages. The number of chiefs varies with the number of sections in the servant village. Generally at least three or four high chiefs have authority and overlordship over the respective sections of the village. One of these high-caste chiefs will be high chief of the whole village and the local village chief will be his representative. The other high-caste chiefs will have overseership in one section only. In their respective ranks the high chiefs may call upon the local chiefs for any services due their particular estate.

The servant village is very much like a high-caste village. It is divided into sections and subsections. There are chiefs, usually three—village chief, sitting-chief, and chief-of-young-men—just as in the high-caste villages. In the particular subsections of the village, the chiefs have work leaders and section leaders, just as in the high-caste villages. The chiefs and section leaders have overseer authority over their sections and lands associated with their estates. They may collect goods from these lands as does a chief in a high-caste village. However, the collections are invariably for the high chief from the high-caste village. The servant villages also build clubhouses, men's houses, and dance grounds, and they hold large ceremonies as do the high-caste villages. They may have magicians and sacred places. Thus the servant village is generally like all other villages in the high caste, except that it has a servant relationship to an extravillage chief.

The obligations of the servant village to the high-caste chiefs are both general and specific. Specifically, they must bring first fruits of all their crops to the high chief of the respective sections of the village. This may include bananas, yams, or even taro. This marks distinctly the servant villages from the lower serf villages. Lower villages would never give food to chiefs, because their land is considered dirty and contaminated. Servants, however, have good land, which is not taboo and which may be used by the high chiefs. Other specific tasks of the village may be delineated according to the custom between the high chief's estate and the village. In a general sense, however, the high chief may call upon his servant village to assist him in any need he may have. For example, if he begins the construction of a taro patch, he may call upon the members of his servant village to participate in the work. They will be fed but otherwise not paid for their service because they are servants. These same people might be called upon to build the house of the chief, put the roof on it, build the fence around it, and so forth. In the past, they were summoned to fight for the high chief in times of war. They act as general all-around assistants to the high chief, doing his bidding in major undertakings. They do not, however, act as household servants for the chief. Other, lower-ranking serfs are called to do such work.

The high chief reciprocates the services of the servants with food and other rewards for outstanding service. If they perform especially well in war the chief may raise their rank, keeping them an obligated village, but placing them in the high caste and giving them additional privileges and rewards. He may give tattoo rights to the warriors, fishing rights in a particular section of the sea, or even rights to some low-ranking serfs. However, general services to the high chief usually bring only food and some traditional valuables to the servant chief.

Milngay ni Kan 'Serfs'

The serfs have two overlords, the village overlord and the estate overlord. The village overlords are high-ranking members of a high-caste village, most frequently from a village of the paramount or nobility ranks. These village overlords preside over sections of the serf village, with one of their number designated the high chief of the village. His local representative is the village chief. The other chiefs oversee village sections and have local section leaders as their representatives. An estate overlord is any clan estate from a high-caste village that owns land in a particular section of the low-caste village and has given it to a serf for use in return for his services.

The serf village is somewhat different from the high-caste villages. Many do not have men's houses, either because they are too small, or because their chiefs do not permit them to build one, thinking them too pretentious. The high-caste chiefs have authority over all village matters in the serf village. Anything to be done on a village-wide basis is first discussed by these chiefs, and they actually conduct the affair. They are in truth *pilung* 'those who give the word'; the local chiefs are merely representatives of the high-caste chiefs. They carry messages from them to the villages. They lead in village work projects and are responsible to the high chiefs for all village behavior. They have no power to make arrangements outside their village. For example, a *mitmit* 'exchange' in a low-caste village is directed by the high-caste chiefs. All the work is done by the serfs, but the chiefs make all the official arrangements. If one low-caste village wants another village to bring a dance, the local leader must request it through his high-caste chief. The chief relays the request to the high chief of the other serf village, who in turn passes it to the local people. This pattern must be followed, and to try any other way is disastrous for the local leader. One *mitmit* in Gagil was spoiled when the high chiefs of one related village refused to come. In this case, even though all the low-caste village participants were there, they could not perform because the high chiefs refused to preside. The local low-caste leader was refused the right even to plead to the high chief of the other village because he had no right to make such a plea. Only his high chief could make such a request on his behalf.

The serf village is divided into sections, with respective high-caste and local section leaders. As in a high-caste village, the high-caste chiefs must hold council for any major function of the whole serf village. Local sectional affairs, however, may be conducted by the high chiefs without consulting the other council members. High chiefs are overseers of all land and land resources. They do not take tribute from these sources, but rather collect services. Serfs are obliged to build the house of their high chief, build the fence around the house, put the roof on the house, repair it yearly, clean the yard, cut his coconuts, and perform other kinds of general services, particularly for the household. Sometimes special services are required of them, such as cleaning or putting the roof on a village community house like the men's house or clubhouse. In the latter cases, special payment is made for services above and beyond those generally required for use of the land. The overseer also may give the service of his serf to others. In such cases he may pay them for this work in food or other special gifts. The whole serf village is the *fak* 'children' of the high chiefs, and may be required to do whatever they decide in council.

The serf estate is also the child of a high-caste estate from which it receives the land for its food. Based upon the father and child relationship, the overlord/serf relationship has the same kind of reciprocity. The father gives land and food, the child gives respect, service, and obedience. Respect comes in the form of posture, places where the serfs may or may not sit in the overlord's household, separation of food resources, silence in the presence of the overlord, and general humility and obedience.

Services of the serf are well defined. The most frequent service mentioned is the preparation of thatch and repairing the roof of the house of the overlord. The second is the burial of the deceased. Both services usually are done without pay. When the roof of the overlord's house is repaired, traditionally serfs are fed and allowed to take home the leftover food. If the roof of a village building were repaired, then a whole catch of fish goes to the serf village. Repair of the house of an overlord, however, has no such requirement. If the overlord is generous, the serfs may be given a few fish. In the burial of the dead, again no payment is given. The serf may keep certain *macaf* 'valuables', such as lavalava or shell money given to the deceased. In some areas, after a period has passed, the members of the patriclan of the overseer may go to pay last respects at the grave. If so, they may bring fish for the deceased, which the serfs eat.

Other services of the serfs include cleaning yard, picking coconuts, cutting betel nut, and making mats. They also may be required to work with the high-caste women in the gardens on the hilltops, or they may work alone on high-caste land, cultivating gardens for high-caste women. A man may be required to paddle or pole the canoe of his overlord on a trip. These services may be rewarded if the overlord desires, but need not be. The garden work generally is rewarded with fish.

Finally, serfs must observe certain taboos in the high-caste village. They must walk on the paths for the ritually contaminated teenage girls. They must stop when they pass a seated high-caste man or woman and request that they stand so they may pass. They must step off the path in deference to high-caste people coming toward them. They must not go into taro patches for old men in the high-caste villages and must observe numerous taboos and respect patterns. For this behavior, they are guaranteed a relatively safe, adequate livelihood. To violate the taboos is to invite punishment and even death in the traditional culture. Punishment is administered by the patriclan of their overseer, or by their high chief.

8. COMPETITION AND CONFLICT IN TRADITIONAL LEADERSHIP

To analyze the dynamic aspects of the Yapese political field, we must shift our focus from statuses to the occupants of those statuses, and to situations of conflict in which these leaders attempt to gain power, make decisions, or in some way shape the patterns of action in the political field to meet their own interests and objectives and at the same time meet the demands of the people. I have given particular attention to standards of legitimacy and means of gaining and maintaining support.

Succession to Leadership Statuses

The statuses of paramount chief and chiefs of the *bulce'* and *ulun* ranks are, like all Yapese leadership statuses, invested in plots of land. Succession therefore depends upon inheritance of the land. Maybe at one time in Yapese history succession was a mechanical process, with the passing of land from father to son, but the present situation implies that all was not so simple. One of the most important criteria for leadership is age. A young man, regardless of his status as a landowner, is not considered capable of making decisions and speaking with authority. He lacks the knowledge and experience prerequisite for leadership. Age, knowledge, intelligence, and articulateness may preempt the requirement of absolute land ownership, especially if a competitor holds some distant claim to the land. The following cases illustrate some of the dynamics of succession to leadership positions.

Case 1. Succession to Tagabuy Estate

The first example is from Tagabuy estate in Gacpar, the chief estate of the section called Ariap, *ulun* rank, and the first leader of the Banpagael alliance. The line of succession is shown in Figure 20. In the memory of informants, succession passed in a straight line from fathers to sons for four generations. The fourth-generation son, Bugulrow, was adopted from another estate into Tagabuy. He lived longer than his son, Folbuw, and at his death left no heir. His grandson, Betow, was too young, so Gorongnag, a brother, who was from a different estate and had no legitimate claim to the land, spoke for Tagabuy. After Gorongnag's death, his son Cayaem acted as chief of Tagabuy, because at this time Betow had leprosy and was confined to the leper colony set up by the Germans. Betow died, without heirs, before Cayaem. Cayaem named one of his sons after Bugulrow, but that son died. Today, Tagabuy is disputed land between Cayaem's wife Yow, and Fanechoor.

Case 2. Succession to Fite'ec Estate

The estate Fite'ec, overseer of men and leader of Banpagael alliance in Okaw, was left without direct heirs. The land fell to Fanayam, sitting-chief of Okaw. Fanayam, however, was lazy and made no effort

Figure 20. Succession to Tagabuy Estate, Gacpar

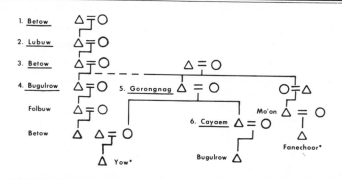

Note: Underlined individuals succeeded to the authority of Tagabuy in numerical order.

* Indicates living persons.

to exercise the power of Fite'ec as a leader in the Banpagael alliance. A classificatory brother, Pong, a chief from the lower-ranking village of Adbuwe', came to Okaw and received permission to build a house on Fite'ec. He then began to work very hard to gain support from the people of Okaw that he might speak for the authority of Fite'ec. He constantly usurped the power and responsibilities of Fanayam, the chief, who appeared uninterested in them. Many of the leaders in Okaw resented the intrusion of a low-ranking man from another village and they arranged the death of Pong's brother in a battle at Gilfith. After this event Pong lived in perpetual fear for his life, sleeping in the rafters of his house at Fite'ec and finally fleeing to Gilfith. Through gifts and services to the people in Okaw, however, he managed to gain enough support to return. On his return he arranged a ceremonial exchange (*mitmit*), publicly declaring his authority as chief of Fite'ec. The other leaders in Okaw supported him in this *mitmit*, thus conceding both authority and legitimacy to him. From that point he worked industriously to increase his power and influence. He arranged and supported the construction of men's houses in the villages of Kaday and Mabu and the building of a young men's clubhouse in Okaw. He consistently used the resources of Okaw to help lower-ranking villages and to broaden his base of power.

Cases 1 and 2 demonstrate that succession to leadership status and power need not come either through legitimate inheritance or through a "name" belonging to that particular estate. When a legitimate heir is lacking or incapable of assuming the authority, other persons with some known relationship to the previous occupant step in. In Case 1 a man with *matam* 'estate father' relationship to his deceased brother's grandson assumed the title and leadership of that grandson's estate. Neither his name nor his land gave him legitimate access to that status, but his age and his position as sibling of the head of the estate made him estate father to the legitimate heir. When the legitimate heir died without children, the estate father passed the land and title to his own son. Case 2 illustrates how an aggressive individual with a sibling relationship to a living heir might use political skills and reciprocal obligations to build a base of power stronger than that of the heir and usurp the authority of the status.

Case 3. Succession to Paramount Chief Status

A third case is succession to the status of the paramount chief of Rull, Ru'way. As in the previous cases, informants remember an ideal pattern of succession through certain ancestors of the land. The complexity of succession arises in the descriptive accounts of leaders actually known to the informants. The pattern of succession is outlined in the genealogy in Figure 21.

The earliest leader remembered by informants was Pitmag who passed the title to his son, Fatamag. Fatamag and his brother Dabcur became embroiled in a struggle for the power of Ru'way, both attempting to arrange the death of the other. Fatamag died, Dabcur succeeded him and then was killed through an arrangement set up by Fatamag and implemented by his brother Tareg, supposedly in retaliation for an earlier killing arranged by Dabcur. Tareg did not succeed to Ru'way, but fled to Yanuf, where he died shortly thereafter, according to one informant, by poisoning. This series of events apparently left Ru'way without a legitimate heir (all of the brothers were childless). At this point the story becomes clouded; two different versions appear, according to which of the present antagonists tells it. One account says that before his death Fatamag had assisted a woman by giving her land. When a child was born to her daughter, Fatamag's brother, Tareg, asked that the child be named after him, because he had no children. This child is the second Tareg on the genealogy. After Fatamag and Dabcur died, Tareg declared that his young namesake should be the next chief of Ru'way. The young Tareg decided that he wanted to be so, but that he would first go to Palau to get stone money to show his worthiness for the task. In the meantime the older Tareg died. Ruwe-

Figure 21. Succession to Ru'way Estate, Balabat, Rull

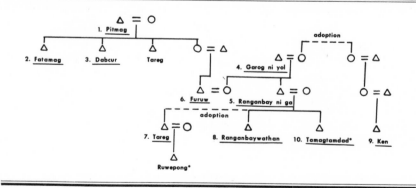

Note: Underlined individuals succeeded to the authority of the estate in numerical order.

* Indicates living persons.

pong, son of young Tareg, declares that his father returned from Palau and assumed the authority of Ru'way.

The other version is that after Dabcur's death, Furuw, a sister's son, was the only one left to speak for the authority. He married the daughter of Gargog *ni yol* 'the tattooed' and incurred such great obligations to Gargog in the marriage exchange that followed that he gave Gargog the land and title of Ru'way. Gargog was already the second-ranking chief of Ru'way, legitimate heir to Mana'ol, chief of Balabat. However, Gargog gave up his authority in Mana'ol to become paramount chief of Ru'way. He was of the correct age, and very intelligent and shrewd, and undoubtedly took the authority of Ru'way while Tareg was on his trip to Palau. Gargog passed the authority to his son Ranganbay *ni ga* 'the elder'. Ranganbay is said to have adopted young Tareg because his wife, who was related to Tareg's mother's husband, desired a child. After Ranganbay died, the authority passed back to Furuw, and then to the children of Ranganbay, starting with young Tareg, and then to Ranganbaywathan. Ken, a classificatory brother of Ranganbay *ni ga*, succeeded Ranganbaywathan, because Tamagtamdad was too young.

In the late 1930s Ken contracted bloody dysentery in an epidemic. At the hospital he called together all the important leaders of Rull to discuss the succession to Ru'way before he died. Ruwepong declined to attend. At this meeting it was decided that Tamagtamdad (about thirty-five years old and legitimate heir) was too busy teaching school for the Japanese to handle the job, and that Mooorow, classificatory brother of both Ken and Tamagtamdad, should succeed to Ru'way. Tamagtamdad objected, arguing that people might say that they were playing favorites and that there were other qualified men, but Ken overruled him. The leaders agreed that Mooorow would follow Ken.

After Ken's death, the leaders again met in council at the men's house for the chief of Ru'way, called Lothok. Mooorow contributed a large sum of Japanese money to purchase fish and rice. They discussed the possibility of one of the estates under Ru'way assuming the authority. In this case Ruwepong, son of young Tareg who held the first ranking of the *wolcath* 'supporting estates', would have spoken for Ru'way. This option was rejected in favor of Mooorow and Tamagtamdad working together to do the job. It was decided that these two would talk over important matters and then Mooorow would speak because he was older than Tamagtamdad. Mooorow was asked to give a valuable piece of stone money to the ancestral ghosts of Ru'way, so he could legitimately speak for its authority. Mooorow and Tamagtamdad then gave four pieces of valuable shell money to the four most important old men present (including Ruwepong, the other claimant to the authority). Small pieces of shell money were given to all others present. Tamagtamdad took the stone money to Ru'way and made the appropriate prayer to his ancestral ghosts on behalf of Mooorow.

The significance of this dispute is obvious. Succession is by no means cut and dried. Rather, it involves some of the most serious and often cutthroat political maneuvering and manipulation. Gargog's succession to Ru'way was highly questionable in terms of the cultural ideal. Important land should never be given away, even under the pressure imposed by the strongest obligation; debts should be paid through other means. Young Tareg lacked legitimate title to Ru'way; his name entitled him to land in Ngolog, and his kinship ties to other lands in Balabat, but he had no direct rights to land at Ru'way. He was also too young. Age and political skill gave Gargog the upper hand, and the problem of young Tareg was solved when Gargog's son, Ranganbay *ni ga*, adopted him into the family. Ruwepong, of about the same age as Mooorow, could have as legitimately succeeded to the title as Tamagtamdad, and in fact Ruwepong had more legitimate claim than Mooorow. He failed, however, to gain support in the community. The most apparent reason for this appears to be associated with the Japanese. Ruwepong's father, young Tareg, was the chief of Ru'way when the Japanese first occupied Yap. They recognized young Tareg as chief of Rull, which he was, and worked through him until he died. After his death, the Japanese, following their style of strict patrilineal succession, declared Ruwepong to be chief of Rull. The Yapese from Rull felt that Ruwepong was too young and Ranganbaywathan was designated the next chief of Ru'way. Both Ruwepong and the Japanese stubbornly refused to capitulate, however, and he maintained his position as the leader of Rull in relations with the Japanese. This conflict in leadership continued through the first years of the American administration until elections were instituted and Ruwepong promptly lost his post.

Ruwepong's behavior in office also undermined public support for him. He became noted for trickery, lying, and high-handed claims of being chief of all Yap. While political deceit is a not uncommon conduct for chiefs, to let it become publicly known is damaging. His claims to the high chieftainship of Yap created a great deal of antagonism in Tamil and Gagil and their chiefs were also instrumental in challenging his legitimacy and support.

Succession to high office then demands consummate political skill. Legitimacy is obtained not only through inheritance rights to land, but also through personal characteristics—age, knowledge, responsibility, articulateness, aggressiveness. Ultimately, the decision of legitimacy rests with a council of old men. Their support must be gained and maintained for effective leadership. One of the primary means of gaining such support is through demonstrations of generosity and an attitude of humility. While aggressive behavior is necessary for a chief, it ideally should be covert, and accompanied by an outward manifestation of humility.

Conflict, Decision-making, and the Council

The paramount chiefs, like the village chiefs, must make major decisions in a *puruy* 'council' with the elders of their village. The chief at Ru'way works through several councils, the choice of a particular one depending upon the matter in question. Decisions with regard to local affairs, important to the section of Balabat called Lan Ru'way, would be decided in a council with seven ranking estates called *wolcath*. Matters of importance to all parts of the paramount chiefly villages would be decided in a council with the leading chiefs of Ru'way, Balabat, and Ngolog. Ru'way also participates in the *puruy ko bulce'* 'council of chiefs' for all of Yap. The following account of the construction of a men's house observed in Lan Ru'way illustrates the working of the Yapese council and the resolution of conflict.

Case 4. Construction of a Men's House

The two presently recognized leaders of Ru'way decided in informal discussion with other old men to build a new *pebaey* 'men's house' for the old men of Lan Ru'way. When it was determined informally that support could be acquired for the project, the two leaders then undertook additional informal groundwork. A carpenter was sought for the project, again informally, and certain individuals were questioned regarding contributions of traditional valuables to pay the carpenter, of timber for the main supports of the building, and of labor. Finally, after determining the feasibility of the project, a formal meeting of the *wolcath* 'supporting estates' of Ru'way was called, during which the aged leader, Mooorow, proposed a men's house for discussion. Since it had already been decided informally before the meeting that a men's house should be built and since the members in attendance, with one exception (Ruwepong), were approving, the meeting legitimized the informally made decision and quieted any opposition through the weight of consensus in council. Members of the council demonstrated their support by offering stone money and other economic resources.

One of the most important stages in the construction of the building was the request for labor assistance from Ngolog and Kanif made by the paramount chief and the council of Ru'way. The obligation to provide such labor is specified clearly in the traditional authority code existing between these villages and Ru'way. Providing such labor, however, is a public test of support and legitimacy for the project, the chiefs, and the villages' traditional subordination to Ru'way. The work on the house progressed to the point where a large body of workers could be summoned to tie together the bamboo supports for the thatched roof. Then the chief and council sent word to Ngolog and Kanif, on the traditional *tha'* channels, requesting their assistance in the tying. A day two weeks away was specified and the chiefs from Ngolog and Kanif sent word that they were coming. In the meantime preparations in both areas began. The chiefs in Kanif and Ngolog informed their subordinate villages to come in support of the labor force from their areas. Kanif also sent word to the *bulce'* estate, Bileydid, in the low-ranking village of Magaf, which spread the word and came in support. The chief of Ru'way and the supporting *wolcath* estates met together to determine the amounts of food, fish, and other resources required to feed the laborers. Word was sent from Ru'way to the chief of Balabat requesting that Balabat bring fish to Ru'way for the work project. Young men from Ru'way and Balabat were dispatched to cut coconuts for drinking, and women from all the households in Ru'way section gathered vegetable foods for the laborers.

The fishing was done in two areas, one of which was set apart for the eating classes and the other for the young men. Food was cooked in four large pots, one for each rank of eating class to be represented (*pagael* 'young men', *piteruw* 'mature men', *matha'aeg* 'taboo', and *garkof* 'titled'), and the food was obtained from two separate taro patches, belonging to the taboo and titled ranks. The women preparing the food observed special taboos related to handling food for each rank. Two turtles were prepared for men of titled rank.

On the designated day, Kanif villagers and their allies came by automobile to the adjacent village of Worwo' where they met the men from Ngolog. Traditional political protocol required that word of coming or going from Kanif pass through Ngolog. Worwo' was chosen as a meeting place because of its central location and highway access. Ruwepong, rival to the leaders of Ru'way, met these two groups in Worwo' and presented them with a bottle of rum. After they began drinking the rum, Ruwepong told them that they should not finish tying the whole building, but should do only one side. He argued that the work was the responsibility of Ru'way and the villagers should do only part, then drink a little and go home.

The chief from Kanif objected, saying they wanted to finish the job. When they arrived at Lothok to begin work, he reported what Ruwepong had said and asked what should be done. The leaders replied that Kanif and Ngolog should do whatever they (Kanif) desired. Mooorow did suggest, however, that they complete half the job and then stop to eat. Then they could finish, should they desire. The men from Kanif and Ngolog insisted on completing the work.

As work neared completion, Ru'way council members withdrew to make a last minute count of food and drinks for the workers. Both Balabat and Worwo' villages had contributed alcoholic beverages. The young men also had been assigned this task because they were engaged in wage work and had money. The total amount of liquor included twelve cases of beer and twenty bottles of whiskey and rum. This was considered far too much for the number of people present and one-half was set aside for a future work party. In the distribution of the food and drinks, portions were set aside for the carpenter, and for Ngolog, Kanif, and Balabat respectively.

During the whole day Ruwepong sat in attendance, but refused to join in the discussions, or with the other old men when photographs of the work were taken. People complained about this, and about his consistent efforts at obstructing the work of the council. Even though not recognized as high chief, he held rights to an estate second in rank to that of the high chief, and was a legitimate member of the council. His refusal to support the council's decision created many awkward situations and much bad feeling. One final incident makes this clear.

On the day of the thatching, it soon became painfully clear that one whole section of the roof was without laborers and thatch. Ruwepong's section, one of the seven supporting estates requested to provide laborers and thatch, had not been notified, again because he chose to oppose rather than support the project. An argument ensued between Ruwepong and Mooorow as to who should bear the responsibility for the failure in communication. Ruwepong asked where Mooorow got his information of Ruwepong's responsibilities and who did Mooorow think he was anyway. Mooorow claimed authority from the previous chief, Ken, and Ruwepong claimed authority from young Tareg, his father. Both men made recourse to past chiefs and sponsors. The conflict was resolved when Mooorow and other members of the council pooled their excess piles of thatch and requested their laborers to finish the untouched section of the roof. Ruwepong again had succeeded in disrupting the normal processes, but at the cost of further isolating himself from the council and his legitimate rights to power.

The building of this traditional men's house provided an exceptional test case for analysis of the dynamics of traditional leadership. The purposes of building a men's house extend far beyond the actual building. A men's house is a status symbol for a village and its chiefs.

Its size and peculiar characteristics set it apart for admiration and comment on the skills, wealth, and capabilities of the people and the chief who built it. A men's house project is also an occasion to demonstrate political power and alliance through labor and resource tribute, and, finally, its completion provides an opportunity for a *mitmit*, or village exchange.

The process of decision-making described above is an excellent example of good mobilization of political capital. In the initial decision to build the house, exploratory moves were made and commitments gained before a public declaration of intent was made. Possible opponents of the program were excluded from the early contacts, thus denying the opposition time to mobilize an opposing force. A meeting was then called, the outcome of which had been predetermined, for the purpose of formalizing the decision and silencing the opposition. The decision was given formal support and the project was begun.

During the time I was in Yap, I observed discussions in two other villages of tentative plans to build a men's house. The outcomes, however, were quite different. In both cases no informal groundwork had been done. No one dared suggest that a men's house be considered, but only hints were given such as "We'll need a lot of tin," or "We should fix up the dance ground." One council appointed a committee to investigate potential support further and the other decided to conduct minor work projects to judge the degree of support. In both cases the ideas died. The committee never met and the exploratory projects were unsuccessful and short-lived. Both cases lacked the determined leadership evidenced in the Ru'way council, in which concrete commitments were obtained before publicly discussing the matter.

The Rull case furnishes some useful insights into the political process. The rival leader first of all refused to support the project, not on its merits, but because it denied his claims to leadership. As a means of asserting these claims, he tried to undermine support for the project. By giving a bottle of rum to the chief from Kanif he hoped to incur some reciprocal obligation and support for his suggestion to stop the work before its completion. The magnitude of the request, however, far outstripped the significance of the gift. The request challenged the whole political framework upon which the project rested, and was summarily denied as both insulting and illegitimate. The chief from Kanif then publicly supported the authority of the other leaders by asking them what he should do. Their answer to "do what you want to do" settled all doubt of support, and the job was finished.

At the same time, the lack of consensus among the leaders from Ru'way was painfully evident and the subject of much talk. Consensus is not only ideally good but politically important. This became very clear in the conflict over thatching a section of the roof. In this instance the rival leader had authority and responsibility for one section of the roof. He and only he could request the labor and materials from the village section over which he was overseer. In his refusal to support the project he embarrassed the other leaders, engaged them in a disgraceful public argument, and forced them to obtain the necessary materials and assistance from their own people.

In summary, decision-making on Yap is greatly dependent upon the support of members of the councils. Preliminary, informal gathering of support among members of the council is primary to effective decision-making. The council gives a decision legitimacy through consensus, and decisions without consensus fail to gain public support and thus implementation. The ideal of consensus is very difficult to attain in real situations and provides an ever-present means of questioning legitimacy and creating conflict. Support of leaders and decisions falls consistently beyond the bounds of consensus legitimacy, engaging the participants in continuous political conflict. One of the traditional expressions of this conflict was warfare.

Warfare and the Councils of Ulun *and* Bulce‘

Yap-wide political maneuvering and manipulation are also a matter of committee rather than of individual leadership. The paramount chiefs participate in two important councils, *puruy ko bulce‘* 'council of chiefs' and *puruy ko ulun* 'council of warriors'. The council of chiefs is the most important in Yap. The high chiefs of Rull, Tamil, and Gagil are members of the council as are the chiefs of the seven *bulce‘* villages. In the past, any matter of national importance to the Yapese was discussed and decided upon by them. The council of chiefs also functioned as the war council for the Banpilung alliance; in matters to be hidden from the Banpagael alliance, Gacpar village was omitted from the meeting. The council of warriors functioned for certain national affairs that were led by *ulun*, and also functioned as the war council for *ulun* villages, omitting the villages of Balabat and Me‘rur when it was desirous to withhold information from Banpilung member villages.

These two councils may operate on Yap-wide or on local bases. If there is a matter of local importance in southern Yap, the matter may be handled by the local *bulce‘* with final word going to Rull. If the issue is of major importance, the word must be passed around to all the *bulce‘* or *ulun* members, as the case may be. If the *ulun* villages in a particular area wish to propose a matter to the paramount chiefs, the word is sent to Gacpar and then to the *bulce‘* through Tholang section in Gacpar. Villages in Rull that are Banpagael pass word to Balabat rather than go all the way to Gacpar. The nature and size of the problem, then, determines the composition of the council and the channel for communication. Local matters of minor importance can be handled by the local leaders. Such matters include village construction, disputes regarding marriage, stealing of property, and so forth. Serious matters such as war, ceremonial exchanges among *ulun* or *bulce‘*, major religious ceremonies, or major disputes require the assembly of the council of chiefs and/or the council of warriors.

One of the prime functions of these two councils was directing warfare. Fighting was very common between Yapese villages. Most villages had a traditional enemy and carried on frequent disputes, raids, and feuds. Often these feuds burst into large-scale fighting, in which alliance members were summoned to assist. According to legend, the first war started during ceremonial games between Gagil and Rull. Men from Gagil were assembled in canoes on the tideflats off Tamil when one of their number took a piece of bamboo and killed someone from Rull. Mass fighting erupted and Gagil lost a low-caste village to Tamil because of it. Gacpar then gave a large slab of stone from Rumung to Ma‘ where the battle had been fought. From this time on, war became an integral part of politics.

The Nature of Warfare

From the beginning, war has appeared to be a method of political maneuvering. Its objectives were generally the death of a particular individual or the destruction of a clubhouse by fire. In many, if not most cases, the paramount chiefs and the *bulce‘* and *ulun* prearranged the war's outcome. One of the best examples of this occurred in a war between the village of Balabat in Rull and Fal in Rumung.

The war was preplanned so that the *tagac* 'renowned warrior' and chief of Balabat named Gargog would kill the renowned warrior and chief of Fal named Lukan. The paramount chiefs sent out word secretly that the Banpagael allies of Rumung should not come to their aid. Rather, they should hide and let Rumung face Balabat alone. On the appointed day, Lukan and six other renowned warriors from Rumung embarked in a canoe to join their allies in an attempt to burn the men's house at Balabat. When they came to Map, they called ashore, but received no answer. Seeing no canoes (they had been pulled inland), Lukan decided that he was late and hurried on to Gagil. At Gacpar he again called ashore, and received no answers, so he hurried on faster. Stopping at Tamil he called again and received no answer. When he rounded the bend and entered the large lagoon and harbor at Rull, he found that instead of being filled with canoes, it was empty, and Lukan knew he had been tricked. However, it is a shame to run away from a battle and unthinkable for a renowned warrior to do so. So he proceeded to Balabat for the fight. Gargog from Balabat advanced to meet the canoe, walking on the low tideflats. The chiefs from Rull and Tamil sat by the clubhouse on the shore watching the battle. The fight began and Gargog was speared in the foot by Lukan. As he sat down to take out the spear, the watching chiefs became panicky and called for help. Two renowned warriors, one from Atiliw and one from Ngariy, were called up to assist. In the meantime, Gargog had removed the spear and then together with his new assistants killed Lukan and his second. The other five in the canoe, recognizing that they were hopelessly outnumbered by the forces on the shore, returned to Rumung. The war's objective was met and the war was over.

This is characteristic of a Yapese war. An objective is set and when it is attained, the battle is over. The setting out of these objectives and the arranging of alliances is done through *makath* 'secret word' that is passed around between paramount chiefs and the *bulce'* and *ulun*. One group will be instructed as to where to gather forces and what to do, the other will be told to withdraw forces or just not appear, as in the above story. In all cases, the balance between the alliances is maintained. If Banpilung wins one war, the next one will be planned in favor of Banpagael. Each will have certain grievances against certain villages or chiefs and the high chiefs will assist in the alleviation of these grievances through war arrangements. For example, the above fight left the people of Rumung with a strong grievance against Rull. At quite a later date, the Banpagael alliance arranged to have Gargog killed in Dugor; when Gargog and Balabat went there to do battle, they were outnumbered and he was killed. In short, everyone wins and no one wins.

Causes of Warfare

The most common cause of these wars was political rivalry between chiefs and villages. Lower-ranking villages struggling to rise would, with the assistance of a friendly high chief, attempt to wipe out their closest rivals. Informants cited numerous examples of uninhabited or nearly uninhabited villages today in which the majority of the population was wiped out by war. Invariably, these were high-ranking villages, attacked by rivals and destroyed. Usually such a village aroused the serious antagonism of a higher chief by trying to climb higher than his village. In retaliation he would support a lower-ranking rival, arrange a nearly disastrous war and destroy the political power of the village. The victorious lower-ranking village and the devastated higher-ranking village would then exchange their relative ranks.

Another common cause of war was revenge. This is quite obvious in the story above of Lukan from Rumung when, in a later battle at Dugor village, the Banpagael alliance killed Gargog to revenge the death of Lukan. Every time a chief or important leader was killed, revenge would be the only thought of his relatives and subjects. In the case of Gargog, his son spent the rest of his life seeking revenge. The son staged several battles with Dugor, but was never satisfied, and passed on the task to his own son, who also fought with Dugor.

War was also a mechanism of social control. The power of the chief rested most strongly upon his ability to eliminate his enemies and rivals. This ability was related directly to his skill at wooing and holding allies. When a village member attempted to make trouble for the chief or for the village, the chief would arrange a war to eliminate him. Case no. 3 cited earlier of the younger brother who tried to overthrow the paramount chief at Ru'way is an excellent example. The chief made arrangements with the *bulce'* village of Kanif to come and kill his brother. The deed was done and the rivalry settled. The powers of alliance were used constantly in this manner. Problems of the village or alliance, which the chief lacked authority to settle according to custom, were often settled by war, arranged and predetermined as to its result.

War was the means of sanction for social, political, and economic crimes. In a case of theft from another village (food, timber, women, or other valuables), the only means of redress was war. A rapid plea by the chief of the offending village, accompanied by shell money and promises of local punishment of the offender, could avert war. The plea was sent out *dakaen e tha'* or 'upon the power of the word of the chiefs'. It would be sent to as many related chiefs as possible to gain their support and then to the village that had been offended. A plea that came in this manner was very difficult to refuse. Without it, however, war was certain.

One example may be given from the village of Bugol in Tamil. Bugol acts as intermediary between Gacpar and Okaw, passing word between these two villages. At one *mitmit* in Okaw, Gacpar sent an important contribution via the chief of Bugol. The chief took one of the shell valuables for his own collection and sent the others on. Gacpar had planted a spy at the *mitmit* to see if the gifts were received properly. When it was discovered that the piece was missing, the chiefs planned retribution against the chief of Bugol. Word was sent to him that there would be a council of warriors in Waloy, Map, with regard to war, and that he should come on a stipulated day. The people of Waloy were instructed to kill him when he arrived. Everything went as planned and in this way the theft of the shell valuable was punished.

Failure to follow customary economic and political rights also re-

sulted in war. One example is cited from Gacpar, concerning rights to
all turtles caught in Map and Rumung. One time Toruw village took
a turtle to Wacolab, Map, rather than to Gacpar. The chief of Gacpar
attacked Wacolab for assuming the rights of the paramount chief.
Wacolab switched in alliance from Gacpar to Teb, Tamil, because of
this war.

Case 5. Rights to Distribution of Bagiy

An example of violation of political rights is seen in the case of
Gamedbay from Okaw who held particular rights in Teb, Tamil, to the
distribution of *bagiy* or lavalava at the beginning of a dance. On a day
appointed for a dance, the people and chiefs of Teb waited for
Gamedbay, but he did not come. Finally, tired and weary of waiting,
Tamanfalethin, paramount chief of Tamil, distributed the lavalava and
began the dance without Gamedbay. When Gamedbay arrived he was
so angry that his rights had been ignored that he killed Tamanfalethin
on the spot, and returned to Okaw. The sequel to this story is very in-
structive in showing the operation of the council and the ranking
system.

After the death of Tamanfalethin, the paramount chiefs of Rull
and Gagil met with the *bulce'* in council in Tamil, at the place of the
high chief of Arib. The paramount chief of Tamil was, of course, dead,
but the chiefs from Teb and the *bulce'* were represented. The meeting
was to decide what should be done about Gamedbay from Okaw; it met
repeatedly for days without a satisfactory solution. No one was very
interested in going to battle with Okaw, because of its fame in fighting.

The Yapese custom is that the low-caste serf of the chief paddles
his canoe for all journeys. In this case, Thapngag from the low-caste
village of Kanif paddled the canoe of Pitmag, the paramount chief of
Ru'way in Rull. He became very weary of the daily journey to Tamil,
for which he could discover no reason, since low caste were not allowed
near the meeting place of the high chiefs. Finally, he asked his chief
why they had to go so often to Tamil. Pitmag related to him the se-
quence of events and the problem caused by everyone's reluctance to
fight Okaw and kill Gamedbay. Thapngag said he would kill Gamedbay or be killed, that he would rather be dead than have to keep pad-
dling the canoe back and forth to Tamil. So, this time at the council
meeting in Tamil, Pitmag said that his serf would kill Gamedbay or
be killed himself. The council agreed to let him try and instructed Pitmag to give him the chance.

Thapngag made arrangements with his own village to fight Okaw
when they went to Lamaer for the religious ceremony (*togmog*) called
Gurgur. The traditional political alliances of that time required that

each village between Okaw and Fed'or take the chiefs and men from Okaw by canoe to the next village, providing them with transportation and tribute for the ceremony in Lamaer. Thapngag planned the attack at Fed'or where the people from Okaw would come on their return to Okaw. Gathering all his men from Kanif and the surrounding allies of serf rank, Thapngag attacked at Fed'or and killed most of the men from Okaw. Gamedbay, however, managed to escape by way of the sea, swimming and walking up the reef north to Okaw. Thapngag found him missing among the bodies and rapidly paddled to Okaw in his canoe. There he waited in the mangrove swamps and met Gamedbay as he swam into the river entering Okaw. Gamedbay offered very valuable shell money in place of his life, but Thapngag refused, killed him and cut off his head, which he took to the paramount chief, Pitmag.

Pitmag and Thapngag then returned to Tamil where the head of Gamedbay was placed before the council of chiefs. Thapngag was called into the center of the council, given a backrest and seat right in the middle of the chiefs, and told that from that moment on his village would replace Okaw in the council of chiefs. Thus Kanif was raised from a serf village to the rank of *bulce'* and became the first-ranking assistant to the paramount chief in Rull.

Functions of Warfare

War, then, is very important in traditional Yapese politics. It consolidates political power, giving the chiefs powers that the ideology of Yapese culture denies. For example, it is bad to kill a member of one's own village, or worse, to kill a member of one's own family. This destroys the unity of family and village. It is also bad to work against one's own alliance. Thus, the ideology is for weak, honest chiefs who have limited power and control. In fact, the power struggle is one of the major preoccupations of the Yapese, from the level of estate to that of paramount chiefs. The unending quest for political power does not mesh with the ideology of the weak, humble, and honest. The use of *makath* 'secret word' and war provides means to deal with rivals within the family and village and to strengthen the power and control of the chiefs.

War exerts pressure for unity and cooperation among the various villages. One of the characteristics of Yapese social structure is the fragmentation introduced by the segmentary nature of the patriclan and nuclear family. Each nuclear family and each patriclan are separate units, each with its own land and resources. Each village is a separate unit, with its own land and resources, and even sections within the village are separated socially and economically from each other. Fragmentation is a fact, unity an artificial construction of external forces upon the social and economic ideal. War, ranking, and tribute relationships bring Yapese villages into organized interaction that results in trade, cooperative enterprise, and ordered relationships for social and religious purposes.

War limits the application of political power. A chief with grand designs very soon will be tempered by other chiefs or lose his life. Gamedbay is a prime example. His political power and right were not nearly so important as the power and respect of all the chiefs combined. To permit him to kill a paramount chief without retribution would in fact make him the most powerful chief in Yap. This could not be tolerated by any of the paramount chiefs and the *bulce'*. The rank given to Thapngag for his valor is an example of the importance attached to controlling such political power and brashness. The dominance of the council is established over the power of the individual chief.

War acts as a method of social control, providing punishment for breaches of custom and moral law, and reward for service and conformity to the power of the council. If a chief works always with the council, he then can depend upon the council for support in time of need. If he works against it, the sting of rebuke is inevitable.

War also functions as a guarantee of rights and privileges as outlined in the political system. If a chief has certain rights to tribute and service, he will receive them without fail because of his right to wage war. Such a war is planned in council where the outcome is decided before it begins. Thus, the threat of war becomes a strong persuasive factor in the fulfillment of obligations and duties to a chief.

Finally, war serves as a sanctioned outlet for aggressive feelings by focusing them upon extracommunity objects or people rather than upon those within the immediate community. The Yapese place a very high value upon the control of emotions and temper. To become angry in public or at a meeting is improper and a subject of much comment and disapproval. To show feelings of aggression toward members of one's family or to people in the same village is almost always, except in carefully defined situations, bad, inappropriate, and ill-advised. War releases these tensions and frustrations upon outsiders who are not faced in daily life. This is recognized by the chiefs in the planning of wars. They know that if the people were aware of the determined end, the war would not be successful and the people likely would turn against the chiefs rather than support them. Therefore, all decisions with regard to the outcome of the war are strictly secret. The people are encouraged to fight with all their valor, to bring honor to their village, and to themselves. Brave warriors are rewarded and honored for their achievements, receiving the title of renowned warrior, or in some cases, the right to tattoo their legs with the warrior's tattoo. This tattoo, a sign of bravery and spirit, should never be seen from behind by the enemy. The "rules of the game" for battle then calls for vigorous fighting, though the outcome is predetermined.

In summary, the council of chiefs and the council of warriors are the ultimate political decision-making bodies in traditional Yapese politics. All important political decisions are funneled into these chiefs who discuss and decide as a group. The power of execution also lies with the chiefs as they instruct the allied villages. The main instrument of administration of decisions is the *tha‘*, and enforcing of decisions is done through warfare, determined and organized at the outset by the councils. The competition between alliances sometimes does breed wars outside the councils of both *bulce‘* and *ulun*, but the balance of power is such that the alliances depend upon each other.

Some Yap-wide economic, social, and religious functions are not governed by the councils, but rather by the paramount chiefs and their respective allies. These occasions are by definition peaceful, but paramount chiefs and their allies are openly competitive, working outside the bounds of the cooperative council. The most important of these occasions are the *guyuwol mitmit* 'village exchange' and the religious *togmog* 'feast.'

At the *guyuwol* exchange, great amounts of food and traditional valuables are collected by the high chiefs and distributed to the visiting guests. The chiefs compete to see who can give the most-difficult-to-obtain and unusual gifts. This is the obvious incentive behind the expeditions to acquire stone money. The chief who brings back the biggest and finest pieces certainly wins in a competitive exchange. Winning not only enhances the reputation of the chief, but also incurs the obligations of the receiving chief. Actual political power is also at stake in these exchanges.

The Mitmit *'Ceremonial Exchange'*

In chapter 5, the marriage exchange was defined and described as it related to leadership in family and interfamily relationships. The same type of ceremonial exchanges are conducted at the village level, with similar political functions. The marriage *mitmit* was seen as an exercise in family leadership, solidarity, support, and interfamily competition to demonstrate relative wealth and strength. The village *mitmit* performs somewhat the same functions for village leaders.

The village exchanges are much larger than marriage exchanges, involving not only the particular village, but all the allied villages and their chiefs, and even competing villages and chiefs. The village *mitmit* are called *guyuwol,* meaning literally to "see the palm of the hand" or the fortune of the village. It is a grand social affair and, when held in the highest-ranking villages, may last as long as two or three months and involve the whole of Yap. *Guyuwol* of such dimension are things of the past, although smaller-scale *guyuwol* are quite common today.

One type of *guyuwol* is the *ma'af ko pilung* 'anchoring of the chief', a ceremony in which a new chief is installed in a village. The titled estates in the village council meet with the chief and plan a *mitmit*. All the allies are invited and presented with lavish gifts. The ceremony establishes the chief as the leader of the village and signifies to the allied chiefs that he has begun his work. The strength of the chief is tested through the show of his wealth and generosity.

A second type of *guyuwol* is the ceremonial opening of a new house. The first phase of this occasion is called *m'ug*, in which allied chiefs, hearing of the completion of the men's house or clubhouse, come with shell money for the unveiling. When these ritual visits are completed the chiefs of the village send out word that the village will prepare a *mitmit* in celebration of completion of the community house. The festivities, called *thumthathar*, include food, dances, and the distribution of shell money and stone money to the villages that brought gifts to the unveiling and to others who attend.

The last type of *guyuwol* is the commemoration of a dead chief. Interestingly, these observances sometimes are held before the death of the chief, at a time when he is near death, but still able to see his own *mitmit*. There are three different kinds: *puruy* 'council', *curu'* 'dance', and *tayor* or *tam'* 'funeral song'.

The smallest of these is the *puruy*. Upon the death of an important chief, the villages that have relationships with his village hold council meetings and then send the most valuable red-shell neckaces (*gaw*) and mother-of-pearl shell (*yar*) to the family of the deceased. The councils send these valuables as an expression of their sympathy and as their farewell to the dead. Sometime after the funeral the family arranges an exchange in which they return all the shell valuables and give many baskets of cheap shell money as a "thank you" to the councils. The original gift is returned because no one family could possibly be rich enough to give equivalent or more valuable gifts to all the councils who contributed. Included with the money are additional valuables and plenty of rum and beer. Women do not participate and the men do not dance or feast. Food may be prepared if the village and family desire.

If the village so desires, a larger *mitmit* may be planned requiring far more effort, wealth, and resources. These two exchanges are the *curu'* 'dance' and the *tayor* 'funeral song'. If dances are planned, the requirements are less rigorous than for the song. In either case, however, the work is great. The villagers thoroughly clean their homes and the village paths, repair the men's house and dance ground, and gather valuables and gifts of food. The leaders send word and arrange protocol for all visiting chiefs. The higher ranking the village, the more numerous are its allies and the greater the number of arrangements. Yapese say that such a *mitmit* in a high-ranking village requires almost two years to plan and as long as three months to execute.

Perhaps because of the difficult preparations involved, high-ranking villages have not held dance or song *guyuwol* for several years. However, low-caste villages do make funeral song *guyuwol* for their high-caste chiefs on a much smaller scale. An example from the low-caste village of Tenfar will illustrate the principles of the *guyuwol* and the relationships between villages entailed.

Case 6. Funeral Song Exchange in Tenfar

The low-caste village of Tenfar in Gagil held a funeral song exchange for the deceased high chief of Tenfar who came from Wutyum estate in Leng village. A *mitmit* cannot be held for a low-caste chief, but a low-caste village may hold one for its high-caste chief and overlord. In this case the chief had been dead for some time, but the *mitmit* was planned because the village had incurred some debts to the neighboring village of Binaw for a similar ceremony in Binaw and the people of Tenfar wished to liquidate these debts and incur some of their own. The affair began with a petition to the present chief in Wutyum to plan such a *mitmit*. After he consulted with other chiefs, he granted permission and plans were made. The village was cleaned, new houses were built to shelter the guests, and a new sitting platform was built near the men's house. Related villages were then invited to come and to bring songs for their dead chief to Tenfar. *Tayor* 'songs' may be described as both chants and dances; they are performed by the women of the invited villages.

Three villages and their chiefs were invited to come and bring songs. The first village invited was Binaw, which has a *wolbuw* 'gift' relationship with Tenfar. They exchange reciprocally things needed by both villages. The second village invited was Thol, also in *wolbuw* relationship. The third village invited was Go'col, who had a *tug* 'intensively competitive' relationship with Tenfar. Each village was to contribute five songs, one of which would come from an "uninvited" village. Each of the "uninvited" villages contributes on the basis of a relationship to an "invited" village called *mundilak* 'to throw a spear'. This term implies the throwing of a song from a distant village through a related village to the *mitmit* village.

In the village of Tenfar, piles of stone money were placed in the dance ground, with one pile for each song and some extra piles to repay old debts to the related villages and debts from the high-caste chiefs of Tenfar to the related high-caste chiefs from the other villages. In all, twenty-five piles of stone money with an average of seven pieces a pile were placed in the dance ground. Each visiting village was assigned a certain place to sit and certain piles of money for their songs.

The village of Tenfar began the day of the *mitmit* by bringing many strings of mother-of-pearl shell to the young men of the overlord village of Leng. This money was carried by the men of Tenfar, strung out in single file, and placed before the young men of Leng. Another line of gift-giving to the people of Binaw and their chiefs followed, and then the official ceremonies began.

To begin the songs, the high chiefs of Tenfar took single valuable pieces of mother-of-pearl shell to the high chiefs of the village giving the song in a ritual called *puyor* 'release song'. When the *puyor* was received, the visiting chiefs were asked if they had anything to do. The high chiefs of the visiting village looked over the valuables and then returned them to the high chiefs of Tenfar. Other mother-of-pearl shells were sent as *siro'* 'please excuse us' to the chiefs of Tenfar and word was given that they were ready to begin. The *siro'* was returned and, after the chiefs were finished, the women began their song. While they performed, the men from Tenfar and their chiefs took strings of mother-of-pearl shell and large bundles of lavalava and placed them on the pile of stone money set aside for that particular song. The parade of men continued until all valuables for the song were deposited. Then individuals from the host group began to repay personal debts to friends from the village giving the song. This series of events followed through each song until the end of the *mitmit*.

As was mentioned earlier, each of the visiting villages presented five songs. The village of Binaw was first, then Thol, and finally Go'col. Each gave their own version of the respective songs in the series of five. The series was as follows:

> 1. *tayor ni pilung*—asking pardon from the chief of Tenfar. One woman performed this song alone with those seated nearby assisting.
> 2. *tan tayor*—explaining the relationship between the performing village and Tenfar. Three women chanted with the assistance of those nearby.
> 3. *tayor ni diyaen* (pregnancy tayor)—done by women from the *mundilak* villages (Muyub to Binaw, Muyub to Go'col, and Dilak to Thol). This was done by many women who explained in song how they were able to participate by their relationship to the respective village.
> 4. *tayor ni rugod*—begging for and receiving turmeric, shell

valuables, pigs, and other old traditional valuables. This was done by the teenage girls.

5. *tayor ni bulyal*—begging for bread, biscuits, corned beef, makeup, pomade, combs, towels, soap, perfume, rum and beer for their fathers, cloth, and anything else they could think of. Performed by the young immature girls.

The first three songs were quite serious and reserved, in accord with their subject, while the last two were quite rowdy and fun. The first three were presented on the first day and the last two on the second day of the *mitmit*. After all the songs were finished and the men had stopped giving gifts, the women of Tenfar then were permitted to give shell valuables and other gifts to women of related villages. The *mitmit* closed with a final exchange of mother-of pearl shell by the chiefs to signify that the ceremony was finished and it was time to go home.

The competition in giving was clearly illustrated in this *mitmit* by a canoe filled with cases of beer, bread, and bottles of rum. This was given by Tenfar in payment for a previous debt to Thol in which Thol came with a paper boat filled with such items. Lavalava and several sheets of the *New York Times* were strung from the mast to remind the people of Thol that they had given a paper boat and were receiving a genuine one in return.

Competition between chiefs was also evident. The chiefs of Go'col refused to attend because they felt they should be first in the order of the songs. The songs from Go'col were not sung, and Binaw and Thol were asked to repeat songs in order to fill the gap and cover all the stone money. An interesting sidelight is that Go'col is uninhabited presently and the songs from Go'col were to be performed by women from the other villages who were already present at the ceremony. Because the high chiefs of Go'col refused to attend, those songs could not be performed. The power and the competition between high-caste chiefs completely overruled the willingness of the low-caste people to perform the songs.

Thus, the *mitmit* functions to provide ceremonial recognition of and allegiance to high chiefs. It is an occasion for declaration of legitimacy of both rank and leadership. Solidarity among villages of the same rank is demonstrated by the mutual exchange of gifts and services (in this case, the songs). Competition between rival villages is channeled into a peaceful contest of generosity and display of wealth. It is significant that political status and relationships are spelled out specifically in the different songs presented in honor of a dead chief.

Rank and jurisdiction of political power are demonstrated through the ritualized exchanges of the *mitmit*. Conflict arises when some chief attempts to alter the relationships in his favor. The example cited in Case 5 in which one chief preempted the jurisdiction of another ended in warfare. Case 6 shows chiefs refusing to participate at all, rather than submit to a lower position in the order of events. Thus, while the *mit-mit* provides a ritualized means of peaceful competition, traditional alterations in the political alignment come through warfare, and not by peaceful means. *Mitmit* may be used to incur obligations for future assistance, but realignment of rank and jurisdiction comes only through warfare. Since the German administration forced an end to warfare, the traditional system of competition and rank has remained static, and political adjustments to population decline and other changes have become nearly impossible.

9. THE SITUATION OF CHANGE

The Agents of Change

Early European Contact and Depopulation

The first European contacts were spaced far apart and were extremely brief in duration. They had very little impact on the culture. Early in 1526 Yap was "discovered" by a Spaniard, Diogo Da Rocha. Two years later in 1528 Alvaro de Sayavedra visited Ulithi and possibly Yap. In 1543 Ruy Lopez de Villalobos journeyed to both Yap and Palau. The next recorded European contact was in 1686, almost 150 years later, when Lazeano arrived and called the island Carolina. Later, in 1712, Yap was visited by De Eguiy Zabalaga and then again in 1791 by a Captain Hunter. It was not until 1869 that the J. C. Godeffroy and Son Trading Company established Yap's first "permanent" German trading station (Müller 1917:1–7).

It is significant that the 350 years of sporadic contact had very little direct effect on Yapese leadership and politics but a profound indirect effect on population. European diseases spread from Guam through the travel of the Carolinians, including the Yapese, so that before European traders arrived the Yapese had developed a "theory" for the devastating epidemics, crediting them to the evil works of rival chiefs and their conspiring magicians. Depopulation already had made serious inroads by the time of extensive European activity.

While the early European visits had been very brief and chronologically far apart, around the 1850s European traders such as Cheyne, Tetens, and Kubary began coming to Yap and to maintain frequent sojourns among the natives. Then in 1872 David O'Keefe arrived in a Chinese junk (Müller 1917:5). Several stories say that he had washed up on the shores of Gagil at some earlier time, following a shipwreck, was restored to health by an old powerful magician, and determined to return at a later date. At any rate, when he arrived in 1872, he immediately set up a copra and trepang trade. He had observed that the Yapese were not motivated to work by the traditional European methods, but that they were intensely interested in acquiring huge pieces of a stone that they brought from Palau by canoe. He arranged to bring by ship from Palau pieces of these stones in exchange for the copra and trepang. Significantly, this changed the productive habits of the Yapese. They turned to copra and trepang production in order to acquire the traditional valuables. It became easier to get larger pieces of stone money, but, because of the Yapese system of competitive giving, the larger pieces soon became less valuable than those obtained earlier by canoe.

The Spanish and German Administrations

During the late 1800s both Spain and Germany claimed Yap as part of their respective empires. A bitter rivalry between the two countries climaxed in August of 1885. On August 21 two Spanish vessels arrived in Yap, carrying a governor, soldiers, convict laborers, two priests, horses, cattle, water buffalo, and stones for the governor's house and the church. They were five days looking for a suitable site, landing the animals, and planning their flag-raising ceremony. Meanwhile, on August 25 the German gunboat *Iltis* sped into port, landed, and raised the German flag in the name of the kaiser. When the Spanish realized what was happening, they raised their flag and attempted to claim first rights, but finally they relented and the matter was submitted to Pope Leo XIII. In December of 1885 the pope confirmed Spanish claims to sovereignty on the condition that the Germans be allowed to trade freely and establish enterprises such as fishing, plantations, coaling stations, and so forth. (Müller 1917:6–7).

The significance of this period lies in the introduction of building construction by Europeans and organized Catholic religion. Six new churches were built on Yap, and several priests and monks of the Capuchin order took up permanent residence (Hezel 1970:2–5). In terms of trade, new goods were introduced, which the Yapese appropriated for traditional uses. One example was a bottle given at a *mitmit* as the ultimate gift by a chief. Guns and cannons were appropriated rapidly for war.

In 1899 Spain lost the Spanish-American War. The Germans then purchased the Carolines and Marianas from Spain. They appointed a German governor and established an administrative center on Yap.

They built roads, a communication station, and the Tagreng Canal, which shortened the distance between Map and Rumung to the Tamil-Colonia area. In 1903 the first German hospital for the Yapese was built using Yapese labor. The Germans created new political districts, but used the traditional Yapese political organization for leadership. They recognized six paramount chiefs.

The Germans stopped traditional wars and discouraged the *mispel* (mistress of the clubhouse) system. They fined Yapese leaders for infractions of rules in traditional money. Since stone money was too big to move around, ownership always had been a verbal acknowledgement. The Germans began marking the pieces accumulated as fine payment with an X so that everyone would know they were owned by the government even though they remained in the same place. During this period they established the first Yapese constabulary with a Yapese police force. They also trained Yapese to be soldiers and to fight for Germany should the need arise. Some Yapese were even sent to Saipan for special education. The German administration also stopped the import of stone money from Palau.

Some positive directions taken by the German administration included working through the traditional nets and chiefs in matters relating to administration and for the mobilization of native labor for construction projects. That they did so reinforced the Germans' power, but introduced some problems, as the Germans had no way of providing the traditional food as payment for work on these projects.

The Germans permitted traditional exchanges (*mitmit* and *guyu-wol*) in Ngolog in 1907, in Leng in 1909, and in Wonyan in 1917; these are recorded in the historical files of the Yap district administrator. The Germans also levied taxes and built up the trading potential of all the islands under their jurisdiction. Yapese were sent to travel on merchant ships, and in 1909 ninety-eight Yapese went to Angaur in Palau to work in the phosphate mines.

The Japanese Administration

In October of 1914 the Japanese navy seized control of Yap. By 1915 they had constructed permanent garrison headquarters; they governed the islands for six years until 1922 when a civilian Japanese administration replaced them. In terms of foreign contact, the Spanish influence had been largely religious with Catholicism replacing the traditional Yapese religion. The German influence had been largely in the areas of economic development and trade. The Japanese emphasized colonial expansion and military bases. Yap did not prove to be economically advantageous to the Japanese; they established a few small farms and tried mining but found it unprofitable. As World War II neared, the Japanese established military bases, building additional troop garrisons and constructing two airfields.

Many changes were made during the Japanese administration. They established a leprosarium at Pakel. They erected and staffed a five-year language school, which all children were required to attend. The most promising students were sent to craft schools on Palau, the administrative center, where agriculture, carpentry, nursing, mechanics, and other practical occupations were taught. The Japanese sent many Yapese outside of Yap to plantations and phosphate mines in Fais and Angaur, and forced others to work at military installations. They also arranged "culture tours" to Japan for traditional Yapese leaders, so that they could see the cultural "advantages" enjoyed by the Japanese. These tours, however, proved relatively ineffective in changing Yapese habits.

The political impact of Japanese rule was the emasculation of island-wide leadership authority and power. The government appointed district chiefs to dictate administrative policies and decisions to the people. Some Yapese were educated and placed in minor support positions, such as policemen, but they were never allowed to hold positions of leadership. The Japanese prohibited the practice of traditional religious rites and ridiculed traditional religious practices. Consequently, the Yapese people turned almost completely to Catholicism. The Japanese destroyed the meeting sites of the traditional councils and stopped the last practicing *mispel* 'clubhouse hostesses'. They prohibited *mitmit* 'exchanges' and the exercise of the Yap-wide political alliance structure as much as possible. The village chief, however, was allowed to continue to oversee the building of community houses and the administration of local affairs. With the advent of the Second World War, many villages were moved to "safer" areas and more military installations were set up to combat the expected invasion.

The American Administration

In 1944 the Americans bombed Yap. At the end of World War II the U.S. Navy occupied Yap from September 1945 until June 1951. The navy had to arrange for the evacuation of the Japanese troop contingents and to establish an administrative framework in order to meet the needs of the Yapese and a sizable population of Chamorros from Saipan who had been relocated to Yap to work as laborers by the Japanese. Most of these Chamorros returned to Saipan in the early years of the American administration.

The navy allowed the Japanese access to Yapese labor for their gardens and food supply until they were evacuated. Once the Japanese were repatriated, however, the Yapese returned to their home villages.

The navy also requested Yapese labor for road building and repairs, but on a voluntary basis rather than under the conditions of forced labor the Yapese had experienced under the Japanese.

The early postwar wants of the Yapese were quite limited. When asked what they wished in terms of reconstruction, they requested only the repair of the roads. Water shortage was also a recognized problem, however, and the navy contributed pontoons for water storage. Some Yapese sought trade goods such as kerosene, lamps, nails, mosquito nets, and blankets. One chief requested lumber for building boats, as the Japanese had destroyed all canoes, boats, and timber. The naval administration records show that there were about eighteen private businesses on Yap during the postwar period, but most, if not all, were Chamorro-run concerns.

In the area of social change, the navy tried, without success, to stop the traditional separate eating customs by presenting the chiefs with mess kits for each member of their families. They also failed in trying to set up P.T.A.s and Father's Councils. They did bring in movies, however, which were an instant hit. There was also an increase in the drinking of fermented coconut toddy, which the Japanese had prohibited. The navy discouraged drinking, but was not able to stop it entirely. They encouraged laborers to move to town to work for wages, and built a hospital. Upon completion of the hospital, the administration issued an order that all babies were to be born in the hospital.

The general policy of both the military and the civilian governments from 1946 to 1956 was to leave the Yapese alone. Education was offered but attendance not required, schools were staffed by Yapese teachers and American supervisors. A few students who had higher levels of achievement attended secondary school and the most ambitious left Yap to attend high school, either at Pacific Islands Central School or Xavier High School in Truk. A very few attended college or went on for further professional training (primarily in medicine).

Economic development was also low key. Contact with outsiders was limited severely through government regulation of transportation, land policy, and investment. The Yap Trading Company (today Yap Co-op Association) was the only chartered trading company, and other businesses were very small duplicates.

In the social sphere the Yapese were kept apart from the Americans. Liquor was prohibited except in the American club and most Yapese were not invited to enter. The Yapese continued to live in their village communities, with only a few moving to the town to work or attend school.

In the mid-1950s, radical changes began to occur. In 1956 an island-wide referendum approved the importing of beer. A quota of five hundred cases a month was set, then raised to one thousand cases. Waiting lists, rapid gulping of one's supply before friends came, price scalping, advance orders, and sellout in advance became common. The quota system was finally dropped in the hope that consumption would level off, but it did not. In 1968, $138,000 was spent to import alcoholic beverages.

As the number of jobs or educational opportunities increased, more people moved to town. Problems of drunkenness, delinquency, and crimes accompanied the expanding population of the town. Other economic improvements increased the movement of people into and through the town.

In 1962, the former Japanese airfield was rebuilt to service regular flights from Guam. A Coast Guard Loran Transmitting Station was built in Gagil and roads were extended from Gagil to Gilman. The importation of supplies and goods increased, thus fanning the flame of economic wants. Tin roofs replaced thatch, and clothes replaced loincloths and grass skirts. Stoves, bicycles, watches, boats, motors, cement floors, and block walls expanded the new material wealth. Many people in town obtained electricity and then electrical appliances. In 1962 there were only 3 private motorbikes and no private automobiles on Yap. In 1968 there were 160 Yapese-owned motorbikes and 73 Yapese-owned automobiles or trucks, all used in traversing thirty-six miles of unpaved road.

In 1964 the Yap High School was erected and American contract teachers hired to staff it. In 1965 the Yap Radio Station, WSZA, began broadcasting. In 1966 Peace Corps Volunteers arrived, seventy strong for six thousand people, to assist in education, public health, and economic development. In 1968, Air Micronesia was given new contracts to provide DC-6 service three times weekly and a million-dollar hotel (as yet unbuilt) to attract tourists. Mili Lines from Saipan received a contract that same year to provide more frequent shipping of supplies from both the United States and Japan.

The Pattern of Political Change

After World War II the naval administration worked initially through the Japanese-appointed chiefs. Naval administrators solicited one representative from each municipality to live in town so he could be contacted for administrative matters. Frequent appeals for labor were made through the chiefs for road building and to work for pay on the military base.

The navy also requested a list of those over eighteen years old who might qualify to vote, and in July 1946 elections were held for the positions of chief. Five of the ten acting chiefs, who had been appointed by the Japanese, were defeated. All of them lost to higher-ranking chiefs in their traditional districts, signifying the revival of traditional Yapese power. Under the U.S. administration, the chiefs were made the main focus of all administrative matters, including mobilization of labor, distribution of goods provided by the navy, and the establishment of a system of courts. Each chief was appointed judge in his own district, and policemen were hired to make arrests.

These changes were not without problems, however. The chiefs were unable to enforce navy orders because of lack of local support and lack of an effective police force. The local police did not have the power or the courage to arrest their friends and relatives. The naval administrators then became quite angry at the chiefs because they could not control the fighting, drinking, and other social problems. The chiefs were lectured on sanitation, the benefits of the hospital, and the need for education. People were scolded for owning "shanty" houses and allowing disorder in both villages and towns. The production of handicrafts was encouraged unsuccessfully with "money" as the inducement.

In June 1947, the military governor of Guam directed that a local government with its own council and laws be established for each municipality. A magistrate would be elected head of the district to administer and handle misdemeanors. A local head tax ($2 for each adult male) was recommended to provide maintenance funds for public buildings and schools. Existing policemen would keep their jobs. A naval administrator reported that ten thousand books were coming from the United States to provide materials for a beginning four-grade school program. In 1948, after four typhoons devastated Yap, the Chamorro population moved to Tinian. This wiped out the business population of Yap and removed the last significant group of outsiders from the island.

The naval administration provided a vital injection of life into the traditional framework of Yapese politics. Their basic philosophical approach was to respect the traditional institutions and leaders, particularly if they were cooperative. The first "elections" held by the navy enabled the various local councils to meet and select their own leaders on the basis of traditional requirements and then pass the word along the various local *tha'* 'channels' as to which "chief" should be elected. This constituted formal recognition of the power of the traditional chiefs, and through administrative declarations and labor requirements, provided a practical application of traditional channels for specific political and economic goals.

One symbolic aspect of the revival of traditional activities is the reappearance of large *mitmit* 'exchanges'. In 1952 these ceremonies were held in Dugor village and Adbuwe' village respectively. The exchange held in the latter village is important because it celebrated the completion of a large men's house, which must have taken at least two years to plan and build. As soon as the Yapese discovered the noninterference of the American administration in traditional cultural matters, they resumed especially those activities that were political and public. This included eating class feasts, community house construction, and *mitmit*. However, two significant areas of political life—tribute and religious feasts—failed to emerge again. Catholicism had achieved solid support by the end of the war, and tribute relations had been prohibited for so long that the chiefs lacked both the power and support to revive them. The one exception was the service of the low caste, which was still required and achieved through threat of eviction from land.

At the same time the naval administration spawned new leadership statuses. Some Yapese acted as interpreters and assistants to the administration. Others worked to create a new school system and a department of public health. Some became skilled leaders in the labor and police forces. These men and their positions were forerunners of a more complex American-derived political framework. In a real way, Yapese began to take effective roles in the foreign administrative complex.

With the changeover to a civil administration under the U.S. Department of Interior in July 1951, the incipient new leadership positions became firmly established. An administrative hierarchy was defined that included such divisions as administration, budget and finance, public health, public works, education, police and security, and even a district court with Yapese judges. In effect, the civil administration set up a self-sufficient administrative government, in contrast to the navy's, which had been heavily dependent upon local chiefs.

The civil administration formally instituted a council of magistrates in December 1952, replacing the council of "chiefs," which had been the focus of administrative support for the navy. Magistrates were "elected" from a group of four candidates named in each municipality. The new official was called magistrate because "chief" implied a hereditary position, "which is not true in this case" (Yap District, Office of Political Affairs 1952). In matter of fact, however, the membership of the old council of "chiefs" and the new council of magistrates was identical; the leaders were the traditional chiefs, supported by the traditional councils.

The role of the magistrates council led progressively further away from the traditional exercise of power. Magistrates were responsible for such things as levying taxes to support schools and teachers; establishing boards of education and selecting students for study outside of

Yap; organizing labor forces for government projects like causeway repair and to collect and distribute food to outer islanders in the hospital and during the aftermaths of typhoons; providing support for government programs such as sanitation, education, and roads; enforcing administrative regulations regarding fires, collection of trochuses, and so forth; and the formulation of municipal ordinances. Quite frequently they provided tours of the islands and parties for visiting dignitaries. American administrators dominated meetings, setting the agenda and directing the business of the council. The Yapese working directly in the administration became more powerful and influential with the Americans than the chiefs for whom they translated.

By 1956 the functions of the council had become quite complex. Committees were established for agriculture, public roads, education, health, and municipal ordinances. The legislative functions of the council had expanded to include ordinances regulating such things as firearms, liquor, taxes, and even prices for food sold at the farmer's market. The traditional chiefs who for the most part made up the council had acquired a great deal of new power. In 1956 terms of office were increased from one to three years.

The administration aimed to transform the council into a chartered legislative body. A committee of magistrates was appointed in 1957 to review the possible reorganization of the council to this effect, with a suggested formation of ten local municipal governments in its place. The council rejected the chartering of municipal governments, stressing rather the existing island-wide council. The council decided to maintain its own identity and at the same time establish a new legislative congress. District Administrator Robert Halvorsen documents the basic strategy adopted by Yapese leaders at that time.

> November 1958 the special committee for organization and chartering proposed the separation of legislative and executive functions on the basis that, though separation is not essential at this time, such action is better for future development. The committee presented a proposed charter of the Yap Islands Congress which required only a few minor additions and changes for completion. The approved charter was presented to Mr. A. J. Roboman, President of the Council and one of the leaders in organizing the Congress, by the chairman of the United Nations Visiting Commission in February, 1959. First elections of congressmen are to be held in April, 1959, and the first session will convene in May, 1959. The Yap Islands Council will continue its executive function within the framework of legislation enacted by the congress. (Yap District, Office of Political Affairs, Political and Social Development File 1958)

The Yap Islands Congress, as separate from the council, opened a whole new area for leadership. The leadership emphasis of the congress, as opposed to the council, was upon education and skills relevant to the new American political ideology. The members of the congress tended to be younger than council members and more active in other aspects of administration. Two representatives were selected from each municipality, tripling the number of elected leaders.

Perhaps most crucial to the leaders, however, was the fact that control of the budget and funds had passed from the council to the congress.

> It is anticipated that the first session or two of the Congress will be slow and perhaps difficult until procedures and relationships between the two bodies are better understood and established. The Council, accustomed to making appropriations from time to time as unforeseen needs arise, will have to learn to live within a budget enacted into law by the Congress. The Council will also have to learn that other legislative powers now rest with the Congress. (Yap District, Office of Political Affairs, Political and Social Development File 1958)

As time passed and the legislators became more cognizant of their power and functions, their power and prestige also increased. The sessions became more creative, and legislators developed into leaders as important issues were debated and decided. In recent years, members of the council have complained that they are mere employees of the congress and bemoan their loss of financial and decision-making power.

The prestige of the congress further increased with its most recent reorganization in 1968 to the Yap District Legislature. This new body consists of one representative from each municipality, two members-at-large elected from Yap, and eight members from the various outer islands. Several factors make this group a higher elite than its predecessor. It is more select, outer islanders are for the first time represented, and decisions are now applicable to the whole district rather than just Yap (see Meller 1969 and Lingenfelter 1974 for further details in the development of the Yap District Legislature).

The highest (and newest) positions of leadership are now found in the Congress of Micronesia, officially chartered in 1965 and originating from an earlier Council of Micronesia established in 1956. The Congress is divided into two houses; the upper, now referred to as the Senate, and the lower, the House of Representatives. Each district in the Trust Territory of the Pacific Islands is allotted two seats in the Senate, while seats in the House are based on population. Yap District has two senators, one representative from Yap proper, and one representative from the outer islands.

The role of the Congress of Micronesia each year becomes increasingly more important. Significant decisions are being made for all of the Trust Territory and economic appropriations and support are much greater each year. The Yapese members of the Congress actively participate in this new territory-wide elite and enjoy high prestige in their own home district.

Thus, the American administration has not only stimulated traditional political activity in Yap, but has channeled and directed it into totally new forms of leadership, decision-making, and administration. In the process, however, new definitions of leadership, leadership statuses, and authority have preempted the old. The desire for status and prestige is carried over from the traditional values, but it has been redirected toward new rewards: positions in the Congress, the Legislature, the council, or the administration. Furthermore, the power of leadership lies in these same positions, motivating old chiefs to press their sons into further education and obtaining college degrees. At the same time much of traditional political life remains. All of the major statuses and institutions for villages and regional nets persist today, except for the religious rites and warfare, supplying viable alternatives for political action. Yapese mix and match traditional and new alternatives to plan the most promising strategies for political success and to find the most satisfying solutions to their contemporary problems. The ideal solutions combine the best of both worlds, but reality finds the new alternatives gradually, but certainly, eroding the foundations of tradition.

10. NEW STRUCTURES IN THE POLITICAL FIELD

C hange in the political structure was relatively unimportant through the end of the Japanese administration and into the early years of the American administration. The changes that had been instituted either negated or redefined already existing statuses. The German administration utilized the existing forms. The Japanese administration ignored the Yapese almost completely, superimposing its all-Japanese administration over the old German districts. It remained to the American administration to create a totally new political structure and ideology based upon American concepts of representative government and democracy.

Elements of the Political Community

The village residential units have formed the basic building blocks of all political structures in the recent history of Yap. Their importance has varied with the respective administration, but in all cases it has been recognized. Thus throughout the consecutive foreign administrations governing Yap, the village's political identity has been relatively undisturbed and provides a significant reason for the persistence of the traditional patterns.

The German administration established the ten districts of Yap as the basic political units for government. These districts were based upon the traditional political order, which included a traditional net and a high-ranking village, which would act as leader and provide the focus and leadership for German administrative decisions. Nine of the ten districts were led by a village of the *ulun* or *bulce'* rank, with the only exception, Rumung, rationalized on a geographical basis (it is an island to itself). Rumung also has a leading village, but not of the highest rank. The lesser Yapese nets were divided and/or incorporated into larger districts to provide a viable work force for German interests. These political districts were retained through the Japanese and American administrations. The Americans renamed them municipalities, but preserved the same local names and composition established in the German period.

The municipalities are united together at a higher level, the Yap Islands, which form a political, cultural, and linguistic unit as distinguished from the outer islands in the district. Although the outer islands from Ulithi to Satawal were under the political domination of Wonyan and Gacpar villages, they are separate from the Yapese and without voice in local Yapese affairs. The Yap Islands, then, form a separate political unit within the larger field of the administrative district.

Yap District is the largest unit of the political field to be considered here. It is primarily political, comprised of two major cultural and linguistic groups, the Yapese and the Carolinians. The Yapese reside primarily in the Yap Islands, while the Carolinians inhabit the atolls from Ulithi to Satawal in the east. A small community of Carolinians reside permanently on Yap, while others come to Yap for short periods, particularly when medical care is needed. A third cultural group, about three hundred Palauans, live permanently in the town of Colonia. They are not significant in Yapese or district politics, but contribute to the skilled labor force in the district center.

Although beyond the scope of our discussion, it should be noted that the Congress of Micronesia is becoming increasingly influential and important in the various local districts of the Trust Terrtiory. Decisions of the Congress have impact in all of the districts as the Office of the High Commissioner and the Department of the Interior increasingly pass decision-making responsibility to the Congress. A body that once performed largely ritual acts of approval and distribution of minor funds has become an active legislature with power to tax, make laws, and formulate policy for all of the Trust Territory. The local members of the Congress of Micronesia are given considerable prestige and recognition, concomitant with their new positions of power and responsibility.

New Political Statuses in the Village

On the village level, statuses in the political field remain largely unchanged. Decision-making and administration are still the province of old men and chiefs, as defined by the traditional authority derived from the land and the estate. The only new status is that of village representative on the municipal council, an American-instituted position. Each village selects a representative to municipal council meetings who participates in making and administering decisions. Generally one of the traditional chiefs of the village is appointed to this position by a council of old men. In the early days of the council, the representatives were all chiefs, but presently the situation varies from village to village, municipality to municipality. For example, in Weloy municipality, four villages selected unranked men to represent them and another four selected men from among their traditional landed chiefs.

The authority of the village representative to the municipal council is derived from his representative status. He carries the wishes of his village to the municipal council and to the magistrate. He in turn represents the decisions of the council and the magistrate to the village. He acts as an administrative assistant to the magistrate, carrying word of decisions and administering them in his village. His duties may include collecting food for municipal entertainment functions or summoning labor for a municipal project. An example from Wonyan village, Gagil municipality, illustrates how the representative works through traditional village politics. Word was passed from the magistrate to the village representative regarding a meeting for all the men of Gagil. The representative carried the message to the acting chief-of-young-men in each village section, who then went from house to house passing the word of the meeting. This same procedure is followed for announcements by the traditional village chief.

Traditional Yapese political statuses have persisted because the authority has been distributed according to village and estate land units, rather than being vested in a particular political family or lineage as found in other areas of Micronesia and Polynesia. To destroy the Yapese hierarchy it would be necessary to destroy the villages and estates as social and political units. The authority belongs to the land and not to the people. People die, but as long as land and concepts about land persist, the statuses and authority patterns of Yapese politics will persist. Traditional chiefs are legitimate because the concepts about the land are still considered legitimate.

Nevertheless, today the authority of the traditional village chiefs is being challenged seriously. The traditional extension of power outside the village has been truncated by the cessation of warfare and assumption of power by foreign administrations. Certain authorities, useful to the foreign powers, were retained but very rapidly changed in form and meaning. The only overt demonstration of traditional extravillage power today are the ceremonial *mitmit* and the exchange of traditional valuables for political or social ends. However, in the undercurrents of Yapese politics most procedures and activities follow traditional norms and channels.

The crucial factor in challenging traditional authority is local support. The Yapese say that when a chief loses the support of his people, he is no longer a chief. It is somewhat prophetic that today many legitimate village chiefs have lost local support. The reasons for this loss, however, lie beyond a chief's personal power or skills. Depopulation was certainly very important. Many large villages that formerly had a complex hierarchy of chiefs and subordinate leaders have been reduced to as few as six or seven families, an obviously inadequate number of personnel to maintain village prestige, work projects, and other political functions.

Wage work is even more important a factor in the erosion of the chiefs' support because it entails a completely new way of life. Instead of pursuing traditional subsistence activities in the village and being available for community projects, men are leaving the villages to work for wages in town (Colonia). This means either a shift in residence or daily commuting into Colonia. A commuter's day begins at 6:30 A.M. when the bus leaves for town and ends at 5:30 P.M. when it returns. With a five-day work week the wage earner has little time on weekends to care for his family's needs, to drink and have fun, and no time to support the traditional chief in village projects.

In the 1968 census, 482 out of 901 males between the ages of twenty and sixty-five held regular wage jobs. Of the remaining 419 men, 122 worked part-time as storekeepers, handicraft workers, stevedores, or produce representatives for the farmer's market. Only 297 men followed traditional subsistence patterns and were available to support the chiefs of about one hundred villages. And of these 297, many engaged in part-time copra production for cash income.

These figures show that labor support for traditional village projects is almost nil. An example from Balabat village in Rull municipality illustrates this point. Balabat, with twenty-two households, is the third-largest village in Yap. The paramount chief of Ru'way and supporting leaders from Balabat decided to build a new men's house for the chief. The labor force consisted of a traditional carpenter brought from another village and four men, all above sixty years of age. They regularly complained about the young men not coming to help, but in the next breath excused them because they were working in town. They joked about the old men doing young men's work, but it was obvious that the joking was more painful than funny.

Other villages are enduring similar experiences. Skeletons of traditional clubhouses stand all over Yap, due in large part to the lack of support in the villages to repair and maintain them. The excuse given is that there are no more low-caste people to do the work, but the people do not really care whether it is done or not. Their life-style has changed and the clubhouses with their traditional roles are outmoded. In some of the more remote areas, the labor force is still at home and the clubhouse is still a normal part of life. However, roads now reach every municipality of Yap except Rumung and even the more traditional villages are becoming victims of the commuter syndrome.

The new life-style has far-reaching implications for Yapese culture. Politically, wage work has brought about adjustments in values and spheres of orientation. The wage worker is mobile, moving in and out of the town, interacting with Yapese from all over Yap. This is in direct contradiction to the traditional village orientation. Traditionally Yapese did not travel except on very special occasions. It is still true that many Yapese women and children have not traveled to areas of Yap outside their own districts or even beyond adjacent villages. Men traveled infrequently until the advent of roads and motor vehicles. Today one-half of the adult male population of Yap interacts daily in town. This reorientation has not erased local loyalties, but shifted their focus from a village to a municipal level. A person from Gagil rides the bus with people from Gagil, thinks of himself as being from Gagil, and interacts with people from other villages in Gagil. In town social or drinking circles, people from municipalities tend to group together. Village boundaries, while not forgotten, have become less important and it is in the larger sphere of the municipality that much social interchange beyond the family level takes place. Certain cases of intense intervillage rivalry provide exception, but even these rivalries do not stem the frequent social intercourse between members of traditionally hostile villages.

Adjustments in values follow this shift in orientation. People still say that village solidarity is good, but most are too busy to support it. Local village projects are considered good; to say otherwise would be heresy, but primary concern is given to municipal roads, municipal buildings, and municipal projects rather than to the village community houses, dance grounds, group fishing, and other group tasks. Municipal and Yap-wide leaders are more important than traditional chiefs, and, by implication, power has passed from landed leaders to elected leaders. A primary example of this is the situation in which a traditional chief, acting as the representative of the magistrate, receives support from his village for a municipal project, but not when he acts as chief and leader of a village project. Finally, one finds in present-day Yap an emphasis on intramunicipal social relations that overrides the traditional village or village section barriers of interaction. These changing values yield subsequent feelings of political as well as social unity.

New Statuses in the Municipality

The American administration has stimulated or mandated the creation of new statuses at the level of the municipality. Each municipality has a magistrate, a secretary to the magistrate, a municipal council with representatives from each village, and a legislator. Other new statuses in the municipality have arisen to fulfill particular administrative needs. Boards of education have been formed to rally public support for the school programs. Agricultural representatives have been appointed to coordinate the market program and to assist in agricultural improvements. Other development programs such as those sponsored by the Yap Community Action Program (Office of Economic Opportunity) require local municipal leaders. New organizations also have developed at the municipal level. Some municipalities have women's clubs, which participate in farming projects, sewing, and other domestic skills, as well as socializing on a municipal-wide basis. Young men's organizations, with constitutions and officers, have been formed to pursue recreational and constructive objectives.

The status of magistrate is the most important in the municipality. He is an elected representative to the Yap Islands Council of Magistrates and the leader of his local municipality. He serves as administrator of directives from the district administrator, the Council of Magistrates, and the legislature. He is the primary executive officer for work projects and for the spending of legislated appropriations for his municipality. Apart from his executive tasks, he acts in an advisory capacity to the district administrator and to the legislature. Facilitating cross-communication between the people and the policymakers is one of his primary roles. His work includes project planning for his municipality (cleaning, building, repairing, forming clubs, and so forth) in cooperation with the Yap Islands council, District Legislature, and district administrator. He also hosts visitors, and directs school and health programs and dances. In short, he acts as the leader and representative of his municipality in all matters relating to it.

Each magistrate has a secretary, whom he appoints at the time of his election. The appointment is generally approved by the municipal council, although legally it is not required. The secretary ideally records all important matters discussed in the municipal council and assists in keeping the vital election statistics of his municipality. He also acts as messenger for the magistrate to members of the municipal council and to the people, and supports the magistrate in the administration of decisions.

Each municipality is represented by an elected legislator in the Yap District Legislature. These legislators have no direct authority in the municipalities, except as members of the law- and policy-making body of the government of Yap. Rather, the legislator proposes municipal projects to the legislature and solicits funds for them. His other municipal functions are to communicate the legislature's actions to the magistrate and the people.

The municipal council is the municipal-level equivalent of the traditional village council. Each village in the municipality, regardless of rank, has a representative on the council who is paid one dollar a meeting for his services. Originally these councils formulated municipal ordinances, collected taxes, and provided labor support for municipal projects. The legislative functions have since passed to the legislature and the councils now provide channels of communication between village, magistrate, and legislator. One of the important, but not legally specified, functions of these councils has been to select candidates for elective positions. This practice was initiated under the naval administration when the administrators required that more than one candidate be offered for election. The councils designated candidates for the positions, a practice that has carried over into the present, though this procedure has been supplanted by submission of petitions to an election clerk.

The other new leadership statuses in the municipalities do not carry the authority of those in the government. The board of education has very limited powers, designed mostly to coordinate public support for school programs of the administration. Agricultural representatives confine their efforts to agricultural matters and are limited in that agriculture is no longer the primary concern of the Yapese. Club leaders coordinate and direct the functions of their own groups, which often include members from all the villages, of both high and low rank, in the municipality. The clubs may provide very powerful interest groups and thus affect the political process.

Legitimacy of New Municipal Statuses

Magistrate, secretary, legislator, and councilman are statuses mandated by a foreign, dominant government to meet the legal and administrative requirements of that government and to support a new style of life involving new economic, political, and social forms. Legitimacy of these statuses rests not on some traditional framework of referents but upon the dominant government and the situation of change.

At the same time, certain characteristics of these statuses derive support and legitimacy from the traditional field. For example, the status of magistrate is elective, permitting the exercise of traditional values in selecting leaders. The status is placed in a political context with the other statuses of secretary, legislator, and local councilman. In this manner, the traditional value of distribution of power is duplicated in remarkably similar fashion. The magistrate, secretary, and legislator parallel in form the statuses of village chief, chief-of-young-men, and sitting-chief, and their functions are also remarkably similar; the magistrate is the chief executive, the secretary is his administrative assistant, and the legislator is the councilor and representative with regard to laws and appropriations, and matters affecting the people as a whole.

The magistrate, secretary, and legislator cooperate with the municipal council, again following the traditional custom of cooperation with the *puruy* 'council'. While the municipal council, contrary to custom, includes representatives from the lowest-ranking villages, members from these villages do not flaunt their newly acquired power but rather behave in a quiet, subservient manner. Furthermore, the council representations fall along the lines of the *tha'* 'channels of communication', and one of the primary functions of council members is the communication of decisions and demands. The structure of new political statuses so nearly duplicates the traditional structure that legitimacy is derived from the traditional values, a duplication that has proved very important in maintaining support. (This, it might be added, was purely accidental on the part of the American administration, which followed an American format and did not intentionally seek to duplicate the Yapese system.)

Another factor in the legitimacy of new statuses is that their authority lies for the most part beyond traditional politics and therefore it does not supplant traditional leaders. In the earlier discussion of the traditional elements of the political field, the village was observed as the most important unit of organization, tied by the slender bonds of the *tha'* and by force through the sanctions of warfare and religion. The villages have remained undisturbed, but they are now incorporated into larger, permanent, geographical units—the municipalities.

Foreign powers formed the municipalities for their own political ends. The geographical units, however, were not arbitrary, but, as noted earlier, were based upon traditional political relationships to facilitate administration. The municipality became quite like a village with its ranked subsections and internal rivalries—in fact, a supervillage. The American innovations of magistrate, secretary, councilman, and subsequently legislator statuses neatly duplicated Yapese political ideals to reinforce the supervillage, or municipality, concept.

The new supervillage requires new kinds of community services, administration, rules of behavior, and leadership statuses. Such projects as the building of municipal roads, schools, and docks, the forming of municipal clubs, competition between municipalities in dances or various sports lie beyond the sphere of traditional authority. Newly defined leadership statuses are required. At the same time, traditional statuses have remained unchallenged, although the cessation of warfare and the demise of religious and tribute relationships have altered their authority.

The occupants of the new statuses are not prohibited from holding traditional ones, thus the leading traditional chief of the highest-ranking village in a municipality may well be the magistrate. Conversely, a lower-ranking person may be chosen magistrate if the people support him and the traditional village chief does not lose face because of his selection. Since the new status is not defined in land and the standard rule of succession is elective support rather than inheritance, the position of the traditional chief remains secure, although his lack of power may be psychologically disconcerting.

The argument may be summarized by stating that Yapese acceptance of the new political structure is directly related to its structural similarity to the old system, and that the new structure successfully fused segments of the traditional political system into a larger superstructure along the lines of traditional fission and fusion. The village units, while not based upon kinship, define their mutual political relationships in kinship terms, and the fusion of the smaller village units into a larger municipality logically extends the system. Furthermore, the Yapese think about the municipality as a land unit, just as they conceptualize the smaller units of village, section, and estate. People from the same land, that is, municipality, are kinsmen because land, not blood, determines the relationship. The new municipal statuses find support through structural parallels to traditional village statuses and supplement these traditional statuses with authority assignments directly related to the situation of change.

New Statuses in the Yap Islands Government

The Yap Islands Council of Magistrates coordinates the municipal organization into a Yap-wide government. An executive committee elected from among the ten magistrates provides leadership in the council. It includes a president, who presides at all meetings and is the chief executive officer of the council; a secretary, who makes and maintains records of meetings and acts as assistant to the president; and a treasurer, who receives all island funds, disburses them as directed by the council, and submits reports of his activity. (This office has been supplanted by the district treasurer in a mandate by the legislature.) The executive committee acts in advisory and liaison capacity to the district administrator during the interim between council meetings. They also meet in advance of meetings to plan the agenda.

The Council of Magistrates was originally quite active. Its authority included the passing of laws, the collection and appropriation of funds, and the sponsoring of projects such as building intermediate school dormitories, rallying public support in "copra weeks" to make copra for public school funds, paying teachers' salaries, regulating alcoholic beverages, and providing economic assistance to outer islanders. The working of the council was based upon traditional ideals of decision-making and distribution of authority. A comment by one district administrator suggested that matters that could easily be handled in committees were still brought before the whole, following the traditional idea of council meetings and consensus in policy-making.

Since the formation of the legislature, the decision-making power of the council has gradually passed to the legislature, and the council has turned more to a functionary, administrative, and advisory role. The executive committee still functions as the chief liaison and advisory group to the district administrator. The president of the council is the speaker/leader on important occasions such as U.N. Day or celebrations for and entertainment of visiting dignitaries. All magistrates, and particularly the executive officers, along with other community leaders, occupy important positions as chairmen or members of various boards or committees.

The legitimacy of the council and executive committee lies in both the sanction of the American administration and the traditional values and concepts of the political field. For over ten years the council functioned as the legislative and executive power in the district. At the peak of its power and efficiency the administration urged a separation of legislative and executive authorities through the formation of a legislature. The process and consequences of this act will be discussed in detail later. The point here is that initially the council received full American authority and support as the Yapese branch of the American-instituted government.

Like the municipal structure, the Yap Islands Council of Magistrates falls into the traditional ideology of Yapese government—that is, three leading chiefly statuses and a supporting council or *puruy*. Although it does not meet the requirements of the dual alliance system, this is not necessary because a balance of power is maintained through the opposition of the alien administration. Power strategies, while still important among Yapese leaders, focus upon the American administration, rather than upon competing local groups.

Constituents define the status of magistrate as chief or *pilung* and the magistrates are referred to as such. They meet in council with three executive officers and seven supporting members, matching the numerical ideals of the traditional council for *bulce'*, which had three paramount chiefs and the seven chiefs from the seven *bulce'* villages. While council members are not necessarily from *bulce'* villages, they invariably come from the highest-ranking village in their respective municipalities. Thus the structure of the council and its cultural definitions placed it into the legitimate traditional framework of the Yap political field.

At the same time, the authority of the council applies to the situation of change rather than to traditional matters. Schools, roads, visiting dignitaries, and administrative decisions lie beyond the traditional field. The status of magistrate forms a cultural bridge between the two political spheres. Yapese define the position of magistrate in traditional terms, but authority in terms of responsibilities for the American government. The individual magistrate may in fact hold both traditional status and the magistrate status and function in both spheres; or he may lack a traditional title, but because of the prestige of his new authority defined in traditional status terms, he may be able to maintain support for actions in the traditional field.

In contrast, the legislature is viewed as an American innovation, defined in American terms and operating on American principles. Its power and authority are defined in peculiarly American ways and its operating procedures require American skills such as parliamentary procedure, the writing of bills and resolutions according to an American legal format, and the knowledge and use of English. The definition of the status of legislator is couched by the Yapese in terms of these skills.

Yapese view a legislator as one knowledgeable in the ways of Americans, having some proficiency in English and prolonged contact with American leaders. He should be skillful in dealing with Americans so as to obtain all the benefits possible for his local constituents. His status is truly new, having no traditional precedent, nor forming any logical extension of the traditional structure of political relationships.

The leadership of the legislature, president, vice-president, and secretary, represent new Yap-wide political statuses carrying considerable prestige and authority. As in most American-designed organizations, the president presides, the vice-president takes charge in the absence of the president, and the secretary maintains records of all sessions of the legislature. The three act as an executive committee to prepare and publish the agenda of business for each session and to act in an administrative capacity for the legislature when it is not in session. This practice is a carry-over from the council and is not normally part of an American-style legislature. The committee was instituted as a convenience and an educational device for the administration. The Yapese knew nothing about legislation and legislatures. The administration trained and guided the executive committee and the other legislators followed them. These assignments provided the executive committee with some additional power over legislative policy not held by their peers. Perhaps even more important, however, is the influence these executive officials acquired through their positions as leaders of the legislature. They were able to influence fellow legislators, American officials, and many of the people they represented. After the legislators gained experience and were trained by Peace Corps lawyers in the use of legislative committees, the role of the executive committee declined (see Lingenfelter 1974).

The authority of the legislature as a body is best observed through the decisions made by the group. The tables below show the types of decisions made in three sessions of the Yap Islands Legislature, May 1967, November 1967, and May 1968.

Table 18 shows a steady increase in the decision-making activity of the legislature. Members were elected to two-year terms and the 17th session represents their first term. As members became accustomed to their responsibilities and the legislative procedures, the amount of business considered and passed actually doubled, showing increased legislative skill.

Table 19 clearly shows appropriations to be the primary concern of the first session of the year, and, in fact, of all succeeding sessions (Table 20) until all money acquired through taxes and Trust Territory allocations was distributed. The second most frequent set of bills considered concern revisions of statutes in the legal code. However, some of the more important decisions occurred in other areas. Study commissions, supported by the legislature, were established to point up areas of primary concern to the people of Yap. It is significant that commissions were established to study the problems of the district legislature and municipal governments, tourism and its implications for Yap, physical planning for the Yap Islands, and the Micronesian wage scale; in addition a committee was appointed to study the functions and duties of the Council of Magistrates. These obviously are some of the issues

Table 18. Legislative Activity—Yap Islands Legislature

	17th Session	18th Session	19th Session
Total Proposals			
Introduced	31	38	44
Passed*	25	30	37
Defeated	—	1	4
Changed	—	—	1
Filed	—	—	1
Tabled	—	5	1
Pending	6	2	—
Total Bills			
Introduced	58	55	82
Passed*	38	19	52
Disapproved by administration	8	—	3
Approved by administration	30	—	47
Were amendments and remained as acts	—	—	2
Pending	9	23	12
Defeated	2	—	14
Filed	4	—	3
Converted into resolution	—	2	1
Rules introduced as bills	2	3	—
Tabled	2	7	—
Changed into proposal	—	1	—
Rejected	1	—	—

NOTE:

Data are summaries from Yap Islands Legislature 1967–1968.

* Proposals that are passed become resolutions, and bills become laws.

the Yapese would like to consider carefully and over which they wish to exert some authority and control.

The proposals provide another indicator of the interests and values of the legislators and their constituents. Community and economic development are highest on the list of priorities, reflecting the desire for accelerated change and improvement. This supports the generalization made earlier about the shift in values to wage work and its concomitant benefits and opportunities. The high frequencies of resolutions about government reflect the continual Yapese interest in politics. The negative aspects of Yapese values can be seen in Table 21, Bills Defeated.

Like most legislatures, they dislike reducing taxes and thereby reducing funds, but are reluctant to raise taxes and lose popular support. Recreation and sanitation fall low on the list of priorities. Bikinis and miniskirts, while considered immoral in this topless culture, are not to

Table 19. Summary of Laws and Resolutions of Yap Islands
Legislature

	17th Session	18th Session	19th Session
Laws			
1. Appropriations	17	5	32
2. New Regulations—Yap Islands Legal Code	2	5	—
3. Amendments of Yap Islands Legal Code	3	6	5
4. Committees	2	1	3
5. Government organization	7	2	3
6. Licenses	—	—	1
7. Tourism	—	—	1
8. Taxation	3	—	—
9. Other	4	—	2
Resolutions			
1. Economic development	7	5	9
2. Community development	2	—	6
3. Road improvement	2	2	2
4. Local government	6	9	7
5. Medical facilities	—	—	3
6. Expression of gratitude	3	2	3
7. Education—political and otherwise	2	5	2
8. Political development	—	2	2
9. Ownership of land and sea	—	2	1
10. Typhoon relief assistance	—	3	—
11. Other	3	—	2

be outlawed, for to do so would deny the men one esthetic pleasure that may come with tourism.

The authority of the legislature may be summed up from these bills and appropriations. Any important issue affecting the welfare of the people is subject to legislative investigation and decision. The power to make far-reaching decisions is obtained through legitimacy and sanctions from the Trust Territory government and the Congress of Micronesia. At the same time, the Trust Territory government has the final word. The local district administrator may veto all acts of the legislature, and the decisions of the group must accord with the Trust Territory Code, which defines laws of the administration binding for the whole territory. The legislature is limited also by the small local tax base. The district administration may provide additional support for legislative decisions and projects, and in many cases has done so. This financial endorsement of the legislature increases its power and legiti-

Table 20. Summary of Legislative Appropriations—Yap Islands Legislature

	17th session	18th session	19th session
Local Government			
A. Legislature			
1. Per diem for legislators	$ 6,000.00	—	$6,000.00
2. Clerical and maintenance salaries	360.00	$1,200.00	4,921.00
3. General expenses and entertainment	2,887.00	—	3,887.00
4. Construction and maintenance of legislature building	10,213.56	300.00	100.00
B. Council			
1. Salaries of council members	8,999.90	—	9,000.00
2. Salaries of secretaries	7,176.00	—	7,176.00
3. General expenses and entertainment	1,000.00	—	1,387.00
C. Treasury			
1. Staff salaries	5,565.80	—	5,565.80
D. Yap museum—staff and expenditures	1,842.00	—	1,332.00
E. Others			
1. Salaries for municipal councils, police, culture teachers	5,491.20	200.00	5,711.20
2. Yap-wide community projects	—	—	2,650.00
3. Yap housing authority	—	—	5,000.00
4. Legislative planning boards	—	—	490.00
5. Funds for assistants and observer to Congress of Micronesia	—	—	1,498.00
Education			
A. Local	5,061.60	—	1,200.00
B. Abroad—transportation and scholarship	936.00	—	1,000.00
Agriculture			
A. Salaries of 16 local agents	6,500.00	—	9,750.00
B. Other general expenses	667.80	—	619.66
*Municipalities**			
A. Rumung (one project)	—	—	666.66
B. Map (nine projects)	6,286.00	545.00	4,452.68
C. Gagil (three projects)	—	—	10,277.50
D. Tamil (three projects)	—	—	10,061.00
E. Fanif (two projects)	6,000.00	—	8,666.66
F. Weloy (two projects)	1,700.05	—	400.00
H. Kanfay and Gilman	500.00	—	—
G. Delipebinaw (one project) (three projects)	1,250.00	—	3,000.00
I. Rull (no projects)	—	—	—

* Types of Municipal Projects—19th Session
  1. Roads, bridges, passages $24,661.00
  2. Water catchments, dispensaries, buildings $21,418.50

Table 21. Bills and Proposals Defeated, 19th and 17th Sessions, Yap Islands Legislature

19TH SESSION—BILLS DEFEATED	
Bill Number	*Purpose and Title*
1–5–68	Lower sales tax
12–5–68	Require sanitary dwellings
13–5–68	Require magistrates to hold monthly meetings
14–5–68	Rental income of government from legislature
15–5–68	Prohibit bikinis and miniskirts
17–5–68	Establish recreation advisor
23–5–68	Establish planning commission for local government
25–5–68	Place curfew of vehicles at Gilman
30–5–68	Levy head tax
31–5–68	Levy tax on Tuba
55–5–68	Extend electricity to South Rull, Kanif, and Gilman
72–5–68	Pay expenses for tourist commission
73–5–68	Establish sanitation week
76–5–68	Require a toilet in every home
19TH SESSION—PROPOSALS DEFEATED	
3–5–68	Establish commission for traffic
8–5–68	Prohibit construction of new hotels on Yap
14–5–68	Change zoning laws for location of bars
24–5–68	Establish traditional values commission
17TH SESSION—BILLS DEFEATED	
11–5–67	Establish salaries for Yap Island legislators
21–5–67	Establish $50.00 bond for non-Yapese

macy, but at the expense of its power to act independently of the administration.

Conflict between the Council of Magistrates and the legislature is inherent in their opposing sources of legitimacy. The council, as already noted, achieves legitimacy and considerable support through its structural similarity to the traditional ideas of status and government. On the other hand, the legislature actually supplants the council in the important areas of appropriations and decision-making. The legislature, in fact, established two commissions—one to explore municipal forms of government and the other to study the functions and duties of the magistrates—to search out justifications for the council's existence. The rationale put forth in justification of the investigation is that council members are really employees of the legislature and therefore the legislature should define their responsibilities.

The magistrates are keenly aware of their loss of power, their new employee status, and are quite unhappy about it. The change, however, was gradual and the results not foreseen until it was too late to change. Furthermore, the pressure levied by the American administration in favor of a legislature could not be denied. With the creation of the legislature, decision-making power passed from older traditional Yapese to younger, American-educated and -indoctrinated Yapese.

Local support for the legislature is obtained through the weight of the administration and through the legislature's power to appropriate funds. Each legislator gains prestige and support in his own municipality by his effectiveness in acquiring funds for municipal projects and appropriations are actively sought for these and other beneficial projects. Municipalities compete with each other for prestigious office buildings and other displays of power and wealth. Over $37,000 was appropriated to eight of the ten municipalities for municipal projects in 1968. This outflow of money is a primary factor in maintaining public support of the legislature.

Another factor is the changing values of the Yapese. In 1958 magistrates and traditional chiefs were the unquestioned leaders of the village-oriented Yapese, but by 1960 the scene had obviously changed. Today with the shift to wage work, town life, and wider social and political interaction, the traditional forms are no longer adequate, nor applicable, to the situation of change. Traditional leaders lack the skills required for participation in the new decision-making processes.

New Statuses in the Yap District

The Yap District Legislature was chartered by the Fourth Regular Session of the Congress of Micronesia in August 1968 (the only legislature in the territory chartered by the Congress) and approved by the High Commissioner of the Trust Territory. The resolution proposing the legislature was submitted by the Yap Islands Legislature and approved by the leaders in the outer islands of Yap District. With the formation of the new District Legislature, the Yap Islands Legislature was dissolved in October 1968.

The District Legislature calls for twenty elected representatives from Yap District. Of the representatives from the Yap Islands, ten are elected from their respective municipalities and two are elected at-large. The two at-large representatives from the Yap Islands are especially influential, not because of actual power, but because of the implications of Yap-wide support. At the first election held in November 1968, these two statuses were sources of multiple political struggles.

The authority exercised by the District Legislature is the same as previously discussed for the Yap Islands Legislature, except that the geographical base of the authority has been expanded to include the whole of Yap District. Consequences of this expansion have been increased prestige of the legislature, a broadening of its base of power, and an increased feeling of responsibility on the part of Yapese legislators. With the addition of the outer islanders to the legislature, Yapese legislators became more conscious of their duties and of the demonstration of their political skills. The marked improvement in attendance of the Yapese at the first session of the legislature in June 1969 was indicative of this new attitude.

The legitimacy and support of the District Legislature parallels the earlier discussion of the Yap Islands Legislature, at least in Yap. The effect of outer island representation has yet to be analyzed because of its incipient nature.

The second set of new statuses found at the district level are the congressmen to the Congress of Micronesia. Yap District has two senators and two representatives, one from Yap proper and the other from the outer islands. These positions have great prestige, representing as they do Yap to the rest of Micronesia and to the Office of the High Commissioner of the Trust Territory. Their authority includes participation in decision-making affecting all of the Trust Territory, as well as the representation of their home islands at the Trust Territory level. Thus, they are directly involved in making such important decisions as the future political status of all the Trust Territory, and also the smaller, closer-to-home problems of their individual districts. With the levying of taxes by the Congress, funds are available to support large projects not fundable at the local level. One such appropriation for a road in Delipebinaw/Weloy municipalities was approved and funded for $154,000, more than triple the total funds appropriated for projects in the 19th session of the Yap Islands Legislature, May 1968. The congressmen also bring considerable expertise from their experience in the Congress. Senators Petrus Tun and Francis Nuuan were especially influential in the increasing effectiveness of the Yap Islands legislature in 1967 and 1968.

The legitimacy of these new statuses derives from American definition and support, finding no precedent whatever in traditional Yapese politics. They are statuses created to meet the situation of change in a world where in a twenty-year period travel by outrigger canoe has been replaced by jet aircraft, and hundreds of miles of sea are crossed in less time than it takes to go by boat from one end of Yap to the other. Support for these statuses is maintained through the sheer prestige of the position, which is highly valued in Yap, and by the implications and benefits of decision-making from that higher level of government.

The third set of new statuses at the district level are those found

Table 22. Yap District Administration—Yapese Statuses

Job Title	Pay Scale Classification
A. *Administration*	
1. Office of the District Administrator	
a. Assistant to the district administrator	C–1
b. Senior administrative clerk	B–7
2. Administrative Support Services	
a. Senior administrative clerk	B–7
3. Budget and Finance	
a. District customs officer	B–9
b. Assistant district finance officer	B–7
4. Communications	
a. Radio operator, supervisor	B–8
5. Property and Supply	
a. Assistant district supply officer	B–7
B. *Education*	
1. Administration	
a. Assistant district director of education	C–1
b. Administrative aide	B–9
2. Elementary	
a. Superintendent of elementary schools	C–2
b. Principal	B–8
3. High School	
a. Vice-principal	B–8
b. College graduate teacher	C–1
C. *Health Services*	
1. Hospital and Field Services	
a. District director of health services	C–5
b. Hospital administrator	C–1
c. Medical records technician	B–8
d. Medical supply officer	B–8
e. Senior laboratory technician	B–10
f. X-Ray technician	B–10
g. Pharmacist	A–11
h. Medical equipment technician	B–10
i. Nurse supervisor	B–11
j. Head nurse	B–10
2. Sanitation	
a. Chief district sanitarian	B–10
D. *Resources and Development*	
1. Agriculture	
a. Agriculture extension agent	B–9
b. Assistant district agriculturist	B–7

Table 22. (Cont.)

Job Title	Pay Scale Classification
2. Economic Development	
a. Assistant economic affairs advisor	B–6
E. *Public Affairs*	
1. Political Development	
a. Political affairs officer	C–1
2. Radio Broadcast Station WSZA	
a. Broadcast station manager	B–9
b. News director	B–8
F. *Community Development*	
a. Community development officer	B–11
b. Adult education assistant	B–7
G. *Protection to Persons and Property*	
1. Police Department	
a. Chief of police	B–12
b. Police captain	B–11
c. Police lieutenant and fire chief	B–10
2. Legal Services	
a. District prosecutor	B–7
b. District public defender	B–9
3. Judiciary	
a. District court judge	—
b. Clerk of courts	—
H. *Public Works*	
a. Leader carpenter foreman	A–13
b. Leader plumber	A–11
c. Leader heavy equipment operator	A–11
d. Leader foreman heavy equipment mechanic	A–13
e. Leader welder	A–12
f. Machinist	A–11
g. Leader boat operation	A–11
h. Leader power plant	A–11
i. Leader foreman electrician	A–13
j. Leader electrician	A–12

NOTES:
Status positions in which Yapese individuals were actually serving at the time of the research are given. American statuses and outer island statuses are omitted from the table.
See Table 23 for definition of pay scales.

in the district administration. These statuses and their respective assignments (Table 22) exhibit a marked emphasis on specialized skill. New professions and professionals are found particularly in health and education, but also increasingly in the economic and legal spheres. Politics always has been a Yapese profession; however, new forms have come into being in the administration and in other areas previously discussed. At a lower level, a variety of new statuses occur in the areas of clerical and administrative functions and technical and supervisory skills. These are often very specialized, such as broadcast station manager, chief of police, pharmacist or X-ray technician, and require special education and skills. Finally, the crafts and trades (carpenter, mason, electrician, mechanic, welder) provide opportunities for the assumption of leadership positions, as men who are especially skilled and capable achieve supervisory positions. The authority assignments of each of these statuses falls in the area of special skill and the application of that skill, and outside the traditional culture.

Education is the crucial factor in the achieving of these new statuses, and the more education acquired the higher one rises in rank. Tables 22 and 23 show the relative valuation of skills as designated in the Micronesian pay scale of the Trust Territory. Education and experience are the primary differentials in the scaling of statuses and pay ranks. College graduates are rewarded with the highest pay and professional status. To achieve the same level without a college degree one must have a similar amount of educational experience on the job or related to the job and then assume a position of administrative responsibility. Minimal education for clerical-helper positions is set at ninth grade, and for the higher positions a high school diploma is desired. In the trades and crafts a minimum of four years apprenticeship is required before one may become a journeyman. A further input of American values is seen in the pay distinctions between the trades and crafts and the clerical, technical, and administrative positions. Regular clerks and technicians receive an almost equivalent wage rating with the highest-skilled tradesmen, and supervisory positions in administrative desk jobs receive much higher wages than do trade foremen.

Not all of these new statuses have direct political significance. Technical skills, for example, do not have authority assignments outside the practice of that skill. They do, however, often provide indirect support for political objectives. A medical doctor is elected senator on a campaign promise to provide a hospital in the outer islands. A head nurse in the hospital is elected legislator-at-large, with the hospital providing an area of personal contact with people from all over Yap. A carpenter foreman is elected president of the legislature. A job in the administration based on some particular skill may provide indirect

Table 23. Definition of Administrative Pay Scale Ranking
(7/2/67)

Schedule	Minimum Annual Beginning Pay Scale
1. A-*Schedule—Craft and Trade Skills*	
a. A:1–4 Unskilled labor	$ 686—$ 956
b. A:5 Trades helper	$1060
c. A:6–9 Intermediate apprentice	$1164—$1476
d. A:10–14 Journeyman	$1580—$2121
2. B-*Schedule—Clerical, Technical, and Administrative Skills*	
a. B:2–3 Helper	$ 686—$ 894
b. B:4–6 Assistant	$1040—$1310
c. B:7–9 Clerk, technician	$1456—$1768
d. B:10–12 Highly skilled technician or supervisor	$1955—$2329
3. C-*Schedule—Professional Skills*	
a. C:1 College graduates; especially trained admin. leaders	$2800
b. C:2 Master's degree, or advanced professional education	$3240
c. C:3–5 Advanced professional degree or demonstrated capability for executive responsibilities	$3740—$5300

SOURCE:
Compiled from *Micronesian Title and Pay Plan, 1967, Yap District*

advantages for political goals, even if it is only the fact that an administration job provides opportunities for contacts with Americans and thus in the eyes of voters the jobholder is considered capable of dealing with them.

On the other hand, certain administrative statuses have direct political authority. The assistant to the district administrator is very influential in policy-making and administration by virtue of his role as advisor and interpreter to the district administrator. He acts as a channel of communication between the district administrator and the people, interpreting both the interests of the people and the interests of the district administrator in the process. Another important status is that of political affairs officer. He is the supervisor of elections and administrative liaison officer to the legislature and Council of Magistrates. One of his most important duties is the dissemination of information on political affairs in both Yap and the outer islands. Other influential political positions include the community development officer, education administrators, and police and court officials. The community development officer has considerable political influence through advising and assisting other leaders in the various community development projects. Educators build a broad base of influence in their Yap-wide work with young people and teachers. The police and courts assure the enforcement of law and the effectiveness of the legislature and council as law-making and administrative organizations.

Legitimacy of these positions is defined by the administration through its assessment of what it requires and values as important in them. Support of these new statuses is given through payment for services and sanctioning of administrative policy and action by the chief executive or district administrator. The people accept and support these decisions and actions upon the weight of authority that obtains when something is done in the name of "Am," the colloquialism for administration.

In summary, all of the new statuses at the district level and many at the Yap Islands level have neither equivalent nor precedent in the traditional culture of Yap. Land is an irrelevant question when talking about the statuses of senator, assistant to the district administrator, senior medical officer, or carpenter foreman. These positions require foreign-derived skills that are intended to meet new economic, social, and political wants in a changing culture, and future leadership capabilities will be defined in terms of these new skills. Thus we conclude with two coexisting spheres of political ideology—those derived from the values and structures of traditional Yap and those introduced by a superordinate American administration. While certain areas of structural similarity have been observed, it is a foregone conclusion that these two spheres will in some way conflict. The significant question is how the Yapese attempt to resolve these conflicts through choice and decision-making in the situation of change.

II. LEADERSHIP
AND
DECISION-MAKING

The study of change is not simply a matter of documenting substitutions of new elements for old; it is rather a study of process, involving choice and decision, conflict and resolution, and phase development of new political patterns. Political change on Yap is a very complicated phenomenon intermingling the demands of the American government, the new desires of the Yapese, the constraints of tradition, and individual strategies and choices as each leader and each constituent wends his way through the maze of politics to achieve his own personal goals and his particular interpretation of group goals.

The study of traditional leadership and current changes in Yap is essentially a study of political activity. Following Swartz, Turner, and Tuden (1966:7–8), political activity is everything that is "public," "goal-oriented," and involves a "differential of power among individuals of the group in question." Political activity occurs in the context of a political "field," rather than in a synchronic structure, that is filled with tension, and characterized by strategic maneuvering between individual and corporate competitors. These antagonists seek both the public good and their own private interests, and may in the pursuit of these goals alternately support or challenge one another.

Political activity within the field is premised upon demands. The objectives of such activity are to satisfy these demands and to fulfill group and individual goals. The inevitable variance in interpretations of both private and public good create conflicting expectations and a state of perpetual, but often suppressed, tension among the adversaries within the field. When situational demands force public action, these tensions emerge in the ensuing political *event* as conflict- and goal-directed strategies.

Political events occur at focal centers or *arenas* existing within the field in which the principles interact. Each arena has its own normative structure defining the parameters of action and standards of legitimacy. The conditions influencing any action in any arena, however, come from the broader scope of the field. The outer boundaries of the field are marked by the extreme limits from which demands originate or from which support is mobilized to make or implement political decisions. These boundaries vary with situation and time.

The concept of "field" does not preclude structure, but rather identifies it as the normative framework of dynamic phenomena. The following conceptual categories have been utilized throughout this work for analysis of structure as it occurs in the various arenas of the political field.

> *Political community*—the largest decision-making group in which differences are settled by peaceful action based upon shared standards and structures (Easton 1959:229).
>
> *Regime*—the "constitutional order" including the definition of statuses and their structural arrangements, the assignments of authority to statuses, and standards of legality (Easton 1959:228).
>
> *Leadership status*—defined as a position whose role is making political decisions, but which may or may not be part of regime.

Concomitant with these structural concepts are several categories utilized for the analysis of activity in the political field. These include

> *Officials*—occupants of political statuses, or leaders;
>
> *Government*—the organization developed by the officials to make and execute decisions and to conduct the general administration of affairs (Easton 1959:228);
>
> *Decisions*—pronouncements with regard to goals, allocations, and settlements.

These concepts have supplied the basic framework or model for our look at both the traditional and contemporary processes of Yapese politics.

To explain political change on Yap, one must explain the nature of interaction between inputs from the traditional and modern spheres of politics into the field of tension and process. Interaction between these spheres is examined in the areas of structure, leadership, and decision-making.

Change in the structure of the political field, for example, of the sort brought about by American-style administration, councils, legislatures, and democratic processes as documented in the previous chapter, is imposed upon a traditional base of politics, and cannot be effectively analyzed apart from that base. The traditional base is most prominent at the local level, yet determines the occupants of many of the statuses in the new structure, and furnishes restraints on procedures for reaching and implementing decisions. Key concepts for insight into the dynamics of these changes include alternate assignments of authority and the traditional and new mechanisms for achieving legitimacy and support in all activities in the political field.

When changes occur in the structure of a field, changes may also occur in the methods of recruitment and the criteria for selection of leaders. Force (1960) documents such changes in Palau, and the same may be expected in Yap, for Yap is experiencing similar pressures for change. Certain questions follow: How important are new interests, or demands, to the emergence of a new elite? What effect do the new structural positions introduced by the alien power have upon the selection of the elite? To what extent and in what manner have the methods of recruitment and the selection of leaders changed (from traditional ways) and what implications does this have for the creation of a new elite? To what extent is there leadership mobility, if any, from lower positions to higher, both in the traditional and the emergent leadership situations?

Finally, the decision-making process, including the standard procedures for reaching and implementing decisions as defined in regime, and the nature of choice in that process, is fundamental to the study of change. Choice is made on the basis of anticipated gains to be achieved within a socially prescribed framework of acceptable behavior. To predict the direction of choice, it is necessary to specify the nature of constraints and incentives. Through such specification, we can determine the range of possible choices and predict patterns of behavior. Following the ideas of Barth (1966, 1967), it is useful to examine constraints and incentives in terms of statuses, rules, transactions, and values.

Complex patterns of behavior, or roles, are generated both from statuses and from a set of situationally determined rules (Goffman's requirements of "impression management" [1959]). In an analysis of the Yapese political field, political choice or decision-making is restricted by the limitations of status and by the recognized procedures and impression behavior appropriate for an occupant of that status. These two factors, however, are only part of the choice or decision-making situation. Most interpersonal relations are transactional in nature, involving a reciprocal flow and counterflow of prestations. It is this transactional nature of behavior that provides the dynamic of the model.

Transactions necessarily involve values. People value certain ends and are thus motivated and/or restrained to behavior that will hopefully accomplish those ends. The evaluations of a group do not remain static, but are continually revised both in terms of comparative rates of payoffs and in terms of consistency and integration. The rates are subject, in economic terms, to the cost-demand price mechanisms of the market and to the ecological and strategic restraints (values, statuses, rules of behavior) in the system. Consistent evaluations, which are based on the previous experience of members of the community, generate institutionalized patterns of choice and behavior.

The potential of predicting change in the political field lies in the analysis of the decision-making processes. By applying these concepts to Yapese data we hope to see if the "events" of change fill the requirements of the transactional strategies of the model, and if from these strategies and from the specification of ecological and strategic restraints of the society we can predict the institutionalization of patterns of change.

The New Political Elite

In the competition for status, change in the methods of recruitment and selection of leaders becomes of primary importance. New methods of recruitment should precipitate both leadership mobility and the formation of new elites. Some questions considered here are: 1) How do contemporary Yapese recruit and select their leaders? 2) Do these methods lead to the formation of a new political elite? 3) Do they create avenues for individual mobility in the political hierarchy?

Selection of leaders for new status positions is accomplished primarily by election, application of objective requirements such as a test, or by appointment. The first two techniques are foreign to the traditional ideology of Yap politics. Leadership selection was limited by rights to land and kinship relationships, subject to the consensus decisions of a council. Appointment to leadership positions could be made by the council in a case of land left without heirs, but not otherwise. Testing was unknown.

Since the majority of new leadership statuses are filled by the elective process, it provides the most fruitful area for analysis. The naval administration set up the first elections to decide the chiefs who would represent each municipality. The traditional chiefs of the leading villages were nominated by a council of chiefs and duly elected by the people, setting a precedent for municipal leadership. In 1952 the civil administration established election procedures in which each municipality submitted four candidates for magistrate. Ten names on a petition were adequate to establish candidacy. Voting was by secret ballot marked in a private booth, and ballots were placed in a locked box. Each voter, previously ascertained to be mentally capable and over eighteen years old, was called forward by name from a registry to cast his ballot. Campaigning was not done publicly, instead the results of the election generally were decided in a council of municipal chiefs before election day and word passed around to the people as to how they should vote.

Election procedures were not formalized until 1968. Voters now are required to have resided in Yap for one year and to be eighteen years of age or older. Candidacy, instead of being established by the magistrates and village chiefs as in the past, is obtained by submitting a petition with the required number of signatures to the election commissioner. Ballots are secret, submitted after being approved by the local registrar of voters. Votes are counted by an established board of elections and the district administrator declares the official results.

A careful examination of the results of past elections in Yap yields very important insights into the process of leadership selection and the emergence of a new elite. Tables 24 and 25 illustrate very clearly the Yapese distinction between the positions of magistrate and legislator, and the importance of traditional title for the magistrate status. In all recorded elections since 1952, a majority of the magistrates have been selected from the traditional hereditary elite of the highest-ranking villages in the municipalities. Only six individuals of the twenty-eight elected over a period of sixteen years and nine elections have been without title. Only one of these six was from a commoner-ranking village and only one was from a second-ranking village in the municipality. The other four were qualified members of the leading villages selected in place of less-qualified titled members or in the absence of qualified members. The two lower-ranking magistrates were elected in the absence of a capable titled individual.

In marked contrast, the legislature shows a minority representation of titled or even nontitled representatives from the highest-ranking villages in the municipalities. Out of thirty-five representatives elected over nine years in five recorded elections, only four have been titled chiefs in the highest-ranking villages in their municipalities, and only eleven of the remaining representatives were from the highest-ranking villages. An additional three should be added to this figure if Rumung, whose leading villages are of the second rank, is included. All four titled individuals and nine of the fourteen nontitled were elected in the first election of 1959. Six of these thirteen were replaced in subsequent

Table 24. Election Patterns for Selection of Magistrates

Municipality	1952	1953	1955	1956	1959	1962	1965	1967	1968
Rumung	TN	TN	TN	TN	tc	TN^a	tc	tc	TN^b
Map	TC	TC	TN	TN	TN	TN	TN	TN	TC^a
Gagil	TC	TC	TC	TC	TC	TC	TC	C	TC
Tamil	C	C	C	C	C	C	C	C	C
Weloy	TC	TC	TC	TC^a	TC^a	TC^a	TC^a	TC^a	TC^a
Fanif	TC	C	TC^a	TC^a	TC^a	TC^a	TC^a	TC^a	TC^a
Rull	TC	TC	TC	TC	TC	TC^a	TC^a	TC^b	TC^b
Delipebinaw	TC	TC	TC	TC	TC	TC	TC^a	TC^b	C
Kanfay	TC	TC^a	TC^a	TC	N	N	N	N	N
Gilman	TC	TC^a	TC^a	TC^a	TC	TC	TC^b	TC^b	TC^b

Total number magistrates each class: TC = 18; TN = 4; tc = 1; C = 4; N = 1; c = 0; s = 0.
Total number individuals elected magistrate = 28

NOTES:
· TC = titled individual from chief-ranking village (*ulun, bulceʻ*)
  TN = titled individual from noble-ranking village (*methaban, tethaban*)
  tc = titled commoner, *daworcig*-ranking village.
  C = untitled individual from chief-ranking village
  N = untitled individual from noble-ranking village
  c = untitled individual from commoner-ranking village
  s = individual from a servant-class village (*milngay ni arow*)
  Repetition of the same symbol for a municipality indicates the same individual was reelected.
  ^{a} indicates a second individual of the same rank as the first
  ^{b} indicates a third individual of the same rank as the first

elections by lower-ranking, but better qualified individuals. In the election for the District Legislature in 1968, only four of the twelve representatives elected were from the leading villages, four were from commoner villages, three from second-ranking villages, and one from a servant-class village.

These figures indicate the formation of a new political elite on Yap. One very obvious contributing factor in this process is the presence of new political statuses or new structures, that is, the Council of Magistrates and the legislature. A new structure by itself, however, is not sufficient grounds for establishing a new elite, as evidenced by the council. It has been argued previously that the formal structure of the council parallels very closely the traditional structures in the political field. It is not illogical then that the Yapese, in a logical extension of the traditional framework and leadership, should select traditional, titled leaders to fill these new statuses. However, when the form and function

Table 25. Election Patterns for Selection of Legislators and Congressmen

	Elections for Legislature					
Term Length	1959 4 yr.	1959 2 yr.	1961 4 yr.	1965 4 yr.	1967 4 yr.	1968 (Dist. Leg.) 2 yr.
Municipality						
Rumung	N	TN	N^a	N	N^b	N^a
Map	tc	N	N	N	tc	tc
Gagil	C	C^a	N	N^a	N	N^b
Tamil	TC	C	C	C	TC	N
Weloy	c	N	c^a	c^a	c^b	C
Fanif	N	c	c	N	c	N
Rull	C	c	c	C^a	C	C
Delipebinaw	C	C^a	c	c	C^a	c
Kanfay	C	C^a	C^a	C	C^b	s
Gilman	TC	TC^a	c	c	c^a	c
At-Large A.						TC
B.						c

	Elections for Congress of Micronesia		
	1964	1966	1968
Senate A.	tc	—	C
B.	c	N	—
House A.	c	c	c^a

Total number legislators and Congressmen each class: TC = 3; TN = 1; tc = 2; C = 12; N = 11; c = 11; s = 1
Total number individuals elected = 41

NOTES:
TC = titled individual from chief-ranking village (*ulun, bulceʻ*)
TN = titled individual from noble-ranking village (*methaban, tethaban*)
tc = titled individual from commoner-ranking village (*daworcig*)
C = untitled individual from chief-ranking village
N = untitled individual from noble-ranking village
c = untitled individual from commoner-ranking village
s = individual from a servant-class village (*milngay ni arow*)

Repetition of the same symbol for a municipality indicates the same individual was reelected.
^{a} indicates a second individual of the same rank as the first
^{b} indicates a third individual of the same rank as the first

of the new structure, for example, the legislature, is sufficiently different to require new skills and new forms of leadership, a new elite is established without regard to traditional structures. Consideration of criteria for selecting leaders illustrates this more clearly.

The objective criteria for selecting leaders show several marked distinctions and priorities between the old leaders and the new. Education is the first requirement of legislators and congressmen, and considerable experience with the American administration and the new ways is second. Extensive education may be substituted for experience, but the reverse is not generally true. The old leaders, or magistrates, however, are exempt in total from the education requirement. Instead it is desired that they have a traditional base of authority, supplemented by age and experience. The rationale for these distinctions is the separate leadership requirements of the statuses. It was recognized very early in the history of the legislature that legislative skills were new, American-derived, and required special knowledge and capabilities. Traditional leaders, recognizing their own deficiencies, selected younger, educated men to fill these positions. In contrast, the magistrate's position is viewed as one of local authority, with primarily executive responsibilities. The primary local groups are villages, with traditional leaders. To mobilize such traditional leaders for municipal projects, a magistrate with traditional authority, knowledge, and prestige is considered most effective. Selection of leaders on these principles is clearly illustrated in Table 26.

The cultural decision, then, as to the formation of a new elite, very much depends upon the requirements of the situation of change. Should the new institutions be adaptable to traditional patterns of leadership, as was the case with the Council of Magistrates, adaptations are made readily. However, should the new institution require new knowledge and skills, the cultural definitions of leadership will expand to meet the new requirements and to provide the necessary leadership. Class barriers for the legislative leadership have been dropped, because of both the scarcity of qualified leaders and the indirect nature of legislative leadership. The legislator does not play an administrative role in municipal affairs, but rather a representative, informative, and advisory one. These duties were recognized as those belonging to second-ranking leaders in the traditional sphere and thus did not conflict with Yapese values in the selection process described earlier. The decision-making power of the legislature, however, was underestimated and has proved a deciding factor in elevating the prestige of legislators to an equal or in some cases greater level than that of the magistrate.

The impression criteria for able leadership are nearly identical for magistrates, legislators, and traditional village chiefs. Informants were

Table 26. Comparison of Experience and Skills, Legislators, Congressmen, Magistrates, 1968

Legislators

Municipality	American Education	Work Experience	Special Skills
Gilman	College grad.	10+ years	Agricultural admin.
Kanfay	Professional	15+ years	Laboratory tech.
Delipebinaw	Professional	10+ years	Law
Rull	—	15+ years	Labor
Weloy	College	2 years	Administration
Fanif	Professional	10+ years	Business admin.
Tamil	High school	10+ years	Legal clerk
Gagil	College grad.	3 years	High school teacher
Map	Professional	15+ years	Business admin.
Rumung	Professional	10+ years	X-ray tech.

Congressmen

Leg.-at-large A	Jap. School	20+ years	Carpenter
Leg.-at-large B	Professional	5 years	Medical tech.
Representative	College grad.	10+ years	Education admin.
Senator A	College grad.	6 years	High school teacher
Senator B	Professional	10+ years	Medical doctor

Magistrates

Municipality	Education	Work Experience	Special Skills	Traditional Title
Gilman	Jap. School	Traditional	Traditional	Chief
Kanfay	Jap. School	Traditional	Traditional	none
Delipebinaw	Jap. School	20+ years	Bus. Adm.	none
Rull	Jap. School	20+ years	Elem. Tchr.	Chief
Weloy	Jap. School	20+ years	Carpenter	Chief
Fanif	Jap. School	20+ years	Carpenter	Chief
Tamil	Jap. School	20+ years	Business	none
Gagil	Jap. School	20+ years	Judge	Chief
Map	Jap. School	Traditional	Traditional	Chief
Rumung	Am. 9th grd.	5+ years	Policeman	Chief's son

asked to rank in order of their preference the members of the Council of Magistrates and the District Legislature. Each informant was then asked why individuals were placed in their respective order. The characteristics below summarize their likes and dislikes of personal qualities in Yapese leaders:

Qualities admired	*Qualities deplored*
knowledgeable	ignorant of custom
articulate	inarticulate
aggressive	domineering
intelligent	precocious
open-minded	stubborn
modest	pretentious
decisive/forceful	indecisive/timid
shrewd	sneaky
credible	untrustworthy
responsive to people	self-interested
generous	grasping
impressive in appearance	common in appearance

Based on the rankings made by the informants, a legislator may be more domineering and precocious than a traditional leader because of his special skills in dealing with Americans, and because of his indirect responsibilities to his people. The magistrate acts more frequently as a leader and administrator, and therefore is more exposed to public view and disapproval. In both cases, however, personal traits are evaluated on the basis of traditional values, rather than on new introduced values. Critical deficiencies may be overlooked should other considerations, such as effectiveness or special skills, be more important and alternative choices in leadership not available.

One of the obvious consequences of the development of new leadership statuses and a new elite has been political and social mobility. The extent of this mobility may be measured in two areas: the composition of the new elite, and the methods of selection. Table 24 shows that executive leadership in the Council of Magistrates is still the primary province of titled chiefs or the highest-ranking villages in a municipality. Legislative and decision-making leadership, however, have been broadly extended to members from all ranks of the high caste and in one case to a member of the servant class. However, the lowest serfs, irrespective of skills, have not been able to achieve even consideration for leadership positions. One member of a traditional serf village, college educated and one of the brightest Yapese students ever encountered by his American teachers, submitted a petition to run for senator to the Congress of Micronesia. He was forced by another candidate and a caucus of high chiefs to withdraw his petition, with some not too subtle threats of physical harm. The same individual was ineffective as a high school teacher, unable to maintain classroom discipline, and finally left Yap for a less negative atmosphere elsewhere in Micronesia.

Leadership in the administration's appointive positions show the same pattern of selection (Table 27). While American administrators know nothing about the class rank of a particular person, their Yapese subordinates do know and are able to influence appointments so that higher-ranking individuals receive the training opportunities and consequently the appointments to leadership positions. Again, within the high caste, job and leadership mobility is as frequent for members of commoner villages as for the chief villages, but members of servant and serf villages tend to be held in the lower-status positions. In areas of direct-leadership importance, such as the police force, or department heads, members of servant and serf villages tend to be excluded. The hospital administrator and a few skilled laborers in public works provide the only exceptions (Table 28). The composition of the elite, then, shows a marked mobility of low-ranking members of the high caste into new leadership positions. The only exception to this rule are those new positions, such as magistrate and secretary, which are defined traditionally. Low-caste villagers, however, are excluded from this new mobility, particularly in areas of political or administrative leadership.

The methods of selection of leaders provide further insight into the process of the new mobility. Political campaigning on Yap is a rather new phenomenon; it was introduced in 1968 at the time of the Yap-wide elections for representatives to the Congress of Micronesia.

Table 27. Distribution of Jobs in Administration, 1968

Division	No. of Jobs	No. of High Caste	No. of Servant	No. of Serf	No. of Other
1. Administration	33	21	2	3	7
2. Public Health	62	47	4	6	5
3. Education	74	59	3	2	10
4. Public Affairs	6	5	—	1	—
5. Resources and Development	30	18	3	3	6
6. Protection to Persons and Property	21	20	1	—	—
7. Operations and Maintenance	123	64	13	17	29

Table 28. Distribution of Low-Caste Yapese in the Administrative Wage Scale

Wage Scale	Average Yearly Wage	Total Yapese Employees	No. Low Caste	Ratio
Professional				
C–1—5	$3000+	8	1	1/8
Clerical				
B–9—12	2000+	8	0	0/8
B–6—8	1500+	40	1	1/40
B–2—5	1000+	121	18	1/6.7
Labor				
A–12—13	2000+	4	1	1/4
A–8—11	1500+	49	11	1/4.5
A–3—7	1000+	68	24	1/2.8
A–1—2	850+	7	2	1/3.5

Previous to these elections, all candidates were nominated and elected locally and the process was controlled by the municipal council of chiefs. One magistrate said that his father, the previous magistrate, decided to step down and nominated him, his son, for the job. The council accepted the designation of the successor without question and spread the word on how the people should vote. In the 1968 election, this magistrate ran without opposition. The reason, he said, was obvious. No one else could perform as well. They would be weak, lacking the authority and prestige of his village and his title as chief of that village. At the same time he is urging his own son to get a college degree, knowing that future leadership will be dependent upon more than the traditional prestige.

The municipal council is the primary means of providing candidate support. The municipalities of Rull and Gilman always select the candidates and victors before the election. In Rull, for example, all of the elected leaders are related through the same family genealogy in Balabat, which holds the paramount chief titles from Balabat and Ru'way. Tamil, Weloy, and Kanfay also have powerful councils of leaders who designate candidates and winners. In other municipalities, however, youth-oriented power groups are forming new coalitions to shape municipal policy. Councils of young men in both Map and Rumung have seized power from the old men and are making policy for their municipalities. The group in Rumung went so far as to elect a young man as magistrate in order to maintain strict control over new economic interests and policies for the municipality. The councils of youth in Map organized around a legislator in a conflict over use of funds. They supported their own candidate for magistrate and won the election. Fanif has developed a council of young men, educated and leaders in the new sense of the word, who have been given the responsibility of leadership by the old men in such matters as elections. The old men feel the young are more capable of handling such decisions in the new situation. In the two other municipalities, Kanif and Gagil, factions have developed around leaders in a conflict between the young men and the old council of chiefs.

These new demands and situations of conflict ultimately result in a change in the elite. New leaders arise on both municipal and Yap-wide levels. The conflict between the old chiefs and the young men is not without precedent in Yapese culture. The paramount chief in Rull stated clearly that the young men can depose the chiefs if they are unworthy. The young men and the chiefs are *bagayow*, both required for power. This is adequate reason for youth factions to select an older man for their candidate for magistrate. Rumung is the outstanding exception.

A number of traditional methods are employed in a modern election, particularly in the at-large seats for which all of Yap votes. The council concept has been extended to the Yap-wide elections. One candidate reported that he was asked in 1964 by the president of the Council of Magistrates to run for the House of Representatives seat in Yap, but at the same time he was told that another candidate would win the election. He ran and lost as the council earlier had decided. In 1968 the council again asked him to run, and said that this time he would run unopposed. He did and was elected.

Another technique is the passing of shell money *dakaen e tha‘* along the traditional lines of communication through the titled estates. With the shell money comes a request for support that must be honored. To return the money would break a traditional relationship, so it is rarely refused. The support, however, does not have to be total, but can be partial. Thus the chiefs meet together before the election to decide how to parcel out votes to each candidate for whom they have received shell money. The traditional centers of politics in Rull, Tamil, and Gagil all exchanged shell money for the 1968 election of two at-large legislators and a senator to the Congress of Micronesia. Word was then disseminated to their subordinate villages and traditional allies to vote for such and such a candidate as had been decided by the council. One candidate from Gagil was asked to withdraw from the election after a Rull candidate sent shell money and gave a beer party for a chief in Gagil. The Gagil candidate excused himself, saying that it was too late to withdraw.

The low-class candidate has a decided disadvantage in running for office because he lacks access to the traditional channels. If he is going to be successful, he ideally should gain the support of the high chiefs, and this places definite limitations on mobility. The low-caste aspirant's chances of gaining support from a high chief are very slim, as evidenced in the example previously cited. The only candidate from a servant village to run and consequently win an election was selected by the council of old chiefs from his municipality and placed on the ballot by them. He was selected because of his skills in English and lengthy experience in public service through work in the hospital. He works with the council to decide on matters of the municipality to be brought before the legislature.

Even low-ranking high-caste individuals are at a disadvantage in Yap-wide elections, unless they work through the chiefs. One candidate from a commoner village in Weloy very likely lost the 1968 election for senator for this reason. Another candidate from a commoner village in Tamil worked as closely as possible with the chiefs to win the election. More than one candidate requested the services of a fortune teller to assist in planning a campaign.

"New" techniques also are used to gain political position. In the 1968 election, one senatorial candidate gave ten dollars to an influential chief for the purpose of purchasing drinks for an outer island chief and wooing his votes. Another senatorial candidate was aided by a friend who collected petitions from several outer islands in support of his candidacy. Campaign promises are part of the action, also. In the same election, a third senatorial candidate promised a hospital to the outer islands. A legislature candidate from Map, to gain support, promised a change in the planned routing of a road. Publicity was also important, including radio interviews and even campaign signs. One candidate from Delipebinaw used his private bar to entertain leaders who controlled votes. Another, from Rull, sat on a hill in the center of town, waving, getting public exposure. He also treated people to drinks in the local club in the evening. After the election he made no further appearance at either place.

Gaining support is very important to the rising new elite. Because of the importance of the traditional techniques and the traditional loyalties, a low-ranking person must use every means possible to win the necessary support. One of the most common ways is through the traditional leaders, who thus maintain some degree of control over mobility. The movements of organized groups of young men, however, are becoming increasingly more important in the selection of leaders.

One such group was formed during the summer of 1970 to support the candidacies of a senator and representative to the Congress of Micronesia. These two men were from Gagil and Kanfay municipalities, and hoped by combining their support in northern and southern Yap, respectively, to swing the election in their favor. This coalition was formed to overcome the near bloc-voting pattern for local candidates that occurs in each of these areas. Should these two men continue the coalition and support candidates for other positions, the coalition will become Yap's first political party. Both men were reelected, showing the obvious advantages of combining support.

The intense competition for seats in the Congress of Micronesia and for the at-large seats in the Yap District Legislature is obvious from the voting patterns (Table 29) in these elections. Voting choice is still based as much on traditional loyalties as on the merits of the candidate, but there are enough exceptions to create surprises. To overcome such patterns, a candidate must use every means at his disposal.

In elections for senator from Yap District, the Carolinians have consistently swung the election to the candidate of their choice. This success has drawn outer island problems increasingly to the attention of senators from Yap. Gagil has been able to maintain outer island loyalty at crucial moments on the basis of traditional ties, but even these ties provide no future security for Gagil candidates. Votes in Yap and the outer islands are increasingly difficult to control.

In summary, leadership mobility has been introduced through the formation of new political statuses and, particularly, new institutions that require new kinds of leaders with new qualifications and skills. The traditional authority group for political action, the municipal council, and the communication channels of the chiefs in the traditional *tha'*, however, still control this mobility. Low-caste individuals are excluded from the new statuses, even in the American-controlled administrative structure. Low-ranking individuals in the high caste are at a particular disadvantage if they are not able to obtain chiefly support for elective positions. New methods have been devised to outflank the limitations of traditional politics, a particularly successful method has been the organization of young men into municipal councils. These groups generally are led by members of the new elite—legislators and officials in the administration—and they form effective organizations to shape municipal policy and support leadership candidates. Individuals are faced with new power groups and thus new choices in the selection and support of leaders. It can be concluded that conflicts of interest and new demands by both the people and the elite play an important role in the selection of new leaders and thereby the acceleration of leadership mobility.

Table 29. Election Results—Congress of Micronesia and Yap Legislature, 1968

At-Large Legislature	Votes from Yap Municipalities											Totals
	RMG	MAP	GGL	TML	FNF	WLY	RUL	DPW	KNY	GLM	CLA	
Ayin GGL	54	27	176	77	6	12	16	9	8	4		369
Defngin GGL	21	17	114	81	9	13	18	4	7	9		293
Falmog TML	24	52	39	235	48	57	91	73	37	52		708
Falaw'ath RUL	5	3	7	14	18	14	190	69	40	50		410
Grongfich MAP	28	125	60	17	55	21	24	5	10	0		345
Mangefel FNF	12	36	12	36	205	60	44	31	41	30		507
Tamag WLY	17	48	34	44	74	117	67	37	35	10		483

Representative	RMG	MAP	GGL	TML	FNF	WLY	RUL	DPW	KNY	GLM	CLA	YAP
Mangefel	38	98	20	155	190	128	99	25	61	68	370	1257
Senator												
Moonfel DPW	7	10	22	4	40	23	130	71	45	68	184	604
Nuuan TML	46	55	86	143	13	27	20	2	5	5	216	618
Tamag WLY	5	37	41	13	142	78	22	2	12	1	105	458

Votes from Outer Islands

Senator	NGU	ULI	WOL	IFK	LMT	ELT	SAT	EUR	FAS	F/S	YAP	
Moonfel	5	94	195	14	4	1	111	49	1	51	604	1129
Nuuan	12	74	1	2	0	0	3	0	0	9	618	719
Tamag	3	217	68	122	85	16	14	0	116	11	458	1106

NOTE:
Abbreviations for Yap municipalities are: RMG Rumung, MAP Map, GGL Gagil, TML Tamil, FNF Fanif, WLY Weloy, RUL Rull, DPW Delipebinaw, KNY Kanfay, GLM Gilman, CLA Colonia.
Abbreviations for Outer Islands are: NGU Ngulu, ULI Ulithi, WOL Woleai, IFK Ifalik, LMT Lamotrek, ELT Elato, SAT Satawal, EUR Eauripik, FAS Fais, F/S Faraulep and Sorol.

Legitimacy, Support, and the New Elite

We have already observed the methods used to gain and maintain support for one's candidacy to a leadership status. The next logical step is to consider these concepts in the situations of leadership and conflict. How does a leader successfully gain and maintain support through time? What factors contribute to loss of support and how do changes in legitimacy and support contribute to change in elite composition?

Case Study 1

The establishment of a new youth-oriented power structure in one municipality began in 1959 with the formation of the legislature and the selection of educated, experienced young men to represent the municipality. These young men were selected by the magistrate and the municipal council of chiefs who supported them in their new legislative responsibilities. From 1959 to 1965 several young men gained legislative experience and achieved a new respect and skill for their decision-making and political activities. At the same time, the magistrate took little interest in the activities of the legislature or in soliciting funds for municipal projects. The young leaders developed their own ideas regarding policy and particularly the selection and support of leadership. They became disenchanted with the static nature of the council and the magistrate, and their seeming total lack of interest in political action.

They began to take matters into their own hands. In 1966 two of the college-educated leaders in the municipality created a Young Men's Association (YMA). Its primary functions were recreational and social, but it also provided a formal organization of youth in the municipality that crossed village and class lines and provided support and strength to young leaders in the municipality. The formation of the group was celebrated by a large party to which all of the old leaders were invited. The magistrate as usual failed to attend, living in town some distance from the municipality. The first informal political activity of the YMA occurred near the end of the year when it supported the candidacy of one of its founders in a successful campaign for senator to the Congress of Micronesia.

Shortly before a special election, called for March 1967, the young leaders met in a series of discussions regarding the lack of leadership from the magistrate of the municipality. Other municipalities were making considerable advances in the building of roads and other municipal projects, while their municipality remained in a state of stagnation. The magistrate was about seventy-five years old and rarely visited the municipality. When he did, he had no new positive programs to propose. He refused to discuss possible programs suggested by others and to support the legislators from the municipality. There was no positive activity to meet the new demands of the people, which had been stimulated particularly by the developments in the other municipalities.

The young men chose a candidate, a middle-aged man from the leading village, who was living at the time in another village nearby. He met the criteria of rank and tradition, lacking only an important title. He was educated, with a long history of working with Americans and of holding a leadership position in programs for adult education. The magistrates and the municipal council determined the election slate, so his name was not entered on the ballot. Instead the youthful men, through the YMA, mounted a write-in campaign.

Just before the election a representative of the young leaders met with members of the YMA and persuaded them that the municipality needed a new magistrate. On the eve of the election all of the young men were asked to talk to their parents and friends, urging them to write in the name of their candidate for magistrate. The timing was excellent, support was overwhelming, and the candidate was elected almost unanimously.

The new magistrate was as active as the previous one had been lackadaisical. He started several community projects, such as movies on weekends at the school, collection of money to buy a movie projector for the municipality, community gardening and other projects by the women's club. With the opening of the legislative session in May, he sought and was instrumental in obtaining funds for improvement of roads and a causeway in the municipality. He also was able to obtain assistance from the administration for the resolution of municipal problems. Community development funds were made available for the construction of a recreation field for the YMA.

At the same time seeds of discontent were beginning to grow. While the previous magistrate had been so aloof as to lose support, the new magistrate too often permitted self-interest to interfere with municipal interests. Administration of funds for the causeway construction and repair was tainted by the disappearance of a certain amount of money. The new magistrate became involved in a public dispute with a Peace Corps teacher over a proposal to use the projector fund for another purpose. After a typhoon, administration support was obtained to clear the road down to his house in village B, but the road to highest-ranking village A, and debris in other areas, were left to those villagers to clear out. More importantly, he operated very much as a one-man team. While the previous magistrate had done almost nothing, what he did do was done in the prescribed manner through the council. This magistrate was very active, but consulted chiefly with his younger supporters and did very little through the municipal council. The old magistrate was not unaware of the growing discontent and quietly added fuel to the fire.

In the meantime, new officers had been elected for the YMA and a member of village B had been elected president. Disputes over leadership followed, aggravated by certain individuals from village A who felt that no one from lower-ranking village B should tell them what to do. Bad feeling grew between the young members of these two villages, reinforced by a long history of rivalry and conflict. The new magistrate's residence in B and his support of relatives there became a matter of talk for the old magistrate and the people of A.

The crisis in leadership came when the May 1968 session of the legislature appropriated several thousand dollars for the municipal office. The municipal office had become a prestige symbol in Yap, with several municipalities boasting concrete block structures of considerable size and emptiness. The decision on where to place the office was crucial, since the location boosted not only municipal prestige, but village prestige as well. Several locations were considered: near the school; up on the hill; on a men's house site in village A; and on a men's house site in village B. All were fairly central within the municipality, with the school site and the B site having the further advantage of being on the main road.

Several municipal meetings were held to decide on the site. The old magistrate argued for two sites in A, the men's house site or the school site. The new magistrate argued for the site in B. A test of will and support ensued between the old and the new magistrates and between the people of A and B. After several meetings and vacillation between one site and another, the new magistrate brought the district administrator, the president of the legislature, and the chairman of the legislative committee on appropriations to investigate the sites and offer their opinions. With the new magistrate, they visited the sites in A and B and decided that the good road to and the spacious area around the B site made it superior to the muddy and mosquito-ridden site in A. With such strong external support, the new magistrate won a concession to his site in B. Many people, however, were dissatisfied and unhappy. He had antagonized not only the people in A, but other villagers as well who resented his pushing for a site in B. The old magistrate and the people from A complained that the building was being placed in a second-ranked village. The most important factor, however, was the refusal of the new magistrate to concede in this very important matter of prestige to those people who had supported him en masse.

The magistrate, attempting to preempt further opposition, ordered the building supplies and the immediate commencement of the initial construction. Certain of the young leaders from B supported him, saying that the money would be lost if they did not begin. At the same time, working with his usual single-handedness, he made a very important tactical error. He neglected to follow tradition and request permission to use the land from the traditional *suwon* 'overseer' and chief of the men's house site. The overseer at first followed the custom of complaining to villagers and waiting for an apology from the magistrate. The magistrate doggedly refused, however, stating that the land belonged to the village and could be used as it desired, in this case for a municipal office. The overseer then became very angry, and being rebuffed by villagers as well as the magistrate, proceeded to complain to the old magistrate. The old magistrate, who was a judge, observed the situation as an excellent chance to discredit the new magistrate and to reverse the decision of the office site. He encouraged the overseer to obtain a court order stopping construction and to sue for damages to his land. The overseer, with the aid of the judge and former magistrate, filed such a complaint, and obtained a court order to stop the work.

At this point, the magistrate realized his trouble and requested assistance from the village leaders in B. Sixty dollars and a valuable piece of shell money were collected from the people in B and sent to the overseer as an apology along with a request for forgiveness and support. At the same time, the magistrate ordered that the work continue into the concrete-pouring stage so that the site could not be changed. The overseer was not to be bought off. He took the sixty dollars and refused the shell money, returning it and thus refusing the apology. The return of shell money was a serious breach of customary behavior; it was a declaration of war to be carried on in the court, and for all practical purposes, a renunciation of his village, which was almost totally aligned against him and with the magistrate.

After delays, a summons was delivered to the laborers and magistrate to answer charges against them for trespassing and malicious destruction of property. A damage suit for $3,000 was filed against them. The case was to be judged by an associate and friend of the old magistrate, who had disqualified himself from the proceedings. The new magistrate had obtained an attorney to defend himself and the laborers. On the first day of the court proceedings, the hearing on the trespassing case was postponed, allowing further construction on the building. In the meantime, the magistrate had requested assistance from the president of the Council of Magistrates and the traditional chiefs in Tamil. The overseer was very suspicious, saying that the magistrate was an accomplished liar and very tricky. The magistrate expressed great concern that his reputation was being ruined and asked if a law suit could be filed for such damages. The intent of the plea to Tamil was to settle the case out of court through the arbitration of traditional chiefs. The chiefs in Tamil were traditional adversaries of A and supporters and overlords of B. They argued that they were the highest overseer of the site in question and complained at not being consulted in the first place, according to their traditional right to approve building plans. The president of the council and the magistrate from Tamil represented the chiefs and tried to persuade the overseer to meet the chiefs outside of court and resolve the case. The overseer refused, by now quite pleased at the prospect of collecting $3,000 in damages.

On the day of the new hearing, the charges were presented and the overseer called to the witness stand. He was first questioned by the Yapese prosecutor and stated his case. Then he was subjected to a very grueling cross-examination by the Yapese attorney for the defense. At this point, his confidence began to wane. Old men are not, in traditional situations, subjected to cross-examinations and badgerings. Later he was further shaken by the filing of a countersuit, charging him with false claims to ownership of the land and a request of $5,000 in damages by the "rightful" owners. His actual status toward the land was questionable, and although he was the rightful *mafen* 'trustee', this further shook his confidence. He later agreed to settle the case outside of court.

The overseer was quite unhappy about this decision, but the pressure of Tamil chiefs, his kinsmen, and people from village B was so great that he consented. The court proceedings were dismissed with the understanding that further work on the building would stop until a formal settlement could be made in the village, through the arbitration of the chiefs from Tamil.

On the night of the settlement, the Tamil chiefs arrived at the construction site in village B. Beer, shell money, and stone money were brought by the chiefs of B for the Tamil chiefs, but the overseer failed to appear. The chiefs from Tamil were angry at this discourtesy and immediately decided in favor of the village and the magistrate. They received gifts from B and then presented two pieces of shell money and a piece of stone money named Gamow. They said that construction of the building should resume the following day and that from here on the matter would be closed. They reemphasized that they had highest overseer rights over the land.

The magistrate won the battle but lost the war. His judgement about his reputation was correct: it had been severely damaged, and his support beyond village B was almost totally lost. A compromise would have pleased the municipality, but he chose rather to please his village of residence. The roof was placed on the building, but funds ran out until the next fiscal year. In November of 1968 he lost the election to the old magistrate. Two factions had developed in the municipality around these two leaders and between the villages of A and B.

The overseer has not returned to village B, except for a few hours, since the court case was dismissed. He is an outcast, rejected as a village leader. Traditional lines of communication between villages A and B have been shattered. In 1969 two other court cases erupted as by-products of this factionalism. In one instance two boys residing in A broke into a girl's house in B, were identified and taken to court for trespassing and assault. A plea for leniency and settlement out of court was sent on the *tha'* from A to B, but the shell money was returned, and the offenders sent to prison. A few months later a youth from B was involved in a knife fight with a man from A when both were drunk. The incident was taken to court, and the youth from B was charged with assault with a deadly weapon. Village A refused a plea from B for leniency and settlement out of court. The municipal building is still unfinished and the old magistrate would not complete it in any case. He is as inactive as before, but the factionalism seems to assure his power.

A number of important features of the case above shed light on the dynamics of legitimacy and support. First it is a situation of conflict and struggle for power and prestige between two leaders and two supporting villages. The old magistrate held traditional title and power, the new magistrate held the support of the young leaders. Success in the struggle depends upon support from the other associated villages in the municipality traditionally allied with the village of the old magistrate.

Initial support for the new magistrate was obtained in large part through his association with and selection for candidacy to the position by already successful leaders. This selection responded to the unsatisfied demands of the people in the municipality for active leadership beneficial to the community. His legitimacy as a candidate rested in his position as a landowner in the leading village of the municipality, his age, and his status as an experienced leader in the American administration.

After his election, he employed various methods to maintain support in the community. One of the first of these was economic. Working with the legislators, the magistrate was able to fund and administer a number of community projects. Jobs were distributed to members of different villages for work on these projects, and other jobs were obtained for the youth in the community. The magistrate also saw to it that economic assistance was provided for such things as a ball field or clean-up after a typhoon. He encouraged and supported social activities. This included attendance at parties and church, making and planning club projects for the women, and the institution of movie nights at the schools.

Even more critical, in this case, are the methods not used to gain support, and the means of losing support. One important means of gaining support in Yap is the sharing of power, decision-making, and responsibility through consultation with advisors and the council. Another is the recognition and use of traditional channels such as the council or the *tha'*. This was most clearly illustrated in the reaction of the Tamil chiefs to village recognition of their authority. Both of these elements are capable of providing powerful means of support, but were to some extent ignored by the new magistrate. To ignore these accepted institutions for political action is a sure way to lose support, as was observed in this case.

Support also was lost through faulty impression management and nepotism. The magistrate's mismanagement of funds, personal dominance of meetings, and pressure for support of personal decisions all contributed to an impression of sneaky, high-handed, and self-interested behavior that raised serious questions about his personal qualifications as a leader.

Loss of legitimacy and support may be tied directly to unsatisfied demands. The old magistrate failed to meet the economic and personality demands of his constituents, while the new magistrate failed to meet personality and political demands. Because both men failed to meet the expectations of their constituents, they were subsequently removed from office through the elective process. However, the leader who had undoubtedly done the most for the people was defeated for reelection in favor of the earlier inactive leader. A useful explanation for this phenomenon lies in the transactional nature of support. The activities of the old magistrate were limited and thus disappointment and dissatisfaction were limited, because the potential rewards for support were small. The size of the accomplishments of the new magistrate, however, created much greater expectations. While he was obviously unable to spread the economic rewards beyond their inherent limitations, he created the impression that he had not spread them far enough by distributing them among his family and friends. Furthermore, he did not share the political responsibilities or credits for the municipal programs, and many subordinate leaders felt cheated and disenchanted. Their personal efforts to provide almost unanimous support for his candidacy were considered wasted by a majority of those supporters. Finally, the decision to place the municipal office in B denied a certain prestige to all other villages and leaders of the municipality and created an issue around which the old magistrate could reassert himself.

In conclusion, it may be argued from these data that legitimacy may be defined in terms of objective criteria for leadership and expectations of impression management. Should the leader prove deficient in either of these aspects, support of him will be challenged. The seriousness of the challenge will depend upon the intensity of such expectations and upon other factors of support. Support may be defined as transactional relationships between individuals, in this case leaders and followers in the political field. Following Levi-Strauss (1944), there is a balance of prestations, privileges, services, and obligations between the leader and the group or individual members of the group. Levi-Strauss argues that consent is the only measure of leadership legitimacy for the Nambikuara. I would extend this argument to say that consent is based upon a satisfactory balance of transactions between leaders and followers, with both feeling they have somehow achieved a cumulative gain in the process. It is obvious from the case above that neither leader had effectively met the transactional expectations of their constituents, but the *balance* of transactions was less satisfactory under the leadership of the new magistrate than under that of the old.

Finally, both the present and traditional aspects of the political field employ the transactional model of support. A traditional chief was also subject to withdrawal of support and even deposition from his land and authority. In both spheres of the political field, legitimacy and support are primary factors in maintaining or changing the composition of the elite.

Leadership and the Decision-making Process

Demands, Strategies, Rules, and Payoffs

Two significant problems remain to be considered: the procedures for reaching decisions and the nature of choice in the decision-making process. The concepts of demands, strategies, rules, and payoffs are useful in the analysis of decision-making procedures. Decisions in the political field are basically policy responses to demands of individuals and groups. It is useful to divide demands into two categories: 1) the primary demands of the decision situation, that is, the question at hand, and 2) the secondary demands of status, legitimacy, maintenance of support, obligations of support, factors of power and authority, prestige, and other potential payoffs.

The second area of consideration is the possible strategies present in the decision situation. What are alternative solutions to the primary demands? What alternative means may accomplish the different solutions? Finally, what are the implications of these alternatives for the various secondary demands?

The third area of consideration is regime, or the rules of the game. What are the bounds of legitimate action in the decision-making situation, and how are they specified in the culture? Who may make decisions, that is, are they individuals, groups, occupants of particular statuses? What are the specifications of authority and leadership in the decision situation and what are the methods (rules of order, impression management) for supporting or rejecting alternatives as specified in the rules?

Finally, what is the decision or the payoff? How are the primary and secondary demands satisfied? Does the decision meet the criteria of legitimacy, and draw support from those affected by it? How is the decision implemented or enforced?

The study of conflict and resolution is one area in which decision-making procedures are readily observed. Case study 1 again provides insights into the political process. The precipitation of crisis occurred with the decision to build the municipal office in a particular village. The primary demands were those made by conflicting interest groups attempting to influence the decision in favor of their particular choice. Secondary demands included the potential prestige of the village winning the office and the concomitant loss of potential prestige by others, legitimacy and support of the magistrate in bringing the conflicting groups to a decision satisfactory to all the groups, and the magistrate's obligations to his supporters.

The decision question was "Where shall we put the building?" and the situation yielded four alternatives: in village A, in village B, by the school, or on the hill. When the choice of a site became a matter of personal influence between the old and new magistrates, selection of a site in either village A or B would have been a defeat for one and a victory for the other. The third choice of a site by the school would provide a semivictory for the old magistrate, since the school, although centrally located, was also in his village. The last alternative, on the hill, was considered physically inconvenient for the majority of people in the municipality and thus unacceptable.

The recognized authority for making the decision is the magistrate in consultation with the municipal council. The rules for decision-making include an initial presentation of ideas, and then strategic discussion and compromise until consensus is reached. Leaders in the high-ranking villages are most influential and most talkative. Support may be gained through compromise solutions or through influence of prestigious leaders. Legitimacy is achieved through consensus support.

The decision favored the alternative giving personal victory to the magistrate. The council made the choice under heavy pressure of the new magistrate, with certain influential leaders absent. The decision satisfied the secondary demands of the magistrate's village and certain of his own personal evaluations of payoff. Other interest groups were totally dissatisfied, requirements of legitimacy and support were unsatisfied, but the magistrate felt he would be able to implement the decision and overcome these objections. His evaluation was erroneous however, and he lost his position because of his poor judgement.

The resolution of the land-use conflict shows another set of procedures for making decisions. The conflict between the overseer and the magistrate and the subsequent steps toward resolution are shown below.

Magistrate	*Suwon 'Overseer'*
	1. Complaint of wrongdoing
2. Justification of right	3. Mobilization of support,
4. Shell money plea	court threat
	5. Refusal, filing court order
6. Refused court order	7. Filed damages suit
8. Mobilized traditional	
pressure of Tamil	9. Resisted pressure, pushing
10. Mobilized defense and	suit
countersuit	11. Resistance shaken
12. Required traditional	
settlement	13. Accepted under pressure
14. Formal traditional	
puruy held	15. Nonrecognition
16. Decision won	

The most interesting aspect of these strategic moves to settle the dispute is the continual shifting from traditional to modern procedures for decision and conflict resolution. The overseer made the initial move in hopes of a traditional apology. When the legitimacy of his complaint was challenged and then ignored, he turned to the American court for support to reverse the decision. The magistrate then turned to the traditional *wenig* 'plea' to stop the court action. This move received the same treatment originally given the overseer, rejection as illegitimate. A series of moves and countermoves followed with the magistrate pressuring to move back into traditional channels and the overseer resisting. The crucial shift occurred when the magistrate turned to an aggressive defense attorney who was able to demoralize the overseer with a completely untraditional and somewhat vicious cross-examination. The overseer then agreed to settle out of court and in effect conceded to the magistrate.

This use of nontraditional introduced procedures for making decisions is becoming increasingly more common as demands change. The Yapese quite often move from one technique to another as the situation seems to require. The following case study illustrates how a similar problem is resolved at two different points in time using different procedures, and how the decision-making process changes with the participants and with individual knowledge and skills.

Case Study 2

One of the objectives of the Trust Territory government is "to establish effective legislative, executive and judicial institutions of territorial and local government; develop Micronesian participation in policy making and planning processes of government; and broaden information and political education programs" (Norwood n.d.).

Early in the history of the civil administration planning was begun for the development of a Yap Islands Legislature. The Yapese Council of Magistrates was given the task of deciding what form of legislature they desired. They were not given the choice as to whether they should or should not have such an institution. The primary demands for the decision situation originated with the dominant American administration.

Two basic options were presented to the council: 1) to reorganize the council into a legislature, or 2) to form a new legislature, apart from the council. The first choice would deprive the council of executive power, the second of legislative power. The magistrates were faced with the problem of determining the implications of these alternatives for various secondary demands, such as their status, legitimacy, and support. The most critical issues revolved around the power of appropriating funds and the administration of appropriations.

The magistrates' decision-making procedures were derived from the traditional culture. A committee was appointed to study the alternatives. Its duties were to present the ideas, to discuss thoroughly their implications, and to report to the council. The council made the decision. A majority vote was not part of the decision process, either in committee procedures or in council. Issues were discussed and explained until everyone understood and agreed, at least publicly. Disagreement and discussion were couched in carefully worded statements, so as not to offend another member of the council. Serious disagreement resulted in stalemate, and the issue was set aside until a more opportune time. The deciding of issues often was determined by the influence of a highly respected cadre of leaders whose opinions generally were stated first.

In 1957, after two years of debate, stalemate, and delay, District Administrator Robert Halvorsen pushed the organization of a special review committee to make recommendations. In the next few months, the committee met, reviewed, but failed to proceed further.

> . . . more definitive action by the committee and council appears to have been lacking because of uncertainty of proposed code changes which might affect the status and functioning of the present, recognized and functioning organization. The main points of difficulty came in changes of local government finance and administration. (Yap District, Office of Political Affairs, Political and Social Development File 1958)

The authority to allocate funds and particularly to administer their use at the local level was a powerful instrument for maintaining support and prestige. Magistrates were exceedingly reluctant to give up these authority assignments, and the American definition of a legislative government specifically required that the powers of appropriation of funds and administration of funds be separated. The basic options presented by American administrators to the Yapese are shown in Table 30.

Table 30. Options for Organizing a Legislature (1958)

	OPTIONS	
	Reorganization to legislature	Continuation of council
Innovations required	New municipal government New executive officials New statuses for council	New legislature New legislative officials
Council retains	Old officials Legislative authority	Traditional status Old officials Executive authority
Council loses	Traditional status Executive authority	New status Legislative authority

The magistrates had to evaluate the implications for themselves of alternatives of choice originating from a dominant culture and covering an area in which they had no previous experience. Their evaluation and choice was made on the basis of their experience and the strategic restraints (values, status, etc.) of their culture. The council chose to form a new legislature and to maintain the council as an executive body, because in the system of traditional values, executive power is worth more in prestige than legislative power. The chief gives the word, the council merely supports the chief. But the choice was complicated further by the American assignment of financial allocation to the legislative branch. The magistrates were well aware of the gains in prestige and support to be acquired through allocation of funds. The option desired most, but not offered by Americans, was to retain both legislative and executive functions in the council. The councilmen stalled as long as possible, rejected totally the idea of new municipal charters, and finally opted for a new legislature, with the council retaining the more prestigious executive powers.

In 1968, the sequel to this decision followed, when the Yap Islands Legislature established a District and Municipal Government Study Commission. Ten years after the magistrates chose to retain executive power for themselves, the legislators were making the decisions regarding the formal characteristics of Yapese government. The magistrates, many of whom were in office in 1958, lament their loss of power and their present status as employees of the legislature. Were they able to reenact their decisions of 1958, the outcome might be different as new experience has taught them the considerable power of the legislative branch, for the major policy-making powers have passed to the legislature.

The formation of the 1968 commission was once more a response to outside demands, this time the result of a request from the Trust Territory administration and the Congress of Micronesia that all peoples in Yap District be represented in a district legislature. The Yapese legislators felt that they should hurry and decide what kind of government they wanted before some outside group decided it for them.

The members of the commission included the president and vice-president of the legislature, two legislators, a special assistant to the district administrator, three magistrates, a judge, and the American Peace Corps lawyer appointed by the district administrator. Special guests to the meetings included the political affairs officer from the administration, a senator from the Congress of Micronesia, and another Peace Corps lawyer who was designated secretary of the commission.

The first order of business was to decide upon the form and representation of a district legislature, the second to decide upon a form of municipal government. The procedures of the commission were adopted from *Robert's Rules of Order,* and all decisions were made on the basis of majority vote rather than consensus. The Peace Corps lawyers tended to lead the discussions and to formulate the alternatives, but refrained from voting on decisions as much as possible.

Most of the discussion regarding the legislature centered on representation from Yap and the outer islands. Problem areas concentrated on the number of representatives from Yap proper and how they should be selected—on the basis of municipality, at large, population, or combinations of these. The commission, after prolonged discussion of nine possible options, shown in Table 31, decided in favor of ten elected

Table 31. Possible Representative Alternatives for a Yap District Legislature

Alternatives

| Proposed Total Membership | Legislators from | | | Ratio Yap/Outer Islands |
	Yap Municipalities	Yap at-Large	Outer Islands	
1. 16	10	—	6	62.5/37.5
2. 20	10	2	8	60/40
3. 20	10	3	7	64/36
4. 22	10	4	8	63.6/36.4
5. 24	10	5	9	62.5/37.5
6. 21	10	3	8	62/38
7. 18	10	1	7	61/39
8. 19	10	2	7	63/37
9. 18	10	2	6	66/33

Decisions

A. #4,5,6:   Rejected because of large size and thus expense.
Upper limit of 20 agreed upon by a 6–2 vote.

B. #1:   Rejected by a 3–4 vote. Unit too small, with equal representation for large and small municipalities.

C.   Decided that Yap District Legislature have either 12 or 13 members from Yap, 2 or 3 at-large seats. 7–0 vote.

D. #8,2:   Eliminated on grounds of outer island representation being too large, or not fitting the three areas of outer islands.

E. #9:   Selected over #3 by 4–3 vote. Conflict arose between the value of 3 at-large seats in Yap, and value of 7 or 6 seats in the outer islands.

representatives from the respective municipalities of Yap, two from Yap-at-large, and six from the outer islands. The decisions revolved around problems of the legislature's size and expense; equal representation for large and small municipalities; adequate representation of the three outer island divisions and yet retaining a balance of power in Yap, which would provide the major tax support; and representation of the three largest municipalities in Yap: Gagil, Tamil, Rull, without undue influence by Gagil through its traditional ties to the outer islands.

The second order of business, municipal government, proved the most controversial. The first decision concerned the scope of municipal government, or the basic political boundaries to be established for an effective municipal system. Table 32 shows the alternatives considered,

Table 32. Alternative Boundaries for Municipal Government

Alternatives considered

    #1. Combined municipal/district government

    #2. Yap Islands municipal government and X number of outer island municipalities and governments

    #3. Ten chartered municipalities in Yap and X number of outer island municipalities

Decision

    a. #3 unanimously eliminated

Discussion

    American lawyer listed advantages and disadvantages of #1 and #2

    #1 Advantages

        1. Combined municipal/district government

        2. Smallest, simplest, cheapest

        3. Easier—one district, one government, one policy

        4. Adequate finances, fewer money problems

    #1 Disadvantages

        1. Too central, not local

        2. Requires extension of magistrate system to outer islands

        3. Local taxes, mostly from Yap, would be spread over district

    #2 Advantages

        1. Incorporates magistrates in new government

        2. Yap controls own needs

        3. Funds collected in Yap will be spent in Yap

        4. New leadership and self-government in outer islands

    #2 Disadvantages

        1. Lack of funds

        2. Expensive

        3. Increases proliferation of government

        4. Outer islands may not be ready for new leadership

Decision

    b. #2 rejected by a 3–3 vote. #1 accepted by a 4–2 vote

Table 32. (Cont.)

Discussion

  a. Alternative solutions to role of Council of Magistrates presented by lawyer

    1. Disband council

    2. Maintain council and outer island representatives in advisory capacity without pay

    3. Same as above, but with small pay or per diem

  b. Dispatch received from Trust Territory attorney general rejecting #1 as unconstitutional. Discussion: President of legislature suggested outer islands would prefer one chartered government for the whole district

  c. A magistrate noted two problems with one chartered government:

    1. two languages and cultures make cooperation difficult at times

    2. the problem of the present council of magistrates would have to be resolved

  d. President of legislature suggested that present council could become municipal legislative body, retaining a similar structure to present body.

  e. Clarifying statement was requested from lawyer-secretary to

    1. simplify governing of district

    2. provide Yap control over her internal problems and outer islands control over their internal problems, but share overall policy in district legislature

Question

Why have district legislature and then divide into municipal governments?

Answer

Separation of powers—the way it is done in the United States

Decision

Previous decision withdrawn and #2 accepted as basic plan for municipal government by a 5–1 vote

---

the areas of discussion, and the decisions reached. The secondary demands, the advantages and disadvantages of each alternative, were defined by the American lawyers and accepted as legitimate by legislators and other nontraditional leaders on the commission. The lawyers highlighted the problems of finances and available funds, ease of administration, and the precedent of the district format for the legislature. These arguments precipitated the initial decision for a unified district municipal government. No one thought to raise the obvious traditional considerations, such as different languages, cultures, and spheres of interest and authority, until the Trust Territory attorney general notified the commission that a unified district municipal government was unconstitutional. Then the dissenting minority raised its voice and called the "question" for reconsideration. The commission with little other choice reversed its position deciding for separate Yap and outer island municipal governments.

The next major question concerned alternative organizational forms for a Yap municipal government. The lawyers introduced a number of possible forms and asked members of the commission to select the two they liked most. By this method they narrowed the question to three alternatives shown in Table 33.

Table 33. Alternative Organization Forms for Yap Municipal Government

Alternatives considered
  #1. a. New legislative body formed from present Yap Council of Magistrates
       b. Executive—Yap Islands mayor elected at large
  #2. a. New legislative body called Yap Islands Assembly, council disbanded
       b. Executive—Yap Islands mayor elected at large
  #3. a. New legislative body called Yap Islands Assembly
       b. Executive—Yap Islands mayor elected at large
       c. Yap Council of Magistrates—advisors to mayor and assembly

Discussion
  1. Senator suggests that council could be legislative body and then work for the mayor in the municipalities
  2. Legislator suggests a possible conflict of interest between assemblymen who both make and enforce laws
  3. Magistrate suggests that the mayor may not be supported by people from municipalities other than his

Decision
  A. motion to accept #2 failed in 4–2–2 vote
  B. popularity poll of three choices taken .... #1—0 votes
                                                        #2—4 votes
                                                        #3—1 vote
                                                        —3 abstentions
  C. #1 eliminated 5–1–2 vote
  D. Popularity poll of two choices .... #2—5 votes
                                                        #3—0 votes
                                                        —3 abstentions
  E. #2 accepted 6–1–1 vote

The secondary demands or issues in this case centered on the Council of Magistrates. No member of the commission felt that the council was capable of reorganization into a municipal legislative body or that it was appropriate to attempt it. Nor did they find it necessary to retain the council as an advisory body. At the same time, they did not find satisfactory solutions to the problems of legislation and administration in the options considered. Problems of new statuses, authority assignments, support, and reward were ambiguous and undefined, and no one could offer further elaboration on the implications. The members voted, as shown in Table 33, but could not reach a consensus decision.

Commission members were dissatisfied and undecided, but the voting method of parliamentary procedure forced them to approve something. The discussions revealed much more of the thinking of the members than the votes. They discussed the variation of population in municipalities and dismissed it as unimportant. They argued that each municipality had had one vote in previous forms of government and the same should hold for the new. Relying even more on the past, one member defined the "new assembly" in terms very much like the council. Since the assemblymen would be busy with their municipal duties, each should have a secretary (as do magistrates) to help him. If two assemblymen were elected from one municipality it would in effect create two equal-ranking chiefs and this would not fit tradition. Others countered this argument, saying secretaries were not economical. The municipal government would not have enough money to pay all of those people adequately without appropriating all of its money for salaries.

The commission decided salaries, officers, and certain other formal characteristics of the new municipal assembly in a hasty, rather disinterested fashion. They submitted their decisions and copies of the proceedings to the legislature for consideration and final adoption or rejection.

The legislature approved the commission's recommendations for a district legislature, changing the composition to 12/8, upon request from the outer islands to meet the 60/40 population ratio. The municipality question fomented the same uncertainty in the legislature as it had in the commission, with the council lobbying firmly against the commission's recommendations, and in typical Yapese fashion, was tabled, to be settled at a more convenient time, after considerable thought and some observation as to the functioning of the new district legislature. At the same time, a committee was created to study the functions of the Council of Magistrates.

The Nature of Leadership Choice and Decision-making

Arenas of Decision and Choice

Decisions have been defined as policy responses to the demands of individuals and groups. The demands of a decision situation originate from and are considered at different levels or arenas in the political field. This is an important consideration, for each distinctive arena may define different strategic considerations and methods of action for similar kinds of decisions. For example, building construction may be the focus of political action and decision at the estate, village, municipality, and Yap-wide levels. Each level has its own specified leadership statuses, methods of succession, authority assignments, rules of decision-making, and standards of legitimacy. Leadership at each level also includes specific interaction relationships with leaders at other levels. In the construction of the municipal office of Case study 1, participation was required of leaders at the Yap-wide level to appropriate the funds, and at the village level to mobilize support and supply labor. The precipitation of conflict occurred between a village chief and the magistrate. The resolution of conflict required participation of municipal leaders, Yap-wide leaders from the Council of Magistrates, traditional chiefs from another municipality, and the foreign-instituted, but Yapese-led court. The principal arena of the decision situation defines the basic framework of decision-making, but does not and cannot exclude interaction with other elements in the political field.

The Nature of Demands

We have also noted the different primary and secondary levels of demands, both of which may be derived from the separate contexts of tradition and change. The primary demands or decision questions frequently are derived from new external pressures from the dominant contact group. The stated objectives of the American administration are to bring about directed changes and development in the areas of politics, economics, health and community welfare, and education. These objectives obviously imply the development of new political and social forms, new statuses and institutions. At the same time, the Yapese people are developing new wants, personal and group wants, derived from the continual contact with outsiders. A municipal office becomes an important new prestige object and symbol. These new wants are placed in the context of other more traditional demands (such as social control, *mitmit*, men's houses, and selection of leaders) and become important in the decision-making process.

Secondary demands likewise incorporate new and old considerations of status, authority, prestige, legitimacy, and support. The definitions of other factors such as natural restraints within the cultural ecosystem and political rewards or payoffs are expanded or changed. Both of the cases considered illustrate this point. The magistrate's case was defined largely in traditional terms, emphasizing traditional village loyalties, leadership behavior, and limited land areas actually suited to the cultural demands of the project. Certain secondary demands—money, and power outside of the council—were derived from new wants. The second case of decisions regarding forms of government illustrated how leaders occupying different statuses and different positions in time view the same demands in a different light. The magistrates who first decided on the formation of a legislature in 1958 based their decisions on traditional interpretations of secondary demands. The members of the commission of 1968 included legislators, administrators, and magistrates with ten years of experience dealing with a legislature. A number of new considerations were obvious. One of these was limited finances. Others included the valuation of the power of the magistrates' position and of the power of legislators, new sources of power, new sources of prestige, and new sources of support.

Another illustration of the implications of one's status in decision-making was observed in the conflict and discussion about merging the Outer Islands High School with Yap High School. One young legislator argued strongly for the merger on grounds of finances, quality of education, supply of qualified teachers, nonduplication of facilities, and other factors fully supporting the American education officer's position. In contrast, an old chief and judge argued that each major atoll should be given a separate high school, regardless of cost, and that merger was out of the question. The differences between the two opinions stem from status, experience, and individual loyalties. The chief was representing his traditional status as "father" to the outer island groups and making his judgements on the basis of traditional ecological and cultural specifications, such as unique atoll identity, distance and cluster of atolls, and interisland socioeconomic dependencies. The legislator was representing his status with its responsibilities for leadership in development and change. He defined the situation in terms of present cultural and ecological limitations (limited finance, logistics, unnecessary duplication of physical plant and personnel) for present objectives. Both were concerned about their particular status expectations and support from their constituents. Elite responsibility and communication to constituents are very important secondary demands, but the definition of action to be taken rests very heavily on the individual's conception of his status and responsibilities.

Strategic Alternatives for Choice

The strategies of the decision situation are another important consideration in analyzing the nature of choice and decision. The alternate arenas of political action are very important in strategic considerations. A construction project at the different levels of estate, village, municipality, or Yap-wide entails different alternatives. Resources and labor are derived from different sources. Mobilization is managed by different leadership statuses and support is gained through alternate methods. At the level of the estate, kinship provides the primary obligations for gathering of resources, labor, and other support, and for supplying direction or leadership. In the village, both kinship and political reciprocity are important, while on the municipal and Yap-wide levels, the primary alternatives for support are found in institutionalized channels such as the Municipal Council, the Yap Islands Council, the District Legislature, the American administration, and the traditional leadership statuses, authority assignments, and transactional alliances.

Within each arena or level for political action are found certain alternate approaches or choices for the decision question. Organizational alternatives are found within the traditional structures. One example of this was the definition of the American-instituted position of magistrate in terms of traditional statuses and structures. The traditional definitions of arena were extended logically to the new land unit of the municipality and the magistrate status was defined in terms similar to those for a traditional chief. Another example is found in the resolution of conflict regarding the new municipal office. The concept of municipal office was derived from the change situation, but the conflict about its location was resolved through traditional channels and procedures.

New strategic alternatives are designated or derived from the change situation. The traditional chief of the men's house site chose the court and a damage suit as the means to achieve his objectives. The process of election is used to depose a traditional leader no longer acceptable. The site of a municipal office is chosen on the basis of such factors as roads and schools, rather than on the traditional requirements of village rank.

The kinds of strategic alternatives are specified by the arena of choice and by the concerns of the participants in the decision-making process. Choice occurs through the weighing of the alternatives in the light of concomitant implications for the primary and secondary demands of the decision situation.

Procedures for Decision-making

The rules or procedures in decision-making have strong implications for maintaining legitimacy and support. The examples above show that alternate rules also exist and may be applied when making decisions. The traditional rules emphasize council and consensus—a time-consuming process including the meeting or wearing down of opposition until consensus and thus legitimacy is assured. The new rules of committee organization and parliamentary procedure are time-efficient, overruling the opposition, but sacrificing legitimacy and support as they are traditionally defined. An example in Fanif was observed in which a council of young men met with the magistrate to decide on a candidate for legislator-at-large. Discussions and proposals were considered through several meetings but consensus was impossible. Too many of the potential candidates were part of the council. The magistrate unsuccessfully proposed a vote several times during the meetings. At last, unable to make a decision, the group told the magistrate that he should decide who the candidate would be and the council would support him fully. The significance of this tactic lay in the implications for support. A vote would have divided the council and weakened support. A different kind of consensus was reached, that is, the council would support whatever decision that its leader, the magistrate, made.

The application of different rules of procedure varies with the decision situation and the requirements for support. In the legislature, *Robert's Rules of Order* set the standard for decision-making. However, should an issue arise against which there is an obviously strong opposition, although not necessarily one in the majority, a careful count of votes will not be made, and the bill would be "defeated." It has been observed that when voice votes are taken and the "Nos" are rather numerous and loud, the bill fails, regardless of the actual count. Decisions in the Council of Magistrates are handled most often in the traditional manner.

Evaluation, Choice, and Payoff

The act of choice or decision and the concomitant payoffs constitute this whole gamut of variables and restrictions. Political choice by current Yapese leaders first of all is restricted by the limitations of their statuses and by the reorganized procedures and impression behavior appropriate for an occupant of a particular status. The individual leader then is beset by rigorous problems of evaluation. He must assess the primary and secondary demands of the situation, particularly with regard to his own position. He must evaluate the strategic alternatives, both traditional and modern, which are found in the specific arena, and then reach a decision within certain predetermined rules and restraints, culminating in choice and implementation and/or payoff. The accuracy of his evaluation has crucial significance for the legitimacy, support, and implementation of the decision. For example, the magistrate in Case 1, having reached a decision which he felt most rewarding to himself and his supporters, found it nearly impossible to implement and ultimately it cost him his status as a leader. The decision by the District and Municipal Government Study Commission is another case in point. Achieved through the parliamentary process of overruling the opposition, the decision on municipal government was unable to achieve sufficient support from the commission to get it through the legislature. In contrast, a decision made by the Council of Magistrates by the process of consensus ten years earlier was implemented fully and a legislature was established that became more powerful than the council that created it.

The process of evaluation and strategy in making decisions is strongly influenced by the potential payoffs sought by the participants. Many of the payoff considerations found in the two case studies discussed earlier are listed below.

Case 1. Magistrates

New magistrate: Power, prestige for self and village supporters, discredit for detractors

Old magistrate: Revenge for humiliation in election, power, prestige, discredit for detractors

Suwon (Overseer): Recognition of rights, money, public apology and justification, discredit for new magistrate

Interest groups: Recognition, sharing of power, participation in decision-making, economic and prestige benefits

Case 2. District and Municipal Government Study Commission

Lawyers and American administration: Political development, education, Yapese participation in choice, implementation of American-style representative government

Magistrates and legislators: Political continuity, personal position, power, prestige, local support, administration support

The patterning of choices through time is a product of the basic experience of leaders making choices. Evaluation of payoffs, of alternatives, and of various kinds of demands is done on the basis of previous experience. Without such experience, decision-making becomes very difficult. This is one of the reasons the magistrates delayed the change-of-government decision for over three years. Most of the magistrates had never seen a legislature, and those who had did not really understand it. The choices were made on evaluations of factors other than legislative power. In 1968, legislators had very little difficulty deciding upon a district legislature organization. They were able to build upon ten years of legislative experience. The same leaders, however, had great difficulty in deciding what form a municipal executive and legislative government should take. Continual references were made to the council, which they understood, but such ideas as the position of mayor created a great deal of uncertainty and indecision.

Experience not only patterns decision-making, but it often creates new choices. One clear example was the election of several traditional leaders to the first session of the legislature in 1959. These leaders discovered very quickly that they lacked the skills and training for such positions and recommended younger, more qualified men to fill the positions.

Barth has suggested that ". . . it will be the rates and kinds of payoffs of alternative allocations . . ." that will determine whether changes will be adopted or institutionalized (1967:668). In the political field of Yap, this is a legitimate assertion. The kinds and amount of rewards of legislative status, in terms of economic and political support, prestige, and decision-making power, have assured its institutionalization and political security for a long time to come. Conversely, declining rates of payoffs gradually deselect traditional choices. For example, the position of magistrate has suffered a marked decline in status rewards and power, to the point of open queries as to why it continues to exist. The same pattern of adoption and demise occurs elsewhere in the context of political change. The enduring leaders are those who bring economic and prestige payoffs to their local areas, while the less skillful fall by the wayside. Even the administrative court system has become institutionalized as more and more Yapese seek and achieve larger payoffs in the resolution of interpersonal conflicts. It may be concluded then that the institutionalization of new political choices for change in the Yap political field is achieved through payoffs that are comparable to or greater than those attainable through traditional alternatives.

ABBREVIATIONS
AND
SYMBOLS

Abbreviations for Describing Kin Ties

Ad adopted
Br brother
Cl classificatory relation in which precise genealogy cannot be traced
Da daughter
Fa father
Hu husband
Mo mother
Si sister
So son
Wi wife

These abbreviations may be combined to produce a precise description of any genealogical relation. For example, FaMoSiSo is father's mother's sister's son; or FaAdBr is father's adopted brother.

Symbols for genealogical charts

△ male individual
○ female individual
= marriage relationship
⊥ children of a marriage

△ ○ siblings by birth

△ ○ siblings by adoption

BIBLIOGRAPHY

Alkire, William H.
    1965   Lamotrek Atoll and inter-island socioeconomic ties. Urbana: University of Illinois Press.

Barrau, Jacques
    1961   Subsistence agriculture in Polynesia and Micronesia. Bishop Museum Bulletin 223. Honolulu.

Barth, Frederick
    1966   Models of social organization. Royal Anthropological Institute Occasional Paper No. 23. London.
    1967   On the study of social change. *American Anthropologist* 69: 661–669.

Belshaw, Cyril S.
    1954   Changing Melanesia. Melbourne: Oxford University Press.
    1964   Under the ivi tree: Analysis of economic development in Fiji. London: Routledge & Kegan Paul.

Defngin, Francis
    1958   Yapese names. *In* The use of names in Micronesia, J. E. de Young, ed. Anthropology Working Papers No. 3. Saipan, Mariana Islands.
    1966   The nature and scope of customary land rights of the Yapese community. Mimeograph for Land Management Conference. Saipan, Mariana Islands.

Easton, David
    1953   The political system: An inquiry into the state of political science. New York: Alfred A. Knopf.

1957   An approach to the analysis of political systems. *World Politics* 9:383–400.

1959   Political anthropology. *In* Biennial review of anthropology, B. Siegel, ed. Stanford: Stanford University Press.

Firth, Raymond
1951   Elements of social organization. London: Watts & Co.
1954   Social organization and social change. *Journal of the Royal Anthropological Institute* 84:1–16.
1959   Social change in Tikopia. London: Allen & Unwin.

Force, Roland
1960   Leadership and cultural change in Palau. *Fieldiana: Anthropology*, vol. 50.

Force, Roland, and Maryanne Force
1965   Political change in Micronesia. *In* Induced political change in the Pacific, Roland W. Force, ed. Honolulu: Bishop Museum Press.

Fortes, M., and E. E. Evans-Pritchard, eds.
1940   African political systems. London: Oxford University Press for the International African Institute.

Furness, William H.
1910   The island of stone money. Uap of the Carolines. Philadelphia: Lippincott and Co.

Goffman, Erving
1959   The presentation of self in everyday life. Garden City, New York: Doubleday Anchor.

Halvorsen, Robert
1955–1960   Political and social development files. Office of Political Affairs, Yap District. Trust Territory of the Pacific.

Hawaii Architects & Engineers
1968   Trust Territory physical planning program, final report, Yap, Yap District. Honolulu.

Hezel, Francis X., S.J.
1970   Spanish Capuchins in the Caroline Islands. Micronesian Seminar Bulletin. Truk, Caroline Islands.

Hunt, Edward E., Jr., Nathaniel Kidder, and David M. Schneider
1954   The depopulation of Yap. *Human Biology* 26:21–52.

Hunt, Edward E., Jr., David M. Schneider, Nathaniel R. Kidder, and William D. Stevens
1949   The Micronesians of Yap and their depopulation. Report of the Peabody Museum Expedition to Yap Island, Micronesia, 1947–1948. Coordinated Investigation of Micronesian Anthropology,

1947–1949. No. 24. Washington: Pacific Science Board, National Research Council.

Johnson, Charles, Richard Alvis, and Robert Hetzler
1960   Military geology of Yap Islands. U.S. geological survey under the direction of the chief of engineers, U.S. Army.

Keesing, Felix
1953   Culture change: An analysis and bibliography of anthropological sources to 1952. Stanford: Stanford University Press.
1958   Cultural anthropology. New York: Rinehart and Co.

Labby, David
1972   The anthropology of others: An analysis of the traditional ideology of Yap, Western Caroline Islands. Ph.D. dissertation, University of Chicago.

Lambert, Berndt
1966   The economic activities of a Gilbertese chief. *In* Political anthropology, Marc Swartz, Victor Turner, and Arthur Tuden, eds. Chicago: Aldine Publishing Co.

Leach, Edmund
1954   Political systems of highland Burma. London: Bell.

Lessa, William
1950   Ulithi and the outer native world. *American Anthropologist* 52:27–52.
1966   Ulithi: A Micronesian design for living. New York: Holt, Rinehart, and Winston.

Levi-Strauss, Claude
1944   The Nambikuara of Northwestern Mato Grosso. *In* Comparative political systems, R. Cohen and J. Middleton, eds. New York: Natural History Press.

Lingenfelter, Sherwood
1974   Administrative officials, Peace Corps lawyers, and directed change on Yap. *In* Political development in Micronesia, Daniel T. Hughes and S. Lingenfelter, eds. Columbus: Ohio State University Press.

Lloyd, Peter C.
1965   The political structure of African kingdoms: An exploratory model. *In* Political systems and the distribution of power, M. Banton, ed. A.S.A. Monograph 2. London: Tavistock.

Mahoney, Francis
1958   Land tenure patterns on Yap. *In* Land tenure patterns in Trust Territory of the Pacific Islands, J. E. de Young, ed. Saipan, Mariana Islands.

Meller, Norman
 1969   The congress of Micronesia. Honolulu: University of Hawaii
        Press.

Middleton, John, and David Tait, eds.
 1958   Tribes without rulers. London: Routledge & Kegan Paul.

Müller, Wilhelm
 1917   Yap. *In Ergebnisse der Südsee Expedition*, G. Thilenius, ed.
        II, B, 2:1–811. Hamburg: L. Friederichsen & Co.

Murdock, G. P.
 1949   Social structure. New York: Macmillan.

Norwood, W. R.
 n.d.   Statement of objectives and policies of the Trust Territory of
        the Pacific Islands. Pamphlet from the High Commissioner.
        Saipan, Mariana Islands.

Radcliffe-Brown, A. R.
 1940   Preface. *In* African political systems, M. Fortes and E. E.
        Evans-Pritchard, eds. London: Oxford University Press for the
        International African Institute.

Schapera, I.
 1956   Government and politics in tribal societies. London: Watts & Co.

Schneider, David M.
 1949   The kinship system and village organization of Yap. Ph.D. dis-
        sertation, Harvard University.
 1953   Yap kinship terminology and kin groups. *American Anthropolo-
        gist* 55:215–236.
 1955   Abortion and depopulation on a Pacific island. *In* Health, Cul-
        ture and Community, B. Paul, ed. New York: Russell Sage
        Foundation.
 1957a Political organization, supernatural sanctions and the punish-
        ment of incest on Yap. *American Anthropologist* 59:791–800.
 1957b Typhoons on Yap. *Human Organization* 16:10–15.
 1962   Double descent on Yap. *Journal of the Polynesian Society* 71:
        1–22.
 1967   Depopulation and the Yap *Tabinau*. Mimeographed paper pre-
        pared for Festschrift for Lauriston Sharp.
 1968   Virgin birth. *Man* 3:126–129.

Swartz, Marc J., ed.
 1968   Local-level politics: Social and cultural perspectives. Chicago:
        Aldine Publishing Co.

Swartz, Marc, Victor Turner, and Arthur Tuden, eds.
 1966   Political anthropology. Chicago: Aldine Publishing Co.

Tetens, Alfred, and Johann Kubary
1873   *Die Carolineninsel Yap oder Guap nach den Mitteilungen von Alf. Journal des Museum Goddeffroy.* 1:84–130. Hamburg.

Trust Territory of the Pacific Islands
1958–1973   Annual Report to the United Nations on the Administration of the Trust Territory of the Pacific Islands, Nos. 11, 14, 16, 19, 21, 26. Washington, D.C.: U.S. Government Printing Office.

U.S. Department of Commerce
1966   Local climatological data: Annual summary with comparative data, 1966; Yap Island, Pacific. Washington, D.C.: Environmental Science Services Administration.

Yap District, Office of Political Affairs
1945–1947   Yap district chiefs' file
1951–1968   Public affairs file
1952–1968   Political and social development file

Yap Islands Legislature
1967–1968   Laws and resolutions, sessions 17, 18, 19.
1968   Minutes: Municipal government study commission. Municipal government study commission file.

INDEX

Administration, Yap district, 2, 16; leadership and mobility in, 227–228; Yapese positions in, 212–216

Adoption: cases of, 38–39; irregular and fosterage, 39–40; types of, 36–37; kinship affiliations in, 37–38; motives in, 37

Agriculture. *See* Gardening

Alkire, William H., 149, 153–154

Alliances. *See* Paramount villages

Authority, 219; district, 203–216, 245, 253–254; household, 41–47; municipality, 200–202, 240, 242; patriclan, 52, 54–55, 57–61, 62, 75–76; village, 116–120, 196–197. *See also* Chiefly statuses; Estate; Paramount villages; *Suwon;* Tribute

Barrau, Jacques, 11–13

Barth, Frederick, 219–257

Beauclair, Inez de, 4

Carolinian(s): islands, 5; district leaders, 210–211, 231–233; representation, 247–248, 251; tribute from, 147–155

Caste. *See Pimilngay;* Rank

Ceremonial exchange. *See Mitmit*

Change. *See* Elites; European contact; Government; History; Leadership; Statuses; Wage work

Chiefly statuses: chief of the village (*pilung ko binaw*), 99–101, 106–108; chief of the young men (*pilung ko pagael*), 101–102, 105–107, 114–116; priest, 103–104; sitting chief (*pilung ni pilbithir*), 102–103, 107; succession to, 112–114. *See also* Decision-making

Children, adoption of. *See* Adoption; Fosterage

Choice. *See* Decision-making, nature of

Clan. *See* Matrisib; Patriclan

Class. *See* Rank

Climate, 9

Clubhouse (Young Men's), 82–83

Communication, channels of (*tha'*): paramount chiefs, 131–134, 138–139; use of, 141, 173, 177, 189, 201, 229–231, 239–240; village chiefs, 100, 102–103

Community. *See* Village

Community centers, 80–85. *See also Pebaey*

Conflict. *See* Factions; Leadership, conflict

Congress of Micronesia, 192–193, 195, 211, 229–231

Construction: cases of, 166–168, 236–239. *See also* Labor

Cooking customs, 21–24

Coral reef, 9, 11, 14

Council of Magistrates: conflict and loss of power, 209–210; decision-making, 254–255; formation of, 190–191; leadership qualifications for, 221–226; and organization of legislature, 191–192, 244–248, 251; original duties of, 203–204. *See also* Decision-making; Magistrates

ABOUT
THE
AUTHOR

S HERWOOD GALEN LINGENFELTER is associate professor of anthropology at the State University of New York at Brockport. He began field research for this work in Yap in 1967, spending the first several months in the field in language study and in completing a household census for the whole of Yap.

After gaining competence in Yapese, he conducted extensive interviews on the traditional political and social organization in all of the municipalities of Yap, but particularly in Rull, Gagil, and Tamil. He gathered information on the contemporary scene by observing legislative sessions, by interviewing legislators and councilmen, and through daily contact and interaction with the Yapese people.

Dr. Lingenfelter completed his research for this work in 1969 and in 1969–1970 served as a consultant to the Trust Territory of the Pacific Islands, participating in social studies workshops in Truk District and in Saipan.

Dr. Lingenfelter is an author and coeditor with Daniel T. Hughes of *Political Development in Micronesia*, published by Ohio State University Press in 1974.